They Called Him Rebbe

The Life and Good Works of

Rabbi Boruch Milikowsky

THEY CALLED HIM REBBE

THE LIFE AND GOOD WORKS OF

RABBI BORUCH MILIKOWSKY

by
RAPHAEL BLUMBERG

URIM PUBLICATIONS
Jerusalem • New York

They Called Him Rebbe: The Life and Good Works of Rabbi Boruch
Milikowsky
by Raphael Blumberg

Printed at Hemed Press, Israel. First Edition.
ISBN-13: 978-965-7108-98-7
ISBN-10: 965-7108-98-5
Urim Publications
P.O. Box 52287, Jerusalem 91521 Israel

Lambda Publishers Inc.
3709 13th Avenue Brooklyn, New York 11218 U.S.A.
Tel: 718-972-5449 Fax: 718-972-6307, mh@ejudaica.com

www.UrimPublications.com

CONTENTS

PREFACE
by Dr. Ethan J. Schuman

THE MASHGIACH HAS EARNED a legendary place in our tradition, approaching that of the Rosh ha-Yeshiva himself. Rabbi Nosson Zvi Finkel, Rabbi Yerucham Levovitz, and Rabbi Yechezkel Levenstein all are almost mythical figures who have earned their sacred reputations over the course of many years and generations of talmidim.

The Talmudical Academy of Baltimore, Yeshivas Chofetz Chayim, was blessed with one such mashgiach for forty years. Rabbi Boruch Milikowsky, the man, parent, teacher, Rebbe and lamdan, lovingly but with a strong hand nurtured his boys, hundreds of them if not thousands.

The volume before you is a celebration of that man. Rabbi Boruch Milikowsky was a master at bringing each student's best attributes to the surface and polishing them to a bright luster. Rebbe, as he was called, labored to draw out the best qualities in every boy.

The idea for this tome was born in St. Louis, Missouri at the table of T. A. alumnus Rabbi Gavriel Munk. Although he was a "dorm boy" and I was home-grown, we shared a common thread inasmuch as our passports to life's journey had borne Rebbe's stamp. Through my conversations with Rabbi Munk I envisioned the opportunity to show my gratitude to Rebbe.

Dreaming an idea can be done while sleeping. Making it a reality can of course be grueling. In the seven years that have passed since its inception, I owe tremendous gratitude to my classmate Raphael Blumberg '73. Raphael has done a spectacular job of interviewing, organizing, compiling and writing. He never faltered or lost his enthusiasm for the job. All positive comments about this work must be directed toward him.

In Jerusalem, Raphael and I met with Jay Pomrenze, who provided the initial seed money to begin the project. I will always remain in his debt for the confidence he showed in this project and the patience he displayed to see this work completed.

Finally, as in so many TA projects, the dedication and commitment of two brothers, Joseph and Emanuel Friedman, must be noted. Their loyalty to the school and their love and devotion to Rebbe have helped to turn a dream into reality.

Author's Prologue

In many of the stories here, students asked that their names not be used. In other cases, I chose to change names on my own initiative. Whenever I changed a name, I placed a single asterisk to the right of that name or simply used a made-up first name.

Generally, the stories included in this book are presented in the third person, in my own wording, but faithfully based on taped, transcribed interviews. Occasionally I thought that an interviewee told a story so poignantly or concisely that I quoted the story in his own words, and when I did so I make that clear in the text. If on a small number of occasions I employed literary license and invented my own dialogues to fit the context, as in "Going to Bat" and "Appendicitis I," I beg the reader's indulgence.

In his introduction to *Tom Sawyer*, Mark Twain claims that he employed six different dialects or accents of English to represent the various characters in his book. Yet while Rabbi Milikowsky is quoted many times in this work, he is not presented as speaking with a foreign accent, although he did, of course. To have presented Rabbi Milikowsky with an accent and to have simulated that accent in this book would have been to render him an object of humor, something he never was during his many years as a professional teacher in Baltimore.

What This Book Is Not
(with apologies to Leo Rosten)
The present work is neither a history of the Mir Yeshiva nor a history of the Mir Yeshiva's move from Europe to Shanghai to America/Israel, nor an in-depth treatment of the great rabbinical figures of that yeshiva. These topics have been dealt with quite competently many times already in both Hebrew and English over many thousands of pages (although a full biography of Rabbi Yerucham Levovitz is still waiting to be written and will require a serious *talmid chacham* to write it). I have allowed myself to include a fifteen-

page summary of the quiet miracles involved in the Mir Yeshiva's flight from Europe. There is absolutely nothing unique about my summary except its brevity and the fact that it focuses in a few places on how the upheaval of those times affected Rabbi Milikowsky personally. Those interested in reading more about this topic may find any of the many works already devoted to it.

What This Book Is

This book is a description of the righteous life led by one righteous man as remembered by his students, friends and his family. I was invited to write this book by a person who felt deep gratitude to Rabbi Milikowsky for having helped him in various ways. If I am able to help him show his gratitude and simultaneously to help others to become better people by learning from Rabbi Boruch Milikowsky's example, then I will have accomplished my main goal.

Raphael Blumberg
Kiryat Arba, Israel
2001–2004

INTRODUCTION
by Rabbi Boruch Milikowsky's Children

OUR FATHER WAS AN OUTSTANDING HUMAN BEING, ben Torah, and educator. We learned so much from him and we know that his talmidim also received a great deal from him. We are sure that everyone who reads this book will also in some sense be touched by his life.

Raphael Blumberg's plan to write a book about our father had our blessing at the onset, and we think he has managed to convey some of the essential elements of his life.

His quest to learn more about our father impressed us immensely; indeed, from this book we learned some things about our father we did not previously know.

We well know how demanding was the work Mr. Blumberg did, locating and interviewing family, friends and students in several parts of the globe. We also know how scrupulously he worked, basing all the stories and quotations of students and family he cites on transcribed interviews.

We were given the opportunity to read the book, make comments, and suggest corrections. We did so, and Mr. Blumberg conscientiously put in the corrections.

We have no doubt that the book will be significant not only for us, the family, and our father's talmidim, but also for anyone who wishes to recognize the essential characteristics of a exemplary person whose life has so much to teach every parent and every educator.

ACKNOWLEDGMENTS

THE PRESENT WORK simply would not exist were it not for the initiative of Dr. Ethan Schuman, T.A. '73. I am grateful to Ethan for choosing me as the vehicle by which to express his love for his Rebbe. Writing this work has helped me to grow in many ways, exposed me to much wisdom and made me a better parent, and I am grateful to him.

Neither could this work have been completed without a serious investment in time and effort by more than fifty people, the students of Rabbi Boruch Milikowsky whom I interviewed. It was those students, too many to list individually, who through their stories and comments provided me with most of this book. Whether an hour-long interview resulted in one story, five, or none, the love of those students for their Rebbe always came through loud and clear. Many of my favorite stories in this book are based on long-distance telephone interviews. I hope someday to meet the interviewees and to offer them my thanks in person.

I cannot, however, forego the opportunity to express my personal gratitude to a number of people from the princely European Torah world who enriched my work by sharing with me their crystal-clear memories. Rabbi Moshe Lidsky, Rabbi Avraham Bayarsky, the venerable Rabbanit Fishman-Wernick and the late Rabbi Meir Katznelson, $z''l$, all experienced greatness, and all are in a class by themselves.

Many people have read this book and helped me to bring it to its final form. Whenever I was uncertain how to proceed regarding a particular point, I had the benefit of long talks with my parents, who helped me to clarify matters, and offered me constant encouragement, until I was able to move on. My dear departed father, Professor Arnold Blumberg (Avraham ben Arye Leib, $z''l$), a noted historian and author of seven books on Jewish and European History, read early versions of the book, offering important comments and criticism. I also had the privilege of showing him the rough draft of the completed version, and here, too, his expertise in writing, editing and proofreading proved very helpful.

My mother, *tibadel lechayim*, Mrs. Thelma Blumberg, herself a published author and school psychologist, also read the book. Her comments were invaluable.

My neighbor and friend, Dr. Yerucham Levitt of Ben Gurion University, read the work, made important comments and corrections, as did my sister, Mrs. Rivka Livnat of Elon Moreh.

Rabbi Milikowsky's younger sister, Mrs. Minna Podberesky, shared with me stories of her life and the life of her brother, making those times come alive for me, and providing information that no one else on earth could have provided.

The four children of Rabbi Boruch Milkowsky, after generously giving of their time to tell me about their father, kindly agreed to read the final work. Here as well the book was greatly enriched and improved by their astute comments, proofreading and grammatical skills, and their first-hand knowledge of their father and his life and times.

I am also grateful to Rabbanit Malke Bina, Rabbanit Frady Koff, and Mr. Joseph Friedman, for their permission to use their personal pictures in the book.

Lastly, I wish to acknowledge my dear wife, Mona, who has always been the rock of stability in our turbulent lives. All that I have is thanks to her.

Raphael Blumberg

Part I

EUROPE

Chapter 1

CHILDHOOD IN VISHNEVO

The Shidduch That Almost Didn't Happen

IN EASTERN EUROPE, a hundred miles south of Vilna and ten miles northwest of Volozhin, lay a small village nestled in the marshy farm country of Belarus, or White Russia. In 1907, before the upheavals of World War I, three-quarters of the town's 2,600 residents were Jewish. Yiddish was the preferred language for the Jews, at least among themselves. Of course, there was plenty of opportunity for them to "learn new languages and meet new people" as well.

For example, in 1253, Vishnevo was conquered by Lithuania from the north, which held it for five hundred years. In 1795, it was conquered by czarist Russia from the east, which controlled it until World War I. More conquests followed, which will be mentioned later in this story. And, of course, the Jews' White Russian non-Jewish neighbors spoke White Russian. In any event, for hundreds of years, the Jews of Vishnevo had been referring to themselves as "Litvaks" ("Jewish Lithuanians"), invoking a whole range of associations connected with dialect, personality and outlook.

Life in Vishnevo before World War I was intensely Jewish and traditional. People attended the Orthodox synagogues, participated in the Torah learning, kept Shabbos and worked hard to earn a living. From 1910 until 1914, Rabbi Isser Unterman, later the Ashkenazic (of European origin) Chief Rabbi of Israel, was the director of a yeshiva in Vishnevo. Jewish children studied in *cheder*. Young teenage boys left town to study in the advanced yeshivas elsewhere in the area, or learned trades and went right to work.

Yet as in other places in Eastern Europe, new ideas were slowly influencing the community. Some of the yeshiva students picked up general educations when they were away from home, and brought back the concepts of Zionism and the Enlightenment. In addition to a regular *cheder*, there was already a "reformed *cheder*" in Vishnevo before World War I. Arithmetic was taught there, as well as Hebrew grammar.

It was in the town of Vishnevo that Shmuel Milikowsky (1892–1942) and Malke Dickenstein (1894–1942) were born and grew up. Whatever the details surrounding Shmuel's meeting Malke and their desire to wed, that wedding almost did not happen. It seems that although the Milikowsky and Dickenstein families had many fine qualities, they were quite different from each other. The Milikowskys had great business acumen. They were bright, philanthropic, businesspeople, realists with a lot of what is called "raw intelligence." Although they prized scholarship – they were Litvaks, after all – they were not book-learned.

By contrast, even if the Dickensteins were not overly educated Jewishly, they had more secular culture and learning and were more Zionistic. They were dreamers and *maskilim* who read philosophy and literature, toyed with the various "isms" of the preceding century and argued over them. Some of them had attended school in foreign cities. Therefore, they tended to look down on the Milikowskys and opposed the match due to the differences between the families. Yet Shmuel Milikowsky stood his ground and was very firm, employing the same persistence he had learned from his businessman father. This approach paid off. Malke Dickenstein's family were so impressed by his persistence and by the good traits of the Milikowskys that they ultimately gave their consent.

Thus, early in 1913, it was decided that two prominent families of Vishnevo, each with its own fine qualities, would unite. At a ceremony attended by all of Jewish Vishnevo and some of its non-Jews as well, eighteen-year-old Malke Dickenstein became the wife of Shmuel Milikowsky, aged twenty-one. Together, they settled down to active lives in Vishnevo, occupied with the various philanthropic and business pursuits of the Milikowsky family.

The first two years of Shmuel and Malke's married life were quiet and peaceful. Shmuel and his brothers continued to assist their father in managing the various business interests of the Milikowskys. These included a dry-goods store, a mill for grinding wheat, textile factories that manufactured fabric and felt and, most important of all, a large farm four miles outside Vishnevo.

Life in Vishnevo during those years was tranquil. Many of the non-Jews in the area depended on the Jews for their livelihoods. Thus for example, the Milikowsky farm employed a large number of non-Jews. This economic dependence helped to ensure amicable relations between Jew and non-Jew, whatever the local White Russians might have thought about Jews in their hearts.

Outside of Vishnevo, however, Jewish-Gentile relations were not so tranquil. On Friday, July 22, 1911, the day after *Tisha be-Av*, a Russian Jewish factory foreman named Mendel Beilis had been arrested on charges of murdering a non-Jewish child to use his blood to make matza. The case quickly aroused the wrath of millions of Jews all over the world, and some prominent non-Jews as well. It was clear that the arrest and subsequent imprisonment were the result of anti-Semitism, and that the charges were not only baseless, but also spurious.

Finally in September of 1913, after sitting in prison for almost two and a half years, Mendel Beilis was brought to trial. On October 28, he was pronounced innocent by a jury of twelve Russian peasants and set free. Thus, October 28, 1913 (27 Tishrei 5674) was a day of great rejoicing for world Jewry.

Yet that same day was also one of great personal joy for the young couple, Shmuel and Malke and their families, for on that day their first son, Boruch, was born. All through his childhood, Boruch's parents would remind him of his link to Mendel Beilis. Considering the trials he was to face later on, it was a link well worth remembering.

In 1914, when Boruch Milikowsky was one year old, the tranquility of life in Jewish Vishnevo ceased. World War I broke out. Soon, German and Austrian troops were fighting the czarist Russians. Many Jewish boys from Vishnevo were drafted into the czar's army. While some answered the call, others went into hiding. In 1915, the military front came closer and closer to Vishnevo as the Germans continued to claim victories against the Russians. During the summer of 1915, as German forces approached Vishnevo, Russian troops set fire to most of Vishnevo proper. The entire population of the town became refugees overnight and had to find new homes, at least until the fighting ended. Some of the Jews found refuge in Jewish villages on the Russian side, while others, especially those whose sons had been drafted into the Russian army, found refuge in Jewish villages on the German side. There was no love lost between the Russian czar and the people of Vishnevo, Jew and non-Jew alike. Shmuel and Malke took their small toddler, Boruch, and found refuge along with the rest of the Dickenstein family in Nikopol in the Ukraine, where they had relatives, and which, for the time being at least, was quieter.

Shmuel, possessing the same good business sense as the rest of his family, always landed right-side-up in new situations. He was still very young, and until now, he had done all of his work under the watchful eyes of his father. Now, in Nikopol, he was on his own for the first time. It was a test of sorts. He opened a market and prospered.

Yet he not only did well financially during those years; he also reaped other, more sublime blessings as well. In 1915, a second son, Avraham Elya, was born, in 1918, a third, Eliyakim, and in 1921 Minna, the first of two daughters.

When Shmuel, Malke and Boruch left Vishnevo, they had no way of knowing how long they would have to spend away from home. Yet the immediate fact that their house had burned down was not the only problem. Intense fighting continued in their area for six years. First the Germans fought the czarist Russians for control of Belarus. At first the czarist Russians prevailed, expelling any Jews who had chosen to remain. Then, in 1917, when the Russian Revolution began, the czarist Russians were forced to abandon the western front and the Germans returned. It was at this point that many Jews returned and began the reconstruction of Vishnevo. A *cheder* for lower grades was reopened in a private home and the synagogue was rebuilt. Then, in 1918, when the Russian Communists routed the Germans and World War I ended, a new war broke out between Russia and Poland over control of Belarus.

Finally, in 1921, the fighting was over. Belarus had been conquered by Poland, its western neighbor. The political situation was now stable enough that Malke and Shmuel felt they could return to Belarus. Unfortunately, just before the family's return, all of the money that they had saved during their sojourn in the Ukraine was stolen. Minna, the daughter born in the Ukraine, recalls that all through her childhood her father would joke with her that she would receive no dowry when she married. He would say: "The money stolen was *your* money. You were born at that time!"

Shmuel and Malke, now with four children, returned to Vishnevo in 1921, short of funds but intent on working hard to recoup their losses. Much of Vishnevo had been rebuilt already and both of them had many supportive relatives in town who were happy to help them get back on their feet so that they could resume the lives that they had known before the war.

First on the agenda was arranging for the education of the older children. Boruch was already seven and Avraham Elya five, and Boruch probably had already had a few years of *cheder* in the Ukraine. By contrast, many of the local Jewish children, who had lived in a war zone, had had no schooling at all for several years. There were thus two options from which Shmuel and Malke could choose. First, there was the traditional *cheder* that had been reopened in Vishnevo in 1918. It would offer a continuation of the education that Boruch had been receiving for the past two years.

There was another option. Following much pressure from increasingly progressive elements, the religious and communal leadership of Vishnevo had recently opened an elementary school based on the Tarbut system, which was fast spreading through the larger Jewish towns. Forty children were already studying there, including some of Shmuel and Malke's nieces and nephews, as well as Shmuel's own baby brother Velfke. The school's board of directors was impressive, consisting entirely of local Talmud scholars, including the town rabbi during the mid 1920s, the liberal Rabbi Eliyahu Tzvi Ephron, who later became Chief Rabbi of Rehovot.

Moreover, the planned course of study looked rigorous since it included not only the regular subjects of a traditional *cheder* but also other subjects such as arithmetic and Jewish history.

The approach was what Shmuel Milikowsky might have called "new-fangled," strongly Zionistic with coeducational classes. Neither element particularly bothered him, and indeed, he later sent some of his younger children to the school.

Yet now there was another problem. In its first year, chaos reigned in the school, as sixteen-year-old girls and nine-year-old boys sat together in first grade, learning how to read. This was nobody's fault. There had been little Jewish schooling in the area for the past several years. Still, since Boruch knew how to read already and had proven to be quite precocious, they decided to send him to the traditional *cheder*. Why waste time in a chaotic classroom learning things you knew already? Why take risks? It was sound logic, and a decision was made.

Had the decision gone the other way, with Shmuel deciding to send Boruch to the more secular Tarbut school, it is doubtful whether Boruch would ever have gone on to yeshiva and become the person he became.

Each morning, seven-year-old Boruch would accompany five-year-old Avraham Elya to the *cheder*, and each afternoon, with their studies completed, they would return home.

Now Jewish Vishnevo, as has been noted, was full of the relatives of little Boruch and Avraham Elya. Each day on their way home, they would pass the house of old Nosson Dickenstein, grandfather of Boruch's young mother Malke. A traditional *talmid chacham* (Torah scholar), Nosson Dickenstein was concerned about the modern winds blowing in Vishnevo. He decided to do what he could to have a positive influence on his two great-grandchildren, Boruch and Avraham Elya, who passed his house each day. Soon he began to invite them into his home each afternoon to play with them, talk with them and feed them. Shmuel and Malke were grateful for the babysitting help, especially during the chaotic early days of their return to Vishnevo when they were trying to get back on their feet, and they had no complaints about a loving grandfather providing their children with lunch.

The relationship continued. Each day, Nosson Dickenstein would wait in front of his home for his great-grandchildren and invite them inside. At some point he began to ask them about what they were learning and later on began to study with them. He was pleased and encouraged by their abilities, and he sought to develop in both of them a love and a thirst for Torah learning.

೭   ೬

In the meantime, Shmuel Milikowsky, twenty-nine years old on his return from the Ukraine, was ready to take on more responsibilities in the family business ventures. Immediately upon his return he took over the management of the dry goods store in Vishnevo proper. Eventually, he also formed business partnerships with his brothers on various other projects. Most significant was the family dairy farm, located four miles outside Vishnevo.

The trip between Vishnevo and the farm was accomplished by horse and wagon along unpaved country roads and took an hour. Sometimes he would drive the wagon himself, and sometimes he would have a worker drive him. Yet it was a trip that Shmuel did not have to make every day. The running of the farm was left to a large, impressive staff of non-Jewish foremen and laborers. Shmuel Milikowsky was a levelheaded businessman, but he had a good heart and he always treated his workers fairly, and they repaid his generosity by doing a good job. Providing employment to so many of the local townspeople likewise went a long way towards increasing the good will between them and the Milikowsky family.

The farm was large. Part of it was on lands owned by the Milikowskys, and part of it was on additional lands that they rented. There were horses and dairy cows, beehives for producing honey, large expanses of land on which hay was grown and sold to the Polish army, as well as sharp Hollander cheeses which were cured in smokehouses until ready. The farm also included a large home where workers lived at the time, but which could house the Milikowsky family comfortably if need be.

After the initial difficulties of their return from the Ukraine, the Milikowskys thus settled down into fairly affluent lives *by the standards of their time and place.* There was no electricity and would be none in Vishnevo until 1938. There were no paved roads. There was one telephone in town, at the post office.

At the same time, Shmuel Milikowsky could usually afford to provide his wife with a maid. Malke's main tasks involved cooking and child-raising, both of which she accomplished with aplomb. Her parents had owned a bakery, and she had learned to be a very fine baker. She was also known as an excellent cook. At holiday time, the children would look forward to her meat and chicken and tzimmes and all the other fine dishes she made. They loved the holidays. The whole family would be together, and they would celebrate very festively.

Shmuel was a strict father. He loved his children very much, and all of his children loved him in return. He worked very hard and tried his best to support his wife and growing family.

Sometimes, Shmuel would take his children on the wagon to the farm. The children would play in the fields under the sun and watch the workers do their jobs, cutting hay, milking cows, and preparing cheeses.

∽ ∽

The years passed. In 1924, a fourth son, Moshe Aharon, was born. Boruch and Avraham Elia, now eleven and nine years old respectively, continued to spend time and to study Torah with their great-grandfather, Nosson.

The Milikowskys were prominent philanthropists in Vishnevo. As the 1920s progressed, the Jewish population of Vishnevo once more began to rise. A day came when the synagogue rebuilt at the end of the War was no longer big enough for everyone, and Shmuel Milikowsky and his brothers played a large role in building a second synagogue.

Outside political influences continued to have an effect on the town. Following the war, all of the Jewish political parties and youth movements that existed outside of Vishnevo were established in Vishnevo as well.

Shmuel and Malke Milikowsky in Europe, with one of Boruch's
younger brothers.

This included religious movements like the Agudah and Mizrachi as well as youth movements like Beitar, He-Halutz and Ha-Shomer ha-Za'ir. The young people of the town, who in many cases had known one another from early childhood and were often related to one another as well, split along political lines and debated one another on the street, sometimes quite passionately.

In many homes, families were divided along political lines. Thus, the younger Dickensteins, even if at home they continued to live religious lives, were all connected to He-Halutz, which was linked to the secular Labor Zionist movement. Boruch Milikowsky, who loved his mother's brothers and sisters dearly, would sit with them in the years before his bar mitzvah and hear them argue their politics.

During the 1920s, before anyone in Poland was thinking about Hitler, Malke Dickenstein Milikowsky's family, including her sisters Elisheva and Matle and her brothers Avraham and Ben-Zion, as well as her parents, began to move to Israel. In fact, many Jews in Vishnevo were doing the same.

Thus, for example, in 1926, Ben-Zion Dickenstein joined a Vishnevo group of He-Halutz pioneers making aliyah. They formed the nucleus of Kibbutz Ha-Kovesh that was initially camped near Petah Tikva. Later, after purchasing land, this group settled and established a new kibbutz, Ramat Ha-Kovesh, north of Kfar Saba.

One sibling, Avraham Dickenstein, ultimately reached a high position in Israeli society. He became the founder of Bank Ha-Poalim and Ampal, American-Palestine Investments, and his friends included many of the early Zionist leaders. Working behind the scenes, he was one of those who helped to establish the financial infrastructure for the future State of Israel.

Another family that moved to Israel was the Persky family, who were wood merchants in Vishnevo. One of their children, Shimon, ten years younger than Boruch Milikowsky, grew up to become Shimon Peres, one of Israel's prime ministers.

Chapter 2

RADIN

IN 1925, WHEN BORUCH WAS TWELVE YEARS OLD, he came to the end of all the formal traditional Jewish education available in Vishnevo. That is, he had come to the end of the Vishnevo traditional *cheder*. For that matter, the Tarbut school did not go beyond sixth grade either. Educationally, he thus had three options: to stop studying and to go to work; to continue in the Polish public school of Vishnevo; or, to go out of town to continue his yeshiva education.

Many boys in town followed the first option or the second. At least one of Boruch's younger brothers eventually went to Polish public school and then went out of town to study agriculture, the better to help out on the farm. To Malke's grandfather, Nosson Dickenstein, however, it was clear that Boruch had promise as a Torah scholar and should continue his Torah studies. He broached the subject with Malke, and she and Shmuel took time to consider whether or not they should send their twelve-year-old away to yeshiva.

The Milikowsky family had a warm, loving, exclusively Orthodox home. The children were raised to love Jewish practice. They ate only kosher food and recited the Grace after Meals, and the men *davened* three times a day. Shmuel Milikowsky had been instrumental in financing the construction of the new synagogue. Yet it was not a home in which Torah permeated the cracks. The walls were not lined with holy books. No one had been telling Boruch from the age of three that he should learn as much as he could to become a great scholar. If Boruch was headed in that direction, it had come from within himself, with more than a little help from his great-grandfather. Had Boruch said he wanted to stop school and get his feet wet in the family business, or learn mathematics and Polish language in the public school, his family would have given him their full support in that direction.

As it is, he was asking for something else. As *Litvaks*, Shmuel and Malke were able to appreciate what he was asking. In Northern Belarus in the mid 1920s, learning in yeshiva was still one way for a Jewish boy to achieve a high academic level and at the same time to attain high social status. The Milikowskys, whatever they thought about the idea *per se*, were pleased that their son Boruch had the intellectual potential that enabled him to consider such an option. They gave their permission and promised their economic and moral support. All that remained was to decide which yeshiva Boruch would attend.

Not far from Vishnevo was a town called Radin. During the 1850s, Rabbi Yisrael Meir Kagan had spent ten years learning in Vilna. At the end of that period, after declining to take a post as a pulpit rabbi, he had settled with his wife in Radin, Poland. There, he opened a small grocery store which his wife managed, while he did the "bookkeeping," watching every penny to make sure no one was cheated. He spent his days learning Torah and disseminating his knowledge to the common people.

As his reputation grew, students from all over Europe flocked to him, and by the late 1860s his house was known as the Radin Yeshiva. Rabbi Kagan, known as the Chafetz Chaim for his groundbreaking book by that title on avoiding forbidden speech, directed his yeshiva for many years. Eventually a *beis midrash* was constructed, enabling two hundred fifty boys to learn together.

In 1925, when Boruch was twelve years old, there were three boys from Vishnevo already learning Torah in Radin. It was probably they who recruited Boruch, and others from Vishnevo, to join them in Radin. Besides its famous *yeshiva gedola* for boys beyond high-school age, there was also a *yeshiva ketana* for high-school-age boys. The Radin *yeshiva ketana* was known to be a successful program that took a twelve- or thirteen-year-old *cheder* boy and within four years turned him into a young scholar able to learn *gemara* on his own and generate *chiddushim*, innovative Torah thoughts. It was a natural way to prepare oneself for the *yeshiva gedolah*.

When Shmuel Milikowsky took Boruch there to begin his studies, the Chafetz Chaim was in his late eighties. Although he was by then physically weak and largely housebound, with thrice-daily *minyanim* held for his benefit in his home, he was still very busy providing advice to a steady stream of Jews who approached him from all over Europe. Thus Shmuel took advantage of his being in Radin to ask the Chafetz Chaim whether or not he should buy another farm in addition to the one he already owned outside of Vishnevo. The Chafetz Chaim answered, "When you put a second tap into a beer barrel, do you get more beer or do you just get the same beer faster?"

Rabbi Shaya Milikowsky, who told me this story, concludes: "I assume that my grandfather Shmuel followed this advice, but I do not know for sure."

Having arrived in Radin, Boruch set to work. He had *rebbeim* who taught him *gemara* each day. At first, the *gemara* was spoon-fed, with the rebbe reciting the *gemara* a few times for the boys until the boys began to know it. Within a few years, however, the boys were being given time to prepare the day's *gemara* on their own, and the *rebbeim* were allowing themselves to give *shiurim* [lectures] focusing on medieval and later commentaries.

Sometime in his first year at Radin, Boruch Milikowsky celebrated his bar mitzvah. He did not go home to celebrate but rather stayed in Radin. The celebration consisted simply of his being called up to the Torah.

When Boruch's younger brother Avraham Elya was approaching bar-mitzvah age, he had to make the same decision that Boruch had made a few years earlier. With Boruch's encouragement and his parents' blessing, he left Vishnevo to continue his Torah studies in *yeshiva ketana.*

South of Vishnevo was another famous yeshiva at Baranovitch. In 1930, when Boruch was seventeen years old, he decided to take off a half-year to experience the Baranovitz yeshiva and to hear the *shiur* of Reb Elchonon Wasserman. The population in Rav Elchonon Wasserman's yeshiva was young, a sort of bridge between *yeshiva ketana* and *yeshiva gedola.* The boys were about fifteen to eighteen years old. Yet Rav Elchonon did not hesitate to give *shiurim* that lasted a very long time, sometimes even for four hours at a stretch! He was so used to driving himself to his limits that in the middle of the *shiur* he would sometimes run out of strength. When this happened, he would say, "Boys, sit quietly! I'm going to put my head down for three minutes to take a nap," or "I'm going to put my head down for five minutes." Boys would always check the clock. If he said three minutes he slept for three and if he said five he slept for five. At precisely the right moment he would open his eyes, raise his head and continue his *shiur*.

When he was young, Rav Elchonon had himself been a close disciple of the Chafetz Chaim in Radin. There are stories about how the Chafetz Chaim used to give ten-hour-long *mussar* talks at Saturday night *melave malkas*. Most students would stay for an hour or two of the talk. Only Rav Elchonon would sit absorbed through the entire ten hours.

Another enormous figure in Baranowitz was Ha-Rav Yisrael Yaakov Lubschansky, the yeshiva's *mashgiach*. At least two elements in the persona of this tremendous *tzaddik* may have had an impact on young Boruch Milikowsky. First of all, Rav Lubschansky was a superb orator, with a powerful sense of humor and great stage presence. He would apply his great oratorical talents to discussing man's beastly passions, making the war against the evil impulse relevant to teenage boys. Second of all, as *mashgiach*, he saw himself as guardian of the welfare of every single boy. He would survey the *beis midrash*, and if boys were missing, he would go to find them himself.

After half a year at Baranovitz, Boruch returned to Radin. He wanted to learn for an extended period of time in the Chafetz Chaim's yeshiva.

If the *yeshiva ketana* in Radin was a demanding program for highly intelligent boys with a fiery love of Torah, the *yeshiva gedola* in Radin was even more so. Every candidate was tested before being accepted into the program. It was a test not so much of knowledge but rather of acquired skills and potential. Each boy was given a specific *blatt* of *gemara* to prepare with the *Rishonim* and *Acharonim*, and he had to prepare himself to answer difficult questions on that material. Needless to say, it was a test that no seventeen- or eighteen-year-old boy could pass without years of serious preparation.

When Boruch started learning in the *yeshiva gedola*, it became clear why a difficult entrance examination was required for admission. At Radin, a boy had to be not only intelligent, but mature and self-paced to do well. The Radin student had to behave like an adult, and he was given the trust of an adult as well. Students at Radin were exceedingly diligent. The *beis midrash* was generally quiet only three hours a night. Many boys learned until midnight, and many others arose at three AM and learned for the four hours until morning prayers.

Twice a week the boys at Radin, even in their first year, would gather together with other boys their own age into groups of ten or fifteen for half an hour and conduct "*va'adin*," which corresponds roughly to what today are sometimes called "*chaburas*." Every boy, when it was his turn, would have to expound on what he was learning, expressing *chiddushim*, innovative Torah thoughts that he had come up with himself. Sometimes a boy would not complete what he had to say during his half hour, and then he would expound several days later during the next available half hour as well, until he had completed his presentation. The boys would stand in a circle during this half hour, dignified young *Litvaks* with their jackets draped over their shoulders, each leaning on his own *shtender*, absorbed in what his fellow student was saying, and no staff member from the yeshiva would be there. The boys would conduct these gatherings by themselves. Boruch Milikowsky was already taking part in these sessions and producing novel Torah thoughts at age eighteen, yet he learned in yeshiva for seventeen more years!

The two *Rashei Yeshiva* were Rabbi Mendl Zachs, a son-in-law of the Chafetz Chaim, who lived with his family on the second floor of the Chafetz Chaim's home, and Rabbi Boruch Feivelovitz, a son-in-law of Rav Naphtali Trop, who headed the yeshiva before World War I. Each would deliver a "*shiur kelali*," a weekly general *gemara shiur* attended by the entire yeshiva. Thus, the boys in Radin, even the eighteen-year-old newcomers, heard a total of two *gemara shiurim* per week. Generally speaking, everyone was expected to understand these two *shiurim*, and if anyone had trouble, they would, without any embarrassment, either ask an older boy or approach the *Roshei Yeshiva* themselves and ask them their questions.

There was also a *mashgiach*, Rabbi Eliezer Kaplan, who besides serving as a sounding board for the boys would also give serious talks on the traditional topics of *mashgichim*, aimed at seeing that the boys put their time in yeshiva to its best advantage. He was married to a granddaughter of the Chafetz Chaim.

Despite his advanced age, the Chafetz Chaim was still teaching formally out of his home a few times a week. Twice each Shabbos, following *kabbalas Shabbos* and following *Shabbos minchah* the next day, he would give a *mussar shmuess*, an ethical talk, in his own home. His home would be jam-packed with boys, standing room only, and during the summer months, the windows would be open with many boys standing outside as well. Any boy from the *yeshiva gedolah* could attend these talks, even in his first year. Moreover, there was no "pecking order" about who got to sit or stand closest to the Chafetz Chaim. It was first come, first served. Those who came earliest would sit with the Chafetz Chaim on one of the two benches in the room – there were no other chairs. Those who came last would squeeze into the foyer closest to the front door.

The Chafetz Chaim was not entirely housebound, however. Sometimes younger rabbis would come to escort him to a waiting carriage to take him to important rabbinic conventions in the large cities of Poland. Occasionally as well, during Rabbi Milikowsky's years, the Chafetz Chaim would make the effort to walk the block to the yeshiva and give talks there. In the last years of his life, he would devote many of the talks he gave at the yeshiva to the topic of *Mashiach*. He would say, "*Mashiach* is going to come. We are supposed to be waiting for him every day, and if we don't take steps to increase our knowledge, we won't understand what he is talking about! We don't know anything about *Kodshim*!" referring to those sections of the *Mishnah* and Talmud dealing with the laws of the Temple. He would recommend that boys include the study of *Kodshim* in their schedule, at least *Mishnayos*. It was at about the same time that Rav Velvel Soloveitchik instituted the full-time study of *Kodshim* in the Brisk yeshiva.

Sometimes the Chafetz Chaim would also invite the illustrious Rav Shimon Shkop to come and learn *Kodshim* with him. He would say, "You and I are both *kohanim*, and we have to prepare ourselves." Rav Shimon Shkop would come to Radin during Rabbi Milikowsky's years and would discuss halachic issues within Kodshim with the Chafetz Chaim. Other great sages who were *kohanim* would come as well.

If Boruch came from a well-to-do family, if his father was involved in at least two thriving family businesses, if until then he could eat whatever he wanted and however much of it he wanted, all of that ended at Radin. In Radin there was no dining room or dormitory. Boys would eat in the homes of *balebatim* (householders) in the community, and they would sleep on straw mattresses in their homes as well. Five boys might eat their three daily meals together in one home, while each boy would have a different home where he slept, with rental money paid to the householder by the yeshiva itself.

The food was poor by the standards and customs Rabbi Milikowsky had known previously, and even more so in comparison to those standards he would later adopt in Baltimore. For breakfast, bread, a little butter, and some tea. Lunch, the main meal, consisted of a bit of meat with soup and some more bread. Many vegetables, such as corn, were unavailable or were rejected as being "goat food." It wasn't much to eat, but many did not care. The ideal was to eat quickly and to run back to the *beis midrash*. Boys in Radin did not feel hungry. Their minds were on something else besides food.

All the same, when Rabbi Milikowsky came home once or twice a year to see his family, they would implore him, when he set out again, to take along a large slab of Hollander cheese from the farm. To have said no would have been to insult his family.

One night a thief came and stole all of the cheeses from the Milikowsky's smokehouse on the farm. The next time that Boruch Milikowsky came home for *Yom Tov* and was told the story of the stolen cheeses, he reported that at around the same time his own cheese, the cheese that the family had given him to take with him to yeshiva, had been stolen as well. From this Rabbi Milikowsky deduced that if it was *bashert,* pre-ordained, that the cheese was going to be stolen, it was going to be stolen wherever it was.

Even though most of the students came from the Belarus region, that is, their families lived not too far away from Radin, the boys did not go home for Shabbos. Instead, they would go home once or twice a year, at Succos and perhaps at Pesach as well. Thus, whoever learned in Radin was literally fulfilling the words of *Pirkei Avos,* that one should "exile himself to a place of Torah."

᠀   ᠀

In 1927, Rabbi Zvi Ephron, Vishnevo's rabbi, moved to Israel and became the Rabbi of Rehovot. He was replaced by Rabbi Yitzchak Weinstein, who remained in Vishnevo for twelve years, until he moved to Israel. Rabbi Weinstein was Vishnevo's last rabbi. Boruch's sister Minna, who was six years old in 1927, became best friends with Rabbi Weinstein's daughter Etyl.

The year of Rabbi Weinstein's arrival, a second daughter was born to Shmuel and Malke Milikowsky, and they named her Drezel Matla. Sometime in the next few years, Nosson, the great-grandfather who had helped Boruch and Avraham Elya so much, passed away. When another boy was born to the Milikowskys in 1930, their fifth boy and last child, they named him Nosson after that great grandfather.

When Boruch Milikowsky came home on *Yom Tov* visits to Vishnevo, he developed a personal relationship with Rabbi Weinstein. Rabbi Weinstein, like his predecessor Rabbi Ephron, was a unique man who would have been hard to label. He was personally identified with the Agudah organization, but he maintained an intense connection with the general Jewish public as well.

Sometimes he would take unconventional steps to keep in touch with the mentality of his flock. One time he traveled the hundred miles to Vilna just to attend a secular Zionist conference that was taking place over Shabbos. When he returned home, he made no effort to hide the fact that he had been there. It was important for him to know what the younger people in his town were thinking and where they were heading spiritually. He was a *talmid chacham* and a *mensch,* and without a doubt served as one of the models of young Boruch Milikowsky.

In 1939, he moved to Israel and took over for Rabbi Ephron as Rabbi of Rechovot. Twenty-five years later, when Rabbi Boruch Milikowsky began to visit Israel from America, he always went to see the elderly Rabbi Weinstein.

Chapter 3

WINDS OF CHANGE

IN 1929, A CRISIS IN THE STOCK MARKET affected economies throughout the world. Jews who had prospered in Vishnevo during the 1920s had to reassess the way they conducted their businesses as people everywhere began to buy less than they had previously. Relations between Jew and non-Jew were affected as well. The local non-Jews could no longer be trusted with as free a hand as before. Thus, in 1930 or 1931, while Boruch was learning in Radin, the Milikowskys made a decision to cease their management of the dry goods store in Vishnevo and to move onto the farm. There they stayed until the arrival of the Russian Communists in September 1939.

The move to the farm involved a number of sacrifices. Henceforth the Milikowsky children would have to travel the hour by wagon to Vishnevo each morning to get to school. Shmuel Milikowsky and his sons could no longer go to synagogue on a regular basis. During those years, when the *Yomim Tovim* arrived, the males of the family went to Vishnevo and spent the holiday with one of the uncles. The rest of the year, they had to pray at home, and they continued to do so throughout the years that they were on the farm. It should be pointed out that many other Jews at the time found themselves in similar circumstances.

The home they moved into was considered large in the relative terms of Eastern Polish shtetls in 1930. It had three bedrooms, a dining room and a kitchen. A four-room house may have been above average in size, but with seven children, there was crowding sometimes. Someone always had to sleep in the dining room. Of course, by 1928, the two oldest boys were out of the house, and much of the year, the two girls had a room to themselves. Still, in the summer, cousins would come to spend time on the farm, and occasionally Boruch and Avraham Elya would come home. Thus, there were times when the two girls would have to sleep in the same bed. Yet no one complained. The Milikowsky children were not spoiled, and they were happy to sacrifice so their cousins could visit. The family lived happily together on the farm during those last ten years.

æ   ∽

In 1933, the Chafetz Chaim passed away. In Radin, pictures were taken showing the enormous throngs participating in the *levaya*. In one picture, standing not far from the coffin, it was possible to see Boruch Milikowsky. A copy of that picture was later hung on a wall in the home of Boruch's parents. They were proud of their son's connection to the greatness of Radin.

In about 1934, within a year of the Chafetz Chaim's passing, Boruch Milikowsky decided to move on to the Mir Yeshiva. He was now twenty-one years old.

The Mir yeshiva was one of the very top yeshivas in Europe. There were many prodigies there. If it was hard to be accepted into Radin, it was even more of a challenge to be accepted into the Mir yeshiva. In fact, one had to be extremely intelligent in order to understand the two weekly *shiurim* given by the Rosh Yeshiva, Rabbi Eliezer Yehuda Finkel, and his son-in-law Rabbi Chaim Shuelevitz. Most of the students were in their mid-twenties or older, and a minority were younger than that. At twenty-one, Boruch Milikowsky was very young to be moving to the Mir. The fact that he was accepted was a mark of his brilliance.

For nine years he had been learning diligently, spending many hours each day in the *beis midrash*, soaking up the Talmud. While memorizing the Talmud was by no means a goal *per se* of yeshiva learning, it often happened when someone had a memory that was far above average. For some yeshiva students, it was a natural byproduct of the constant review which was a large part of the yeshiva way of life.

During the first two years that Boruch Milikowsky was in the Mir Yeshiva, he was privileged to have contact with, and to become close to the renowned *mashgiach*, Rabbi Yeruchem Levovitz, who passed away in 1936. Rabbi Levovitz had first studied with the Alter of Slabodka, Rabbi Nosson Tzvi Finkel, who sent him to study under Rabbi Simcha Zissel of Kelm. Rav Levovitz, like the Alter of Slobodka, was famous for the extent to which he related to each student as a unique individual. He must certainly have had an effect on Boruch Milikowsky, who later became famous in his own right for this same trait.

There are numerous stories about the special way in which Rav Levovitz related to his students. Here is one of them:

During the 1930s there were many students who, having heard of Rav Levovitz's reputation for greatness, came to the yeshiva from Western Europe and the United States in order to benefit from the *Mashgiach's* wisdom. Many of these students, besides having achieved high levels of Torah learning, had also received a secular education, and many of them had advanced university degrees. One particular group of students were from Germany, and they had been schooled in the *"Torah im derech eretz"* approach, which encouraged one to combine Torah study with the study of science and Western culture. For more than fifty years, this in fact had been the accepted approach in Germany amongst the Orthodox Jews, although it was not the approach of the great Eastern European yeshivos.

So it happened that some of the students from Germany one day approached the *Mashgiach* and asked him whether or not it was good for a person to follow the *"Torah im derech eretz"* approach. Rav Levovitz responded by refraining from answering them directly. He said, "I don't have time right now to answer your question." Then, for the next several months, he devoted his *mussar* talks precisely to this question, explaining what the term "Torah" meant to him, and what the Mishnah meant by the expression *"derech eretz."* When those months had gone by, the students had an answer to their question, and the *mashgiach* had succeeded in swaying them to accept the Eastern European yeshiva approach (based on the work *Ha-zeriha be-fa'atei kedem*).

In about 1937, when Boruch's sister Minna, the older daughter, was sixteen years old, she was sent to Vilna for a two-year bookkeeping course. At this point the family was still well-to-do, even if as the 1930s progressed, times in general were becoming harder. The Milikowskys were able to cover the costs of the bookkeeping course and to provide their daughter with an allowance to cover her expenses. Minna lived with a woman in Vilna. She had to pay for her room and her food and clothing. Still, she had to be very careful because her family could not give her very much money. If she wanted to buy a skirt, she had to eat less for several days so that she could buy it. But again, to send your daughter off in the 1930s to a large city to a fine course and to be able to give her a bit of an allowance was well beyond the ability of most of the Jews of Europe.

During his years in the Mir yeshiva, Rabbi Milikowsky continued to go home only once or twice a year, for Succos and sometimes for Pesach. Only during his last two years in Belarus did he come home for a month in the summer as well.

Boruch, who was in his mid-twenties by then, he had two small siblings whom he barely knew. Those summer months were a chance to get to know his younger family members. During at least one of those summers, he also volunteered to help recruit new students for one of the Novardok *Mussar* yeshivas.

In those last years during the late 1930s, he would also bring home a guest. There was a boy in the Mir Yeshiva who didn't have any family. The boy and his brother had been raised in Russia and their father had been a rabbi. Then, when the Communists took over Russia, they came and arrested the boys' father. He was never seen again. When this happened, the boys' mother decided to send the boys away, so she sent them out of Russia with a willing companion. One of the boys came to learn in the Mir Yeshiva. It was he whom Boruch and Avraham Elya brought home for the summer. The family's contact with this orphan, besides providing Rabbi Milikowsky with a perspective on being alone in the world and far from home, also provided the Milikowskys with a warning of what was about to happen in Vishnevo itself.

Chapter 4

THE RUSSIANS

WELL INTO 1939, the Jews of Eastern Europe could still tell themselves that Hitler would refrain from attacking Poland. It was assumed that the Communists – Russia – would naturally side with England and France against the Fascists – Germany – and that this would deter the Germans from starting a war. Indeed, the Russian Foreign Minister, Litvinoff, a Jew from Bialystok, had been pursuing such an alliance. After all, why should the Russians side with the Germans? Surely it was well known that the Nazis considered the Russians, and all Slavs, a subhuman race who should ultimately be made the slaves of the German "master race." Surely it was also known that the Germans despised Russian Communism as a so-called Jewish invention.

All this turned out to be wishful thinking. Stalin evidently had different ideas. He fired Litvinoff and appointed Molotov in his place, ordering him to pursue an agreement with the Nazis. Thus, on August 23, 1939, the Germans and the Russians signed a non-belligerence agreement known as the Ribbentrop-Molotov Pact. Then, on September 1st, the calamity was complete. The Germans attacked Poland from the west, and the Russians attacked Poland from the east, and the Poles, whose army still rode on horseback, could put up no defense against German tanks. Within a month Poland ceased to exist.

Perhaps as many as half a million Jews from the German part of Poland chose that moment to flee eastward into the Russian part. Several months later, the Russian Communists spread a rumor that anyone who wished to do so could receive an exit visa from Russia. Hundreds of thousands submitted such requests. Six weeks later still, all who had submitted requests were arrested and exiled by the Russians to Siberia. The whole exercise had only been a trick to catch and to exile the "enemies of the state." Ultimately, this saved the lives of the majority of those Jews by removing them from the area that the Nazis would control two years later. The Ribbentrop-Molotov Pact, which made so little sense at the time, has been interpreted by some rabbis as the miraculous hand of God that enabled some portion of Polish Jewry to be saved. If not for that pact, Germany might eventually have conquered all of Poland in one fell swoop, and those half million or more would all have died. Exile to Siberia saved many of them.

September 13, 1939, the day before Rosh Hashanah 5700, Boruch and Avraham Elya were in the Mir Yeshiva. Their mother and sisters were on the farm, four miles away from Vishnevo. Shmuel and his other three sons spent the days of Rosh Hashanah, September 14th and 15th, in Vishnevo, as was their custom. The next day, September 16, *Tzom Gedalya*, Shmuel Milikowsky made the traditional visit to his ancestors' graves in the cemetery in Vishnevo, and that evening he returned home to his farm and his family. "You know," he said, "the Russians are coming." The air was thick with the rumor that that day the Russians had taken over the town of Mir, twenty miles to the east – as indeed they had – and were headed in the direction of Vishnevo.

For a landowner and a successful businessman such as Shmuel Milikowsky, such a rumor about the Russians was a source of worry. It was not a matter of a strange new culture or language. Shmuel and Malke both knew Russian quite well because Vishnevo had been under the control of czarist Russia during all the years of their youth. The problem was quite different.

The Russian Communists were notorious for coming into towns and murdering wealthy landowners and distributing their lands to the surrounding peasants. For a man like Shmuel Milikowsky, a rumor about the Communists' imminent arrival could mean impending bankruptcy at best, or death for him and his family at worst.

It was early autumn. The hay was all cut and ready for sale. Over the summer the cows had given a lot of milk. There were a lot of cheeses. Everything was being packed up and readied for market. It amounted to thousands of dollars of merchandise almost ready for sale.

The next day, September 17, began normally. The workers showed up and worked the same as always. Then, late in the day, the Russians entered Vishnevo.

Several more days passed. The workers continued coming to work as usual, yet everybody waited for the axe to fall. Then, one afternoon, one of the farmhands knocked on the door of the family home and said that the workers wished to speak with him. Shmuel Milikowsky calmly walked out with them into the clearing while the family watched from inside, fearing the worst. The workers gathered around their longtime employer, and an appointed spokesman said the following:

"Mr. Milikowsky, you were always very good to us, so we're not going to do you or your family any harm. We've put in a good word for you with the Communists. Just go back to your house. Gather your children, one cow, a horse and a wagon, some of the furniture, something from the house, and go away to Vishnevo. Just go!" There was nothing more to say.

The Milikowskys packed up what they could and loaded it onto a horse and wagon, to begin their last wagon trip from the farm to Vishnevo. Through the years, how many times had they made this trip? How much time and money had they invested in the farm? Now it was all gone. Just like that! They would never see it again.

In Vishnevo, the Milikowskys owned a large home which over the last ten years they had been renting out to the local Polish postal workers as a residence. When the Communists arrived, all the Poles who had lived in the house fled. They were afraid of the Russians. Thus, Shmuel and Malke found their Vishnevo home empty. The Milikowskys were fortunate. They were able to move back into their own home in Vishnevo. Moreover, although the Russians had confiscated the farm, which had been a partnership of Shmuel Milikowsky and two of his brothers, there was still a flour mill in Vishnevo that Shmuel Milikowsky held in partnership with one of his brothers. From the mill they still had a means of earning a living, so they still had something to eat.

Minna now went to work for the Russians in a little town called Ivenetz, and her father Shmuel went to work for the Russians as well. They were both "working," but it was slave labor. They earned almost nothing. If the family was to survive, it would not be based on any work that they did for the Russians during those two years.

There was a large garden behind the house which the Russians had not taken away. There, the family raised vegetables such as potatoes. Between all of these efforts, the family continued to survive and did not starve.

Chapter 5

ESCAPE FROM EUROPE

The Mir Yeshiva Makes Its Move

THE CHAFETZ CHAIM (*Nefutzos Yisrael,* Chapter 8) describes the different ways by which God conducts the world. One of the ways is by "Divine blessing," the orchestration of events in a way that works in our favor. When we pray for success, we are praying for Divine blessing. One example of a Jewish event in history where events worked out fortuitously for the Jewish People was the Purim story. Another is the manner in which the Mir Yeshiva managed to exit Europe intact and survive the Second World War.

Rabbi Boruch Milikowsky experienced these events and they were part of him. Here follows a brief summary of those events, with an emphasis on where Divine providence comes into play:

When the Russian Communists took over Vishnevo in September of 1939, they also took over Mir, Poland, twenty miles to the east, where Boruch and Avraham Elya Milikowsky were learning Torah. If, as we saw, it was hard to survive as a well-to-do farmer under the Russian regime, one can imagine the prospects of three hundred men in their twenties and thirties engaged in Jewish rabbinical studies suddenly finding themselves exposed to the cruel talons of the Russian Communists. In Russia proper, under Stalin, all the yeshivas had been closed down and the yeshiva *bochrim* and *rebbeim* either murdered or exiled to Siberia, many never to be heard from again. Now the Russian Communists had their hands on what was arguably the oldest, largest and most prestigious yeshiva in Belarus-Eastern Poland.

Late at night on October 9, 1939, an English-speaking student in the Mir Yeshiva was listening to a pirate radio station that was airing a Royal

British news broadcast. Suddenly the announcer declared with great fanfare that the Russian regime, having conquered Poland, intended to restore the City of Vilna, which the Poles had cynically snatched from Lithuania in 1920, to Lithuania's control.

Until that moment, Lithuania was still independent and part of the free, neutral world. Furthermore, it had a reputation for relative tolerance to Jews. Vilna, a hundred miles to the north, was at that moment still under Russian control, just like the town of Mir, and could be reached without having to show anyone any papers. In the Molotov/Ribbentrop Pact, in which two cruel countries, Nazi Germany and Stalinist Russia, ruthlessly divided Poland, they also inexplicably decided to "strike a blow for freedom" by restoring Vilna to its rightful owner. Had this bizarre deed not occurred, the Mir boys could never have fled the Holocaust.

The news spread like wildfire. The heads of the yeshiva were informed, and within days an emissary of the saintly Rabbi Chaim Ozer Grodzienski, the unofficial Chief Rabbi of Vilna, arrived with a large sum of travel money and a message that the students of the Mir should all come to Vilna. Sunday, October 15, the *rebbeim* and yeshiva *bochrim* of the Mir all fled to Gorodetz, where they would continue by train to Vilna. Some hired wagons, while others fled on foot. The yeshiva's enormous library was packed in wagons, and many of those *sefarim* were later used in Shanghai to make copies for the use of the yeshiva *bochrim* studying there.

The same occurred in Kaminetz, Brisk, Baranovitch, Lomza, Slonim, Radin, Grodna, Kletz and Pinsk. All the Belarussian yeshiva centers moved to Vilna. And they all waited there, refugees with nothing to eat.

Yet as soon as they arrived, Rav Grodzienski took responsibility for their physical and spiritual welfare. Immediately he arranged for the Mir Yeshiva to move into a spacious *beis midrash* in a Vilna suburb, Novograd, where they would remain for a month. Moreover, through ongoing, superhuman efforts, he made sure that all the refugee yeshiva *bochrim* from all the yeshivas now in Vilna were provided with meals on a daily basis.

Yet despite the efforts of Rav Grodzienski, the move from the Mir yeshiva to Vilna took a psychological toll on some of the younger students.

Cut off from their families and finding themselves in what was considered a large city – Vilna had 200,000 inhabitants – many who had been away from home in yeshiva for most of the year without problem, suddenly felt disoriented and homesick. Under these circumstances, Boruch's younger brother Avraham Elye felt that he had to go home, especially when he heard that the yeshiva was about to move even further away to Keiden. Boruch tried to persuade him to stay with the yeshiva, citing the risks and dangers, but Avraham Elye felt an overwhelming need to see his parents and to be with them. Thus, sometime during the yeshiva's stay in Novograd, he set out for a return trip to Vishnevo. He was never seen again.

When a number of days had passed without his arriving home, both Boruch and his family in Vishnevo began to be very apprehensive. The family knew where he had been staying until then. They gave much of the wealth that remained in the home to a Christian girl to send her to Vilna to find him. When she came back she said she had not been able to find any clues of his whereabouts. The family suspected, but could not be sure, that Avraham Elye had been killed somewhere along the way. They never learned where or how this had occurred.

On October 28, 1939, the small Lithuanian army, with the permission of the Russians and the Germans, moved into Vilna, and all of those yeshiva boys were suddenly free again, part of the free world for a moment. The new Lithuanian authorities immediately took stock of the refugee situation that they had inherited and while they had nothing against yeshivas *per se*, they were unhappy to have so many refugees sitting together in Vilna. They therefore made plans to move all the refugee yeshivas to cities and towns outside of Vilna, but within the Vilna district.

Rabbi Eliezer Yehuda Finkel, the Rosh Yeshiva, wanted specifically to move the yeshiva to Keidan, a city further to the north which had a large, warm Jewish community and a satisfactory *beis midrash* that could house his students. The Lithuanians were displeased with that because while they wanted to take pressure off of the city of Vilna, they still wished to keep watch on all of the refugees inside the Vilna district. In the end, after incessant but unsuccessful pleas to allow the yeshiva to move to Keidan, a large payment finally convinced the Lithuanian authorities to allow the move.

For seven months, from November 1939 until June 1940, most of the students of the Mir Yeshiva were able to continue their studies under the Vilna government in the large, ancient study house of Keidan, as in the best of times, as though there was no world war raging in the south. There was a tradition amongst the Jews of Keiden that the Vilna Gaon himself had learned in that *beis midrash* in his youth.

Of course this was a very difficult period for Rabbi Milikowsky. His brother had disappeared and he blamed himself for having allowed him to go. Naturally, Rabbi Milikowsky in Keiden and his family in Vishnevo had hopes that he would still turn up alive, but those hopes diminished with each passing day. He was not in mourning. He could not be as long as he had no final word about his brother. Yet in some ways his situation was worse than mourning. Each day he awoke in hopes of hearing some good news, and each night he went to bed disappointed.

During this time, the people of Vishnevo were suffering at the hands of the Russian Communists, who on arrival had immediately begun to persecute the Jews religiously and culturally. The *cheders* and the Zionist Tarbut School were closed down. In their stead a Communist school was opened in which the language of instruction was Yiddish, but where nothing Jewish could be taught. Indeed, in the secularized Yiddish that they were forced to use, "Shabbos" was spelled with a *samech*. Some of the Zionist youth in Vishnevo began underground activities and succeeded in making contact with the Zionist headquarters in Vilna. One result of this was that they organized a group of youths to try to reach Vilna. Besides any other advantages of being in Vilna at this time under Lithuanian rule, there was more likelihood of a young Zionist with a British certificate being able to reach Eretz Yisrael from there.

In order for the Vishnevo youths to succeed in their attempt to reach Vilna, it was necessary for someone from Vilna to volunteer to meet them and smuggle them across the border from Poland into Lithuania. The person who volunteered to do this was Boruch Milikowsky. At an agreed-upon time, he went to the border and waited for the group with a few Christian assistants. Unfortunately, unknown to Boruch, one of the girls from the Vishnevo group became ill, and at the last minute the group decided to delay their departure by a week. While Boruch Milikowsky was waiting for them, fruitlessly, at the border, he was caught by the authorities and arrested. Although he was released unharmed soon afterwards, his arrest put an end to the Vishnevo attempt to penetrate Lithuania.

Rav Chaim Ozer Grodienski had done what was necessary to ensure that the refugee yeshiva *bochrim* were fed, and the Mir Yeshiva was well settled in Keiden so that its students were able to continue their studies undisturbed. However, for the Rosh Yeshiva, Rabbi Eliezer Yehuda Finkel, this was only the start of the struggle. From the moment that the yeshiva arrived in Lithuania, he began a twenty-four-hour-a-day effort to move his yeshiva to Eretz Yisrael. To achieve this, several things were necessary:

First, every student in the yeshiva would need a passport. In February of 1940, a student of the yeshiva, Yaakov Ederman, was sent by train to Kovno, where the British Consulate was located. Within the British Consulate was an office earmarked to handle the affairs of the Polish government in exile, which was in London. At the time, Poland did not exist, since it had been conquered by Russia and Germany. Ederman went to Kovno with nothing more than a photograph of each student. With these photos, he succeeded in receiving three hundred Polish passports, without any of the three hundred students having to leave the *beis midrash* for even a moment. There was no great demand at the time for Polish passports. Poland was not recognized by any other country and the passports were considered worthless. This probably made it easier for Ederman to attain them. Yet they later proved to be vital in saving the lives of the Mir community.

Second, Rav Finkel began to make every possible effort to acquire "certificates" from the Jewish Agency to allow his students to enter Eretz Yisrael. At the time, the British imposed an extremely strict quota on Jewish immigration in order to placate the Arabs. The 1939 McDonald White Paper limited immigration into Palestine to 15,000 persons per year at a time when hundreds of thousands could have immigrated. The Jewish Agency had the task of deciding which European Jews could come to Israel, and most of those who received certificates were long-time members of the various Zionist organizations. This precluded most of the yeshiva students from receiving one.

Rav Finkel implored Palestinian Chief Rabbi Yitzchak Isaac Herzog to go to England to plead before the British and Russian authorities to allow the thousands of yeshiva *bochrim* in Lithuania to move to Eretz Yisrael. Although Rav Herzog made the trip, he was unsuccessful in that request, which was his chief one. However, he succeeded in obtaining permission for dozens of great rabbis to come to Eretz Yisrael, and the Communists allowed them to travel by way of Odessa.

As it became increasingly clear that moving the yeshiva to Eretz Yisrael was not an option, the Rosh Yeshiva reluctantly began to explore other options. He sent Rabbi Eliezer Portnoy to Kovno to get advice from the Lithuanian authorities on how best to escape the war zone. The advice he received was to try to move the yeshiva to the Far East, specifically to Shanghai, which was owned by no country. To Rabbi Portnoy and to his contemporaries in the yeshiva community who later heard the suggestion, this advice seemed ridiculous, as though he had been told to go the moon.

Yet there were not many other options. One yeshiva activist, a Rabbi Margolis, turned to the consulates of more than thirty countries in Kovno seeking visas for the yeshiva students. His pleas fell on deaf ears. As the Germans slowly conquered more and more of Europe, the Far East option began to seem less absurd. In April of 1940, the Germans conquered Denmark and Norway; in early May they conquered Holland and Belgium; and by May 19 they had conquered France. There was no longer any western exit from the war.

Nevertheless, in that same month of May, something very strange happened in Kovno, the Lithuanian capital. The Japanese suddenly opened a consulate there. No one could imagine why, at a time when every other consulate was preparing to flee a looming war zone, Japan should open a consulate in Lithuania when they had never had one there before.

The Japanese appointed Chiune-Sempo Sugihara, an enigmatic figure, as consul. When he arrived in the Japanese consulate, he was under strict orders to issue no visas. In fact, no Japanese consulates anywhere were issuing visas. Japan was heavily overcrowded and there was a strict government policy against immigration of any kind.

Yet when representatives of the refugee yeshiva community in Lithuania approached him, describing their life-and-death situation and begging for visas to Japan, he was moved. A genuine humanitarian who had never met Jews before, he could not easily turn down their request, even at the expense of his government position. He took some days to consider and finally answered that he would be willing to give out transit visas as long as another final destination was already stamped in the passport. All that was needed was a country willing to be marked in the passport as the students' final destination.

Enter here Nosson Gutwirth and Leo Sternheim, two Dutch nationals who were students at the Telshe Yeshiva. They recalled that Holland, their birthplace, had control over the Antilles Islands, off the coast of Venezuela in the Caribbean Sea. One of those islands was Curaçao. The two students decided to approach the Dutch Consul in Kovno, Jan Swartendijk to ask if the yeshiva students could be granted visas to Curaçao as a final destination.

At first, Swartendijk argued that since Curaçao required no visa at all, he could not grant one. Yet when the students implored him, making it clear that it was visas in writing that they needed, he agreed to create a special stamp that said, "The Dutch consulate hereby confirms that no visa is required for entry to Curaçao by foreigners."

The students then returned to Sugihara, who accepted the Curaçao stamps and added the stamp of the Japanese transit visa to their passports as well.

At just this moment there was some disturbing, if inevitable, news. In June of 1940, the Soviets, on trumped-up charges of "insubordination," forced the establishment of a Communist puppet government in Lithuania. Communism reigned again. The yeshiva boys, after barely eight months of freedom and seven months in Keiden, were trapped once more. It looked as though their move had not helped them. They had found a way to get papers that would provide them with a way out of Lithuania, but now they were once more under the control of the Communists, for whom a request to leave was a one-way ticket to Siberia.

There was other bad news as well. Since the Mir Yeshiva's arrival in October of 1939, Rav Chaim Ozer Grodzienski had been the yeshiva's patron, undertaking to ensure the physical and spiritual welfare of its students. Now he was deathly ill.

But the yeshiva community did not fall into despair. They moved forward with the plans to get exit visas. Starting on July 9, 1940, Sempo Sugihara and his staff worked around the clock preparing the transit visas for the Polish passports of the yeshiva students, asking only a nominal fee in return. At one point, when the administration of the Mir yeshiva asked him to mass-produce the visas without the yeshiva students' having to come to Kovno to receive them, he agreed. As if that were not enough, there was even a period of time when one of the yeshiva students of the Mir, Moshe Zupnik, was permitted to stay in the Japanese Consulate by himself late at night in order to continue processing Japanese transit visas when the rest of the staff had gone home.

August brought more bad news. The Russians decreed that the Mir Yeshiva would have to leave Keiden on August 5th. Four days later, on August 9th, calamity struck when Rabbi Chaim Ozer Grodzienski passed away. The next day, the Russians officially annexed Lithuania.

Once more, all the burden of seeing to the yeshiva's welfare fell upon the shoulders of Rav Eliezer Yehuda Finkel, the Rosh Yeshiva.

Fortunately, Rav Grodzienski had left matters better off than they had been originally. The American Joint Distribution Committee was providing each student with a monthly stipend, even if the sum was insufficient. When matters deteriorated with Rav Grodzienski's passing, Rav Finkel started taking the allotment meant for himself and his family and putting it back in the yeshiva till. His wife, Rebbetzin Malke, was forced to take her own husband to a *din Torah* (rabbinical court) in order to demand that he return the money needed for the family's survival.

As decreed, on August 5th the new Communist regime forced the Mir Yeshiva to disperse to four cities: Krak, Shat, Remigola and Krakinova. Attempts at bribes and entreaties proved fruitless. One of the yeshiva's teachers was placed in charge of each group of students. Meanwhile, the Rosh Yeshiva chose to remain out of the limelight, all by himself, in a fifth city, Grinkishok, the better to continue his efforts on behalf of the yeshiva.

When the Russians annexed Lithuania, all of the foreign consulates in Kovno were ordered to close down. However, Sugihara still had much work to do to prepare transit visas for the thousands who were requesting them. Reports of his willingness to help had spread, and many who originally had been skeptical were now standing in line to receive the visas. For three weeks, he made excuses for not closing down the consulate. Finally, at the beginning of September 1940, he closed down his consulate and left Kovno. He had issued more than 2,000 transit visas for the Jews in Lithuania.

When Sugihara was asked, "Isn't this dangerous for you?" he said that he could not refuse people who were trying to flee from the cellars of Russia. When he completed his task, he was demoted and transferred to Bucharest. The Yad Vashem Holocaust Memorial Authority in Israel eventually recognized Sugihara as one of the Righteous among the Nations for his work in saving the lives of six thousand Jews.

Now that the students of the Mir Yeshiva, together with many others, had visas to Curaçao and transit visas to Japan, they needed only one other thing in order to escape Communist Russia – exit visas from the Soviet authorities. Yet since the Russian Revolution in 1917, such exit visas had been difficult to obtain and dangerous to ask for. Since Stalin's rise to power in 1935, getting a visa had been virtually impossible. Anyone who dared request such a thing – to flee the "Communist Workers' Paradise of Justice and Equality" – was declared an enemy of the state and exiled to Siberia. Readers will recall what happened to hundreds of thousands of Jews only nine months before, in January 1940, when the Soviets tricked them into asking for exit visas.

Still, it was impossible to live as a Jew in Communist Lithuania. The Nazis were not far off, and there were no guarantees of what the future would bring.

Suddenly the Russians opened "emigration offices" in Vilna and Kovno. Everyone asked, "What is the meaning of this? Is this another trick?" People thought they had a pretty good idea of where such "emigration" might lead to.

A group of senior students from the Mir Yeshiva decided to try the *Goral ha-Gaon*, the lots system of Rabbi Elijah of Vilna for seeking out God's advice by means of a randomly chosen verse from Scripture. The result was the verse, Exodus 19:4: "I will carry you on eagles' wings and bring you to Me."

They understood this to mean that God would save the yeshiva *bochrim* and also that the German "eagle" would let them go.

The Mir Yeshiva was the first yeshiva to submit requests for visas. In November of 1940, two months after the Russian "emigration offices" had opened, the yeshiva administration gathered up the three hundred passports of its students and submitted them en masse to the "emigration office" – really the secret police – in Kovno. It turned out that this time, there would be no streamlining. Every individual applicant would have to come on his own to Kovno to meet the "emigration officials" and to fill out forms divulging much personal information. This was not a good omen.

Now came two months of waiting. The other yeshivas waiting in Lithuania were more cautious. They feared submitting the requests, and some even felt foreboding over the fact that the Mir Yeshiva had submitted requests. Yet in January of 1941 came surprising news. All the Mir Yeshiva's requests had been accepted! Now all the two thousand others holding

Japanese transit visas rushed to apply for exit visas just as the Mir Yeshiva had done, and theirs were approved as well.

It was at this time that the Rosh Yeshiva, Rabbi Eliezer Yehuda Finkel, traveled with his family to Eretz Yisrael. Now that the welfare of his students was assured, he could finally allow himself to take advantage of the certificates he possessed to travel via Odessa to Eretz Yisrael. He still had hopes that from Eretz Yisrael he would be in a better position to help the yeshiva students to come to Israel.

The success of the two thousand in receiving exit visas remains impossible to explain in non-miraculous terms. Somehow, high-level Russian policy regarding emigration had changed, at least at that moment. Eye-witnesses saw the head of the Kovno Secret Police headquarters, an anti-Semitic Jew named Schlossberg, shaking with anger and mumbling to himself as he was forced to carry out that policy, working long days preparing exit visas for two thousand Jews.

Immediately groups of students from the Mir Yeshiva began to prepare themselves for the train trip of more than ten thousand kilometers that they would have to take from Kovno to Vladivostok on the eastern edge of the Soviet empire. The first twenty-five students were charged only twenty dollars, the standard price for Russian citizens making this trip on the Trans-Siberian Railroad. Any student in the Mir Yeshiva could afford this price by selling a few used clothing items, and so they set out on their way. Yet by the time the second group arrived to make the trip, the Soviet Authorities had realized their "oversight." The students were turned away and told that each ticket would cost not twenty but one hundred seventy dollars, the "tourist" price for this trip. They would have six weeks to come up with the money or their exit visas would be void.

Without delay, the Mir Yeshiva administration got in touch by telegram with Rabbi Avraham Kalmanovitz, who had been connected with the yeshiva while it was in Mir. The year before, he had succeeded in reaching the United States and in opening a yeshiva there which he, too, called "Mir." He was also very active in the Va'ad ha-Hatzalah, the rescue committee to aid the Jews of Eastern Europe. He got to work immediately, traveling day and night in search of funds, organizing meetings and making speeches, and very quickly he had organized the money needed to buy each student a ticket at the new price. Thus, from January to March, 1941, all the students of the Mir yeshiva set out for the two-week trip to Vladivostok.

Russian trains were notorious for their overcrowding, their spartan wooden benches, the cold in the winter and the heat in the summer. Yet one odd result of the fact that Mir Yeshiva had been forced to pay as "tourists" was that they traveled the ten thousand kilometers in style, as first-class passengers, in soft, comfortable chairs and in cars with central heating. Because they could not eat the food in the dining car, they were provided with reimbursement to purchase kosher food of their own choosing to eat on board. Yet their tourist status did not affect their preferred form of "recreation." A Western European non-Jew who traveled with the students had the following to say:

> Their behavior during all hours of the day was strange. They never ceased to argue with one another. The arguments, between individuals and groups, stormed and raged all day long. Yet it became clear that these were not fights, but lofty debates between learned individuals, between whom love and brotherhood reigned. The debates went on while all the time the debaters were holding large, open books, and it was clear that these books were the source of the debates, and what those books said also held the resolutions to the debates.... (Translated from a quotation in *Ha-zerihah be-fa'atei kedem*).

The refugees arrived in Vladivostok. There they all were housed in a hotel, waiting for a suitable boat to bring them to Japan. The waiting stretched into weeks. It was maddening to be so close to freedom while still behind the Iron Curtain, vulnerable to Soviet Russia's devices.

Finally it was decided that the first boat that seemed reasonably seaworthy would be hired. That boat was a Japanese transit steamer called the *Amkoza Maro*. Men, women and children in groups of hundreds boarded that boat for the two-day trip to Japan. Each group crammed the boat beyond capacity. People slept on the deck. The boat rocked from side to side. Several days after its last trip, with the last of the refugees safely on Japanese soil, the old boat, now empty, split in two and sank. There was no reason why this should not have happened while hundreds of refugees were crammed into the boat, far beyond its capacity. No matter. The Mir Yeshiva was now safely in Japan.

Chapter 6

SHANGHAI

IN JAPAN THEY HAD PERMITS to remain for two weeks, yet these permits
became permanent *de facto.* This would not have come about without the
monumental efforts of Professor Setsuzo Kotsuji, who was the secretary of
the Japanese foreign minister, Yasuke Matzuoke. At the time, Kotsuji was
becoming more and more attached to Judaism. Ultimately he converted,
taking the name Abraham. He wrote the book *From Tokyo to Jerusalem,* and
when he died in 1973 he was buried in the Sanhedria cemetery in Jerusalem.

When he was in the U.S., several of the refugees of Yeshivas Mir and
other yeshivas wrote a letter encouraging the establishment of a fund to
provide support for Professor Kotsuji in New York. They describe his
efforts as follows:

> During those days of hatred of Israel, which flowed from the lands
> of blood in Germany and which spread to the Far East, Professor
> Kotsuji wandered the length and breadth of Japan lecturing against
> anti-Semitism. He also published a special book defending the Jews.
> He strove greatly on our behalf to attain permits for us to move
> from Vladivostok to Kobe. And after we were already in Kobe, he
> would travel every day to Tokyo to persuade the government to
> extend our visas. He also expended a very large sum of money to
> sway the local authorities in favor of those permits.
>
> For his efforts on our behalf he raised the suspicions of the
> Japanese government and was imprisoned under harsh conditions,
> where he miraculously avoided death. There was no one like him in
> the whole world. There was no one like him in all of Japan, not

during the last two thousand years, and not from then until this very day.

Precisely then Professor Kotsuji appeared, and with indescribable self-sacrifice he produced enormous sums of money from his own pocket to help the refugees. No one knew where he got the money that he used to bribe the local authorities, taking them to dinner in the fanciest hotel in the city. During the revelry of these meals he would implore the high-ranking officials to provide the Jews with permanent resident visas.

In September of 1941, three months before Japan joined the war, it was decided to move the Jews from Japan to Shanghai, where there were already approximately 26,000 Jewish refugees. The visas were no longer any good for their remaining in Japan. The moment Japan entered the war, all the white citizens in Japan were put into prisons and concentration camps. But the Jewish refugees were no longer there. They were in Shanghai.

In Shanghai a question arose. Where would the Mir Yeshiva students learn? They needed a yeshiva. After all, they had learned on the train. They certainly needed to learn in the place they would be for the next five years.

Shanghai had a Jewish community. Yet far from the Jewish community, in the commercial district, amongst the fanciest buildings, was a synagogue called Beit Aharon, or "the Synagogue on the Museum street." Until then, the synagogue had been in almost complete disuse. It was a majestic edifice, fully furnished, with various types of halls, auditoriums and kitchen facilities. It had been erected ten years before these Jews arrived in Shanghai. A Jewish philanthropist from Baghdad, purportedly one of the wealthiest Jews in the Middle East, Silas Aaron Hardoon, dreamed that he had to build a synagogue. Because of that dream, he built that enormous complex, a white elephant whose intended use was unclear.

The refugees arrived ten years later. The largest group was the Mir Yeshiva, with 250 students. It was discovered that the Beit Aharon sanctuary had precisely 250 seats. Photographs of the boys learning showed every seat taken.

When the Mir Yeshiva community arrived in Shanghai, they were herded into the Hongkew section of the city, where 100,000 Chinese natives lived. This section, the most squalid in Shanghai, was also the only section then under Japanese control. Other Jewish communities from western Europe, which were better off than the new refugees, continued to live in other sections of Shanghai.

For the Mir Yeshiva, the first year in Shanghai was the worst. Yeshiva boys sickened from malnutrition. There was little aid coming in from the outside. Still, the Chinese in Hongkew were much worse off than the refugees there. Although the Jewish refugees lived in one-room apartments, the Chinese had seven or ten people in each one-room apartment. They literally had nothing. Each morning, the corpses of Chinese natives who had died of hunger would be found lying in the streets.

The 250 unmarried yeshiva boys of the Mir ate in the Beit Aharon complex where they learned. The twenty-five married families of the Mir Yeshiva ate at home, purchasing food with stipends they received from the yeshiva. Yet it wasn't easy for a Mir kollel wife to go to the grocery in Hongkew. In the words of one kollel wife, "You couldn't walk through the streets holding a piece of bread. If the Chinese saw the bread, you wouldn't make it home with that bread."

They needed *sefarim*. When Shanghai was an international city, many pirate publishing houses sprang up. It was not necessary to worry about copyright since there were no copyright laws. Two Mir boys with initiative availed themselves of one of those printing presses and printed all the books they would need to learn. Every yeshiva brought a *sefer* or two that they would need, and they were all printed at this press.

Rabbi Boruch Milikowsky spent five years learning Torah with his fellow yeshiva students in Shanghai. Naturally, however, it was a time of mourning for him as well. First there was his sorrow over his brother's disappearance, and this involved his own feelings of guilt, which was natural, if unjustified. Later on, it became clear to Rabbi Milikowsky and to most of the other students that there was a good chance that they had lost other members of their own families as well, even if they did not yet know exactly whom.

Rabbi Milikowsky chose to deal with his suffering and angst by means of two therapeutic remedies available to him: hard work and the performance of good deeds, and sometimes the two were intertwined. When the Mir Yeshiva arrived in Shanghai, one of the students, a close friend of Rabbi Milikowsky named Moshe Lidsky, of Slonim, was placed in charge of the kitchen, where food was prepared for 250 students. He immediately hired a Chinese cook, and that cook chose four other Chinese locals to help him. Yet much hard work still remained, besides, of course, kashrut supervision. This additional work was performed by a number of volunteers from the yeshiva itself. Rabbi Milikowsky was one of those who quickly stepped forward to volunteer his services.

There was another aspect to Rabbi Milikowsky's therapy, for which we fortunately have the eye-witness testimony of Rebbetzin Taibel Wernick, the widow of Rabbi Henoch Fishman. Rebbetzin Wernick was a seventeen-year-old girl from Slonim when she left her family in 1941 and fled north to Vilna where, like the two thousand other people following the lead of the Mir Yeshiva, she applied for an exit visa. Despite the success of the Mir Yeshiva in attaining these visas, there was still a tremendous risk involved. In February of 1941, she received her exit permit with a group of eleven people who had applied with her. Yet the same day that she and they got their permits, another list of sixty-four who supposedly were going to receive permits never did. Instead they disappeared, sent to Siberia.

When Taibel Sharashefsky arrived at the Trans-Siberian railway to board her train east, she was not allowed to take anything of value with her. She came wearing a ring on her finger. The Russians removed the ring and gave her a receipt for it, saying, "If you come back within six months, you can have the ring back."

In Jewish Shanghai there were almost no appropriate matches for the Mirrer students, but Taibel Sharashefsky was a God-fearing young woman who had studied in a Polish Bais Yaakov school. Rabbi Henoch Fishman was one of the older and more illustrious scholars in the Mir

Yeshiva in Shanghai. He would say a *shiur* for a small number of students. After he arrived in America, he was asked to give a *shiur* at the Mir Yeshiva in Brooklyn. Taibel Sharashefsky was quickly introduced to Rabbi Fishman and the couple wed.

In a yeshiva community where almost no one was married, the presence of a young couple who soon had an infant worked like a magnet, attracting students of the Mir yeshiva who missed their families, their homes, their younger siblings, the sight of a baby. The Fishmans entertained numerous guests from among the yeshiva community. One of the early guests was Moshe Lidsky, her *landsman* from Slonim, who brought along his good friend Boruch Milikowsky. They became regular guests in the Fishman home. Sixty years later, Rebbetzin Fishman Wernick has clear memories of Rabbi Milikowsky from those days. She says:

> Regarding anything associated with doing favors for anyone, Reb Boruch was the one who was always on the spot. In my private life, I was watching his behavior and I was amazed. He was unforgettable. As far as a *baal chessed* (a performer of kind deeds), you couldn't have anybody more outstanding than he was.

Rebbetzin Wernick provided a number of examples to back up her claim:

If They Don't Have Bread…

Almost her first contact with Rabbi Milikowsky was when she was about to get married. She had come out to Shanghai alone, and she had no relatives with her to prepare her wedding or to be present at it. In fact, she was almost the only one still alive from her family. She had a sister and brother-in-law in the United States, but during that first year, the Shanghai yeshiva community was totally cut off from the outside. Otherwise, her sister would gladly have sent her funds to prepare a wedding, and much more besides. The wedding, as was often the custom, took place on Friday afternoon, and the wedding feast and first *sheva berachos* were going to be a modest Friday night dinner at the home of the Rosh Yeshiva, Rav Chaim Shmuelevitz.

Some marriages, due to circumstances beyond anyone's control, begin with "no-frills" weddings, even if the married life that follows is long and rich and joyful. Such was the case here. It was the Mir Yeshiva's first year in Shanghai and severe austerity was the rule. Yet sometime before Shabbos, there was a knock on the door of the Shmuelevitzes' small apartment. It was Boruch Milikowsky and Menachem Kravitzky, and they were holding a wedding cake. Having sensed that a surprise wedding cake would enhance the joy of bride and groom, they had gone out unasked and arranged that someone, somehow, should bake such a cake. Sixty years later, that bride, Rebbetzin Wernick, recalls how much happiness this small touch brought her on her wedding day.

Helping a Captive

After Pearl Harbor, when Japan officially began to fight the Allies, the Japanese took over all of Shanghai and they made Hongkew a "Designated Area for Stateless Refugees" – in a word, a ghetto. All the western European Jews who had been living in the nicer neighborhoods of Shanghai were now moved into that one-square-mile ghetto, and now they also had to suffer the horrible conditions of the more recent refugees.

There was a curfew, and most Jews were not allowed to leave the ghetto. Yet the Mir Yeshiva students somehow managed to obtain special passes enabling them to continue leaving Hongkew to go to their yeshiva.

One time, however, Rabbi Fishman was thrown into jail by the Japanese. There was some mix-up involving his pass. He was arrested late on a Friday afternoon.

Being thrown into a Japanese jail was no laughing matter. Many people jailed by the Japanese died of typhoid fever. The jail was an open place. It was already after Succos when it was wet and cold.

By the time his wife knew what had happened to her husband, it was after candle-lighting. The jailers let it be understood that if somebody came and threw in a coat and some food to Rabbi Fishman, they would not confiscate it. Who volunteered on Friday night to find these items and to bring them to Rabbi Fishman? Rabbi Boruch Milikowsky. He found a heavy coat and some food and drink, and he brought them to the jail and succeeded in getting them to Rabbi Fishman. Rabbi Fishman's widow concludes the story as follows:

> In the end, my husband spent three nights in jail. He was released on Monday. It was proven to the police that there had been an error. Whatever the circumstances, it was a great miracle.
>
> My husband did get sick and he did get typhoid. He was on the critical list for four months. But he came out of it.
>
> This concern for other people was Reb Boruch. If you want to know who Reb Boruch was, that is who he was.

A Guest Who Stayed Late

It is no coincidence that the Japanese chose Hongkew as their ghetto for the Jews. It was sitting right on top of their main munitions dump. If the Allies ever attempted to bomb that site, Hongkew would suffer. Hence, the hundred thousand Chinese who lived in Hongkew were the poorest of the poor.

Sure enough, in 1944, the Americans began air strikes employing B-29 bombers. The following story, quoted in Rebbetzin Wernick's own words, occurred during August of 1945, just after the Americans bombed Hiroshima.

> I'll tell you a little something about my private connection with Reb Boruch. We used to have air raids in Shanghai. There were air raids during the war! Sometimes people were hurt. And I was hurt in one of those air raids. It was Friday night.
>
> When our apartment building was bombed, there was a crack in the wall. I mean, the house didn't fall down. A picture fell off and a part fell on my leg. A lot of people were killed. A lot of the Chinese were killed and a lot of the German Jews were killed.

Shabbos they had to operate on the leg, and then they brought me back home. I was not allowed to get out of the bed. My leg was in a brace. My oldest son was a year and a half old. I had been told that I was not allowed to move for seven days.

Saturday night we were preparing for the next night for another set of air raids. We didn't know what was going to happen. The boys were very friendly with us. There was Reb Boruch and all his friends. They were here with us always. My house was always full. They were always there. And then it emptied out. By eleven o'clock, only Reb Boruch was sitting there. I said, "Why are you sitting here? It's time for you to go to sleep!" I also wanted to go to sleep. It was late! He said, "What do you think – I'm going to sleep? You're going to stay here by yourself with your husband and your baby? And what happens if we have another air raid? How will you get out of here by yourself? I'm not going home. I'm not going to sleep."

I hadn't said anything. Nobody had asked him. Nobody had told him. Nobody else had volunteered, however close the rest of them were to us. And there was no place to lie down. We lived in one room. It was the ghetto. In one room! There wasn't a spare bed or anything like that. There was hardly a chair to sit on. "No, no!" he said. "I'm going to leave you alone here?"

His room was not far away. Only five minutes. If he wanted to he could have run over to us when there was an attack. But no, he wanted to be immediately on hand. He showed responsibility without being asked, without anyone having to mention anything.

There were other boys living in the same building as we. There were four Polish rabbis living in the room on top of me. Our building had four one-room apartments. Yet Reb Boruch didn't say, "Let someone else do it." He was there!

This was so typical of him!

65

As far as the idea of coming running to offer assistance during an air raid attack itself, that wasn't always possible, as the following story will indicate:

Air Raid

There was another air raid. Reb Boruch and a friend were with us at that moment. Reb Boruch had eaten something and was lying down on the couch. My husband was learning in a house five minutes away.

Suddenly the sirens began to wail. My little boy woke up. Boruch ran over to him and tried to shield him. My little son got so scared that it took a half hour until he got his speech back. My husband was five minutes away, but he couldn't get home. When there were air raids, the streets got closed off. The Japanese air raid wardens didn't let people get in and out. Yet my husband later told me that he was sitting and learning, but he wanted to be learning at home, because he was worried about us. But no, they didn't have a chance. As my husband sat in that room, the ceiling fell down on top of him. They were in a room on a top floor. Yet nothing happened to him! Now do you know what *hashgacha pratis* [Divine Providence] is?

Permit me to conclude this section with a few more words from Rebbetzin Wernick on Divine Providence as evidenced in Shanghai:

In one air raid, a thousand Chinese were killed all around us. The Ghetto was in the middle of the city.

If anybody believes in *hashgacha pratis*, you can see it from what happened to the yeshiva. People in Shanghai died from typhoid. They died from beri-beri. They died from dysentery. Some of the German Jewish refugees died. They had better facilities. They had better food. They had more money. The Mir Yeshiva boys didn't have anything. The second and third year (as the Va'ad Hatzalah managed to arrange money transfers from America) there was already food. The first year was *mamash* starvation!

Yet you know what? No one from the yeshiva was killed. One boy passed away there, but it had nothing to do with Shanghai. His stomach wasn't well before he arrived there. But the yeshiva remained complete. As many as came in, whoever came in, that was who came out! Baruch Hashem!

You could see! I mean, I remember experiencing an air raid. I was standing there. There was no place to run to. So we were standing and watching the way things were flying. Through the window! Because where could you go? There weren't any shutters on the windows. I mean – glass windows and that's all. You saw pieces flying through the air in mid-afternoon.

And the bombs. What did they bomb? The munitions dump. Where did they put the ghetto? On top of the munitions dump. Right? The Americans started to score direct hits. They hit the edge of the munitions dump, and pieces started flying from there. We were there. The Lubliner Yeshiva was there. And a lot of our families. Rav Mendel Kaplan was living there with his family. And pieces were flying all over us. You could see! And one huge piece like the wall of a tank – I don't know what it was – landed on the roof of our building. Under that, one of the Mir yeshiva boys was sitting and learning by the table. Yet the only result was that the key got stuck in the door. That's it!

Chapter 7

THE NAZIS ARRIVE IN BELARUS

AT THE DAWN OF SUNDAY, June 22, 1941, just a few months after the last of the Mir scholars was safely in Japan, the Germans broke their agreement with Russia and attacked Russia's half of Poland from the west, in what was called the Barbarossa Campaign. Soon, they entered Vishnevo. Right away, they made their presence felt in very uncomfortable ways. The first thing they did was to take Elyakim, the third Milikowsky brother, to a labor camp. They passed humiliating decrees such as one that Jews weren't allowed to walk on the sidewalk but had to walk in the middle of the street. After a short while, they began to demand high ransoms of the Jewish community. Then, they would beat the representatives who came to hand over the money. A few weeks later, the Germans began to kill one or two Jews every day on various cruel pretexts.

For a month or so, the Milikowsky family were able to remain in their own home. Then, one night in July, thirty-eight men were taken out of their homes, shot dead, and dropped into a pit which had been prepared for that purpose. Almost immediately, the Nazis confiscated all of the Jewish homes and moved all of the Jews into a ghetto, which included Krave street and the synagogue court.

There was a wall around the Vishnevo Ghetto, with barbed wire at the top. Anyone caught outside was killed instantly. There was a large gate to the street of the Ghetto. There were Jewish policemen and a Judenrat. When the Germans wanted something, they told the Judenrat. Some people worked chopping down trees or making roads. They had a permit to leave the Ghetto. Otherwise, they wouldn't be allowed to leave.

The Jews cooked, cleaned, washed clothes and did all the menial work of the Nazis. Once in the Ghetto, Boruch's sister Minna was taken as well to work for the Germans. Ten German soldiers had a place near the railroad station, about six kilometers from Vishnevo. Minna and her future husband Noah's stepsister used to walk the six kilometers to work every morning. As the winter of 1941–1942 approached, it became very cold. Early one morning, her father got up and tore up a precious blanket. He then proceeded to wrap it around her legs so they wouldn't freeze. Many Jews were suffering from overexposure.

By this point, the Milikowskys were having to sell things in order to obtain food. They sold all their linens, their clothing, pillows, blankets – anything they had in the house. They would have Minna or Elyakim take the items out of the ghetto when they went to work, and they would sell them on the outside in exchange for food. That is how they ate at that time.

The Milikowskys no longer had any savings. Any spare money had always been invested back into the farm, which was now gone. There had been some gold, but it had gone to Boruch and Avraham Elye to cover their expenses in yeshiva.

In the ghetto, one large house which had belonged to one of Shmuel Milikowsky's brothers, henceforth housed all the Milikowsky brothers and sisters and their families. It was not easy to live that way.

During all this time, units of Nazi soldiers were traveling around amongst the small towns of Belarus, massacring them one by one. On November 9, 1941 the massacre of the Mir community took place. All the town's Jews were killed, including Rav Avrohom Tzvi Kamai, the town's chief rabbi and a Rosh Yeshiva in the Mir Yeshiva. Rav Kamai had wanted to go north to Vilna with the Mir Yeshiva, but had decided to stay with his community so as not to abandon them in their time of woe. Now he died with them. Ten months later, the bell tolled for Vishnevo as well.

What follows is a brief essay by Samuel Podberesky, son of Rabbi Milikowsky's sister Minna. The essay, written in 1992, includes one of the few eyewitness accounts of the Vishnevo massacre of September 15, 1942, received from Samuel's father Noah, who was one of the few survivors.

COMMEMORATION

by Samuel Podberesky

Persons of the Jewish faith commemorate the deaths of their immediate family members each year by saying a memorial prayer, the Kaddish, on the dates their loved ones died. Many Holocaust survivors, since they have no way of knowing the exact dates on which their family members were killed by the Nazis, have had to choose the dates for commemoration. However, my parents, who survived the Holocaust with the partisans in the forests of what is now Belarus, know exactly when their families were slaughtered since my father was an eyewitness, the only Jewish eyewitness who escaped death. That date this year coincided with September 15, two weeks before the Jewish New Year and fifty years after the Jewish community of my parent's hometown, Vishnevo, was massacred by the Nazis and their supporters. Fiftieth anniversaries always have a special significance; however, this one took on even greater importance since it commemorated an episode in the greatest crime ever perpetrated against humanity, while the vivid memory of that crime and its witnesses are rapidly fading from this earth. The tragedy and the lesson it teaches must not be forgotten.

To truly comprehend the commemoration and the magnitude of the crime involved, one must know exactly what happened fifty years ago in places like Vishnevo. That town of about three thousand people was no different from thousands of similar towns throughout Poland, Russia and the rest of Eastern Europe whose Jewish communities were destroyed. In 1941, a year before the slaughter, the German army took Vishnevo from the Soviet army. The Germans quickly went about solidifying their control, enlisting the support of local Polish and Belarussian officials and placing the entire Jewish community of one thousand people in an enclosed ghetto in one section of the town. Soon, thirty-eight Jewish men were rounded up in the ghetto, falsely accused of crimes by local gentiles at the invitation of the Nazis, and executed publicly by firing squad after digging their own graves. This was a warning to anyone thinking of resistance. At the time, there was no news of mass extermination and the Jews of Vishnevo believed that if German authority was respected they would survive. Their trust in the intelligence, rationality and humanity of the Nazis and their helpers was misplaced.

My parents' families had lived in Vishnevo for generations. Their families, made up of farmers, storekeepers and artisans, were large. Trapped in the ghetto were their parents, a grandparent, five brothers and sisters and dozens of uncles, aunts, nephews, nieces, and cousins. The families had been responsible and respected members of the community – at least the Jewish community. Since anti-Semitism was ingrained among the non-Jewish population of Vishnevo, it is unlikely that many of the town's gentiles respected Jews.

In 1942, the Nazi leadership decided to systematically exterminate European Jewry. Most people in our country are aware of the concentration camps, such as Treblinka, where millions of people were gassed, worked or starved to death. Relatively few people realize, however, that hundreds of thousands, if not millions, of Jews who lived in smaller towns and too far from extermination camps were killed where they lived by traveling execution units made up of SS troops, Gestapo, and Nazi sympathizers. These units were made up of small contingents of soldiers with several trucks and machine guns. In the spring and summer of 1942, these units murdered their way through what was before the war eastern Poland and what is now northwestern Belarus. Vishnevo was a one-day stop.

By the day of the slaughter, the Jews of Vishnevo had heard rumors that nearby communities had been destroyed. But few could believe the rumors, and most were too old or too young to escape or were taking care of someone who could not withstand the rigors that escape would entail. In any event, escape was only an unrealistic dream: they were a thousand miles behind German lines, the gentile population was made up largely of Jew haters, and most of those who might have helped Jews did not because they feared retribution from the Nazis or their sympathizers. For these reasons and probably dozens more, one thousand Jewish men, women and children waited in the Vishnevo ghetto for their execution on the seventeenth day of the month of Elul, according to the Jewish lunar calendar.

The morning of the seventeenth started out like most other days in Vishnevo – the roosters crowed and the weather was not unusual for that time of the year. The rest of the day, however, was like a scene from hell. Jews in the ghetto were rounded up by German soldiers, local police and other town officials. They were forced to wait on their knees until they were all gathered in front of the two town synagogues. Then, while the town band played, they were marched through the streets to a wheat field just outside of the town. The wheat had been cleared for several hundred yards to provide a clear field of fire for the machine guns that had been set up at the field's edge. The Jews were marched out in lines, one row in back of the other, starting twenty or thirty yards in front of the machine guns. German soldiers and local police blocked any escape to the sides. At an officer's command, the machine gunners opened fire. Some people ran, some could not, and some tried to protect their children or parents. But no one escaped except my father, who had military training and was fast and lucky enough to reach the uncut wheat and flee to the nearby forest. Before nightfall, when he left the wheat field, my father saw the SS troops and their helpers walk among the dead, shooting any living adult they found. They did not waste bullets on the small children they found alive. The dead were then moved to an unfinished wood house nearby where they were doused with gasoline and set ablaze. The children who survived the shooting were thrown into the flames alive. My father hears their screams to this day. The plot was later covered with dirt, and one more small town in Europe was *Judenrein.*

Rabbi Milikowsky was not the only member of his immediate family to survive. His sister Minna was away in a labor detail, outside the ghetto, on the day of the massacre. She and her fellow workers heard that the massacre was taking place, so they did not return home. A Christian girl hid them in a barn.

When they heard that the massacre had happened, they fled the place where they were working. At this point, Minna found a rifle on the ground. There were many rifles lying around because many fleeing Russian soldiers had left their rifles behind. She took the rifle and kept it with her as she decided on her next move.

Unfortunately, her brother Elyakim, who was also on a work detail, had chosen to return to the ghetto just before the massacre to bring the family some flour. He was caught in the ghetto on the day of the massacre and could not escape.

Minna Milikowsky spent several months hiding in the homes of non-Jewish families who had benefited from her parents' benevolence and integrity. When it became too difficult for those families to protect her, she took her rifle and went to the forest to join the Jewish partisans, where she remained until 1944, when the Russians liberated the forests where the partisans were hiding.

That year, she married Noah Podberesky of Vishnevo, who had also been with the partisans and who had been decorated as a war hero by the Russians for his efforts against the Nazis during the war. Alas, her father's prophecy about her receiving no dowry proved only too true. Minna was married two years after her parents and four of her siblings were murdered in the Vishnevo massacre of September 1942.

With the end of the war came new lives for both Minna and her brother Boruch.

Part II

BALTIMORE – THE EARLY YEARS

Chapter 8

NEW LIVES IN AMERICA

AFTER THE WAR, Rabbi Milikowsky's sister Minna and her husband Noah were placed in a refugee camp in Austria. Working with the Labor Zionist Beriha group, they were smuggled south to Italy with the goal of moving to Eretz Yisrael. Minna now had many relatives living there who had arrived safely before the war. These included most of her mother's family, as well as her father's baby brother Velfke, who was now called Ze'ev and lived in Haifa.

Minna was five months pregnant when she and Noah arrived in Italy. It became clear that any attempt they now made to reach the Land of Israel would be considered illegal by the British, who controlled the Mandate. In her condition, Minna was in no position to risk her baby by resuming the lifestyle she had known while running and hiding with the partisans in the forests. She had already had a taste of that while she was being smuggled from Austria to Italy. The couple decided that they had no choice but to change their destination to the United States.

In the meantime, Minna's brother Boruch, who had been out of contact with her for the last six years, had gone with the Mir Yeshiva to New York, traveling via San Francisco. In New York, he found out about Minna's whereabouts. She was in France by then, trying to arrange for her and her husband's immigration to the United States. While continuing to learn in the Mir Yeshiva, he now began to think about ways to bring over his sister.

During this time, the Mir Yeshiva asked him to try his hand at fundraising on their behalf. Rabbi Milikowsky had a pleasant, humble personality coupled with healthy self-esteem, a sharp wit, much homespun wisdom and Torah learning. He also had a good deal of demonstrated skill at dealing with the outside world and profound love for and commitment to the Mir Yeshiva. He was also still unmarried, which would make travel easier for him. He was ideal for the job.

In sending out students as fundraisers, the Mir Yeshiva genuinely wished to raise funds to cover expenses. Yet there was another intention as well. More than two hundred European yeshiva scholars now found themselves in a new world. Giving them jobs as traveling fundraisers was a way to allow them to explore their new environment. It facilitated their deciding where they most wished to continue their lives and what they wanted to do there.

During a fundraising trip to Rochester, New York on behalf of the Mir Yeshiva, Rabbi Milikowsky silently considered opening a *yeshiva gedola* in that area. Later on, he was sent to Baltimore for an extended period of time to handle fundraising there.

During the 1940s, the Jewish Community of Baltimore showed exemplary compassion in caring for and rehabilitating the many refugees who were emerging from Eastern Europe at that time. Rabbi Boruch Milikowsky always spoke with warm gratitude about the fine families that took him into their homes when he first came to Baltimore.

In his first long stay there, the hand of fate placed him in the home of Rabbi and Mrs. Elazar Friedlander. Rabbi Friedlander had received his rabbinical ordination from Rav Nosson Tzvi Finkel, the Alter of Slobodka, and then from Rabbi Avrohom Tzvi Kamai of the Mir Yeshiva. He was the Rabbi of the Sha'arei Tzedek Synagogue on Park Heights Avenue.

During those years, the Friedlanders often hosted the great rabbis who were arriving in the United States at that time, so hosting Rabbi Milikowsky was not a new experience for them. They had hosted Rabbi Yaakov Ruderman for six weeks when he first arrived in Baltimore, as he took the first steps towards founding the Ner Yisrael Yeshiva. Many times they hosted Rabbi Kalminovitz of the Mir Yeshiva on his trips to Baltimore.

When Rabbi Milikowsky was in their home, Rabbi Friedlander held many long talks with him. They had much in common, such as their

Earliest picture of Rabbi Milikowsky on his arrival in the US, 1947.

connection to the Mir Yeshiva. They also engaged in discussions of complex topics of Torah learning. Impressed by the newcomer, Rabbi Friedlander described him at length to his good friend Rabbi Chaim Samson, the head of the Talmudical Academy.

It was thus not long before Rabbi Milikowsky was approached by Rabbi Chaim Samson, Rosh Yeshiva of the Talmudical Academy, and offered a job as a T.A. rebbe. To encourage Rabbi Milikowsky to accept the offer, Rabbi Samson informed him that if he became a T.A. rebbe, T.A. would be able to sponsor his sister's entry into the U.S. Whatever dreams Rabbi Milikowsky might have had about starting his own yeshiva for post–high-school students, his main concern was bringing over his sister, so Rabbi Samson's offer was one that he could hardly refuse.

Rabbi Milikowsky had been learning in yeshiva for twenty-two years. Many of his friends from the European yeshiva world could find no work in America at all or were settling for jobs outside Jewish education, or in such fields as kosher slaughter. Even if the T.A. position was not precisely what he wanted, it was still in Torah education, and he considered himself fortunate to have received the offer.

His dream of opening a yeshiva for older boys remained unfulfilled. In fact, only many years later did he ever tell his sons about this dream. It was not to be. In 1947 he moved to Baltimore permanently and became a T.A. Rebbe.

More Neighbors and Friends

When Rabbi Boruch Milikowsky arrived in Baltimore to teach at T.A., he stayed with the Waxman family, who lived on Shirley Avenue. Rabbi Nosson Waxman was himself employed by the Talmudical Academy. The Waxmans, like the Friedlanders, were Yiddish speakers who greatly appreciated Torah learning, and it was correctly assumed that they would consider it an honor and a privilege to help Rabbi Milikowsky feel comfortable and become acclimated. Rabbi Milikowsky lived with them for several months as he began teaching in T.A. He and the Waxman family became very close.

Mrs. Shulamit Lebowitz, the Waxmans' daughter, who now lives in Jerusalem, was a young girl when Rabbi Milikowsky arrived in her Baltimore home. She greatly looked up to this unassuming Torah scholar who was staying with her family. We get a glimpse of Rabbi Milikowsky's humility from the following story, presented in Mrs. Lebowitz's own words:

> I can remember coming down in the morning to the kitchen – I really got put in my place then. He was sitting there having a cup of coffee, and I spoke to him in Yiddish. I addressed him in the familiar [i.e., using the word *du* for "you"], because that's the way I spoke Yiddish. Whom did I speak Yiddish to? My grandparents and my parents. I said to him, "*Vas vilst du?*" and "*Vas machst du?*", etc. My father walked into the room and he hit the ceiling. He said, "How do you talk to him like that? Who do you think you are?"
>
> Yet Reb Boruch only said, "*Shoin! Nicht gefehrlich!* It's all right." I got the message so well drummed into my head that the next time my grandmother came she went crying to my father, because I was saying *ihr* to her [the formal form for "you"]. It would never have dawned on *him* to correct my Yiddish. What did it matter to *him* how you spoke to him?

It was a relationship that would last for forty years. At one point, Mrs. Lebowitz had the satisfaction of arranging a gemara *chavrusa* between her husband, Abe, and Rabbi Milikowsky. For almost a year, Rabbi Milikowsky was her husband's personal learning rebbe. Later still, Rabbi Milikowsky taught the Lebowitzes' son, Shimon, at T.A.

While Rabbi Milikowsky was staying with the Waxmans, he personally arranged for his sister and brother-in-law to be allowed to immigrate to the United States. He approached a Jewish Hebrew school and convinced them to sponsor Noah Podberesky as a teacher. Thus it was ultimately by his own efforts, rather than those of the Talmudical Academy, that his sister and her husband were allowed into the United States.

When Rabbi Milikowsky had been at the Waxmans for several months, he received some wonderful news. His sister Minna was on her way to the United States! After a short stay in New York, she and her husband arrived in Baltimore in 1947, a joyous reunion took place between the two siblings, who had not seen each other in eight years. The Podbereskys rented a second-story apartment in northeast Baltimore, and after a short while Rabbi Milikowsky said his thank-yous to the Waxmans and moved in with his sister and her husband.

Shortly afterwards, the Pechter family arrived from Europe, occupying the first floor. The Pechters had lived in the same building with Rabbi Milikowsky's sister and brother-in-law when the four of them had briefly spent time in Vienna. It was only natural that they would seek out familiar faces on their arrival in the United States. Mr. and Mrs. Pechter were in their forties and had four teenaged children. The whole family became very attached to Rabbi Milikowsky. As their daughter Jean told me, "We considered him one of the *lamed-vav tzaddikim* (the thirty-six saints responsible for the world's continued existence). He was just one of those rare individuals that you are lucky to have known. I can't praise him highly enough." Rabbi Milikowsky was among the first people that the Pechters met in America, and a lifetime attachment was formed. When Jean Pechter grew up, her own children addressed Rabbi Milikowsky as "Uncle," and when they were little they would hug and kiss him whenever they saw him.

To this day, more than a decade after Rabbi Milikowsky's passing, the two extended families continue to go out of their way to attend each other's simchas.

Chapter 9

MOMENT OF TRUTH

Dateline: 1947

Most T.A. boys know Yiddish, at least passively, from home, from the street or from grandparents, but a growing minority do not know it at all.

T.A. boys try to be careful about what foods they buy. There is no "OU." You buy a box of candy and examine the ingredients. You walk down the street to the Jewish non-kosher deli and buy a grilled-cheese sandwich made with plain yellow Kraft cheese.

On Sunday afternoons, T.A. boys play tennis at Druid Hill Park. There are courts – and drinking fountains – for white people, and others for black people. A T.A. boy plays tennis with a black boy. Someone comes and chases them out. There is no way they can play together!

People are better off than a decade before, but they are not yet well-to-do. Many people still do not own cars. The largest Jewish neighborhood in Baltimore is Lower Park Heights, consisting of stately, tree-lined row houses. T.A. is there. Most Jews have not yet moved to the new "suburbs" that are now being built.

You walk around the old T.A. neighborhood late at night and no evil befalls you, but when T.A. boys go downtown or to Fort McHenry, they put their yarmulkes in their pockets.

Most T.A. boys do not own baseball gloves. They cost too much. The few who do own a glove give it to the first baseman. Otherwise, you catch the softball without flinching and when your hand stings, you don't complain. Gloves are for sissies.

If you live in a different neighborhood, you take the trolley car to T.A. Buses will replace trolleys only in the mid-1950s, when the city tears up the trolley tracks.

Wearing a hat and a suit on Shabbos is called "dressing up nicely."

In 1947, Rabbi Milikowsky began teaching one of the younger grades at the Talmudical Academy. For twenty-two years he had been investing in himself, building himself up as a Torah scholar, working on his character, increasing his knowledge. Now the time had come when he was going to have a chance to pass on that knowledge to others in a formal setting. It was a moment of truth.

It was one thing to sit in a *beis midrash* for hours, working to refine a particular idea as a solution to a knotty contradiction in the Talmud. It was one thing to say a *chiddush* before a group of fifteen fellow White-Russian yeshiva *bochrim* in a twice-weekly *va'ad*. It was something else entirely to stand before a group of twenty American twelve-year-old school boys and teach them the basics of Torah.

Following World War II, the Talmudical Academy sponsored many Torah scholars who had been through the Holocaust in one way or another, brought them to America and gave them jobs teaching Torah. These sponsorships could not have been provided without financial guarantees made by staunchly Orthodox Baltimore philanthropists such as Mr. William Lubin. The high school had opened in 1945, and most newcomers were given lower-grade posts. These rebbeim generally did not know any English, but since the language of instruction at the time was Yiddish, the lack of English did not pose a problem. While some of these rabbis became successful educators, others did not. Some were too scarred by the Holocaust, too angry or still too much in mourning to cope effectively with teaching American children and controlling a classroom. Others were so obsessed with their experiences that every lesson ended up being a discussion of the Holocaust to the detriment of all else. A survivor could not know how he would fare until he was in the classroom situation. One T.A. boy recalls his particularly rambunctious class going through "seven or eight" rebbeim in one year of elementary school. To succeed with children was a challenge, to put it mildly.

Yet even if a rebbe was qualified and talented, the job was still difficult. The student population at the Talmudical Academy has always been eclectic, even more that of day schools in New York. In 1947, this was even more true. The Talmudical Academy was one of the only day schools in the United States and the only one on the Eastern Seaboard outside New York City. The elite among yeshiva students came to T.A. from all over the United States. At the same time, since T.A. was the only day school in Baltimore, Rabbi Chaim Samson, the founder and principal, felt duty-bound to accept all local applicants on virtually an open admissions policy. Thus, in one tenth-grade class at T.A. during this period, there was a boy who learned forty *blatt* of the year's *masechta* [Talmudic tractate] by heart, while there were other, semi-observant boys, whose parents simply wished them to maintain their Jewish identity. Many of the latter group attended City and Poly, the two elite public high schools where all the brightest Jewish boys went, if they were not in day school.

One boy, who had recently survived five years in Siberia, was placed in T.A. by his parents two weeks after their arrival in the United States. He spent two years at T.A.'s high school, his first regular schooling in a classroom setting since the third grade. Then, one day, before starting eleventh grade, he turned to his father and asked if he could transfer to Forest Park High. When his father, somewhat taken aback at this sudden request, asked him why he wanted to leave T.A., he replied, "Dad! There's no girls!"

In a word, the attrition rate was quite high. In T.A.'s eighth-grade class, taught by Rabbi Milikowsky in 1948–1949, there were twenty students, but by the twelfth grade there were only twelve graduates.

Rabbi Milikowsky thus faced a double challenge. He had to enter a new situation, teaching younger students on a trial-by-fire basis, and prove that he was competent. Beyond that, however, he had to find a way to reach out to two distinct population groups and keep both interested. He had to prove himself. Some students, based on previous experiences, expected a broken-down soul who would rant about his suffering. For some students, the fact that Rabbi Milikowsky spoke only Yiddish when he started out was not an issue. He was thirty-four years old and had no beard. He was physically healthy, even giving an impression of physical strength and vigor, both of which he indeed possessed. Moreover, he seemed not depressed, but upbeat. All the same, for other boys, longer in America and shorter on tolerance, Rabbi Milikowsky's newness was itself an excuse to take advantage of a new rebbe who did not yet have his bearings.

Some high school rebbeim spend years taking professional pedagogical courses in preparation for teaching. When it comes time to begin their careers, all they have to do is to learn the *gemaras* that they will be teaching, and every night, they do this in preparation for the following morning.

Rabbi Milikowsky had the opposite problem. He knew many of the standard tractates learned in the yeshivot by heart, as well as what the commentaries had to say on them. Thus, the Torah content was the easy part for him. Obviously he would prepare his lesson plans, but he never had to worry about floundering in class over a text he did not really understand. On the other hand, the American boy was a new experience for him.

The first year and a half were not easy for Rabbi Milikowsky. Some boys, especially those of the weaker, more assimilated group, needed some English in the classroom and he could hardly provide it. His first class, which had grown past the docility of early childhood but which had not yet become serious high school students, did not give Rabbi Milikowsky an easy time. Still, Rabbi Milikowsky was committed to succeeding. He did not become one of the "victims," laid off after a few months. He held on and coped.

The eighth-grade rebbe at the time was Rabbi Hirschel Libowitz, one of the first American *talmidim* to go to Lakewood and himself a great *talmid chacham*. When he left T.A. at the end of 1948, Rabbi Milikowsky was invited to take his place.

Here again, when Rabbi Milikowsky took over the eighth grade, he continued to have difficulties, but there was light at the end of the tunnel. One student reports:

We were not an easy bunch. Of course he was a European, and he didn't know the ways of the Americans yet and we tried to pull the wool over his eyes. Yet gradually, gradually, he got us to learn! He learned how to control us! I remember. We saw that he was very kind. Sometimes he had to shout, but he was very good.

The class was thirty percent non-observant. Somehow there was a concentration of good ball players amongst the non-observant boys. During recess the boys would go outside and play softball on the T.A. asphalt lot. At some point Rabbi Milikowsky asked how to play and joined in some of the games with his eighth graders. If he could not communicate verbally with some of the weaker boys, he could at least communicate nonverbally.

One practice for which Rabbi Milikowsky later became famous was already in place in 1948: He gave sing-song *mussar shmuessen*. With his *mussar* background, how could he not?

Occasionally circumstances worked out "in his favor," so to speak:

There was a boy, not so observant, who was creating problems for the class and for Rabbi Milikowsky. One time, in a fit of anger, he threw a *chumash* on the floor. Rabbi Milikowsky got very upset and castigated him about how this was a forbidden, dangerous thing to do. The next day the boy was taken to the hospital for an emergency appendectomy. The students of Rabbi Milikowsky's eighth-grade class took this as an omen about their own behavior. Rabbi Milikowsky didn't have to say a word!

In any event, as the 1948–1949 year progressed, Rabbi Milikowsky began to achieve greater and greater success. One boy from that class summarizes: "We did like Rabbi Milikowsky very much. I remember that he really went all out, with love, to get the turned-off kids to learn."

Rabbi Boruch Milikowsky had learned Torah in the great European yeshivas for twenty years. He had begun to achieve success in the classroom. He was settled in Baltimore. The war was over and he had been reunited with his sister. The dust had settled. At thirty-five years of age, it was now high time for him to get married.

New Prospects

In 1947, two women had booked passage on a ship sailing from France to New York. The two women were Leah Goldman, aged twenty-one, and her mother, Kreindel. They had spent the past several years living first in Austrian and then in French refugee camps for Holocaust survivors waiting to move to Israel.

During that time, following the war, Leah Goldman had helped to smuggle children out of Poland to go to Israel. The whole process was very involved. She would smuggle them out of orphanages and put them on trains traveling south.

Although Leah had been accepted to immigrate to Eretz Yisrael, the British had rejected her mother. Mrs. Goldman was already in her mid-forties and her traumatic war experience had affected her health. Although they had not been in concentration camps, six years of running for their lives and hiding in sometimes subhuman conditions had taken their toll.

According to their quota system, the British would allow only a certain number of survivors to immigrate Palestine. Great Britain was still playing God even after the Holocaust, not letting Jews immigrate to Palestine, so they said yes to Leah Goldman and no to her mother.

The two women, who had been together throughout most of the war and managed to survive, were not going to separate. So they requested and received permission to enter the United States.

On the Goldmans' ship was an old friend of Rabbi Milikowsky from the Mir Yeshiva, Rabbi Getzel Kagan. Sometime during the trip Rabbi Kagan met and spoke with Mrs. Goldman and her daughter Leah. Rabbi Kagan was impressed by these two intensely religious, highly intelligent women. The daughter, Leah, was an idealistic, accomplished and outgoing woman who had not only enabled herself and her mother to survive but had also contributed to the survival and well-being of hundreds of orphans. They loved Eretz Yisrael but could not go there. Instead, they were traveling to America. Rabbi Kagan filed all of this information away for the future.

A year later, after getting settled in America, he thought of his old friend Boruch Milikowsky, who was already in Baltimore. Like Leah, Boruch was a doer. In Shanghai he had been known for his energetic good deeds and for the alacrity with which he volunteered to help with food preparations. Like Leah, he was idealistic, highly intelligent and had a special attachment to Eretz Yisrael. As a bonus, both Leah and Boruch enjoyed reading Hebrew literature, even if Boruch was more adept at it.

It is true that Leah had not been going out of her way to date yeshiva men. As a refugee from Hitler's Europe, preoccupied with survival after years of narrow escapes from death, she had preferred to date successful businessmen, and since she was an attractive, highly intelligent and outgoing young woman in her early twenties, she had the pick of the crop among this group. On the other hand, Boruch had spent many years in yeshiva. For most American girls at the time, this was an incurable blemish, but for the pious Mrs. Goldman, it was a plus, and Leah was at least willing to give it a try. Rabbi Kagan, who knew both parties, saw in Leah a potential rebbetzin, a practical realist who would enable a Talmudic prince to hold fast to his dreams, even if Leah herself could not have imagined this at the time.

Before they went out, Rabbi Milikowsky made exploratory inquiries about Leah's family and was impressed. He found out who Leah's father had been and how he had died. Leah's father had been known as a *lamed-vavnik*, a saintly figure in a town called Rozvadorf near Cracow in Galicia, south Poland. In a manner reminiscent of the Chafetz Chaim, Mr. Goldman had owned a grocery store which his wife ran while he sat in the back all day, learning Torah. If Mrs. Goldman needed help, Mr. Goldman would come forward and provide it. He had died trying to move more people into a bunker during the German bombing of Galicia at the start of the war.

Leah's mother's father had been a vice-mayor in town, the only man who had a telephone. He was well-known for *hachnasas orchim* (hospitality) in the town.

The only possible snag was the matter of ethnic background. Rabbi Milikowsky was a Litvak and a *misnaged* from Belarus, while Mrs. Goldman and her daughter were Chassidic Galitzianiers. They were descended from Rabbi Elimelech of Lizhensk (Leżajsk), a town located forty-five minutes from Rozvadorf.

None of this was an impediment for Rabbi Milikowsky. He had had Chassidic yeshiva friends in Europe, and there was nothing outwardly Chassidic about Leah Goldman. Indeed, the shadchan, Getzel Kagan, was himself a chassid who had learned in the Mir. In America, most young people were not observant at all, and after the destruction of European Jewry, such differences became inconsequential if not ludicrous.

But Leah's mother was concerned. In Europe, these distinctions had been more rigid. Sometimes, back in Europe, when some siblings in a family became Chassidim while the rest remained Misnagdim, it created such a deep rift in the family that one branch would not attend the weddings of the other.

Thus, Mrs. Goldman wanted advice from a Chassidic Rebbe. She had a connection with the Satmar Rebbe, Rabbi Yoel Teitelbaum, who had recently arrived New York from Europe. She approached the Satmar Rebbe to get an *etzah*, to receive some advice. Should she let her daughter marry Boruch Milikowsky? He was not a chassid! How pious could he be?

The Satmar Rebbe answered that Boruch Milikowsky was a *talmid chacham* and that she should go forward with the match. Rabbi Milikowsky then brought Leah home and introduced her to the Podbereskys, to the Pechters downstairs, to the other families that had hosted him, and to his yeshiva friends in New York. These were all the available family he had. She charmed them all, and on February 15, 1949, Boruch Milikowsky and Leah Goldman were married in a ceremony held in New York. Guests from Baltimore were surprised to see that when it came time for the dancing, the men and women danced separately. For the European yeshiva men who made up the main guest list, there was nothing irregular about this at all, but it was still a novelty for American-born Jews in 1949.

Thus Leah Goldman, who might have ended up a wealthy society lady, became a rebbetzin instead. The stage was set for Rabbi Milikowsky to engage in forty years of devoted service to Jewish education with Leah as his helpmate and partner.

In the meantime, Leah's new husband was about to encounter a second major educational challenge.

Chapter 10

INCREASED RESPONSIBILITIES

UNTIL 1944 THE TALMUDICAL ACADEMY only went as far as ninth grade. Graduates of the ninth grade either completed high school in the Baltimore public-school system or at one of the few yeshiva high schools in New York City. There was a special program during those years for public high-school students in which they returned in the afternoon to learn *gemara* with Rabbi Chaim Samson, the long-time head of the school. Prominent rabbis such as Rabbi Emanuel Poliakoff and Rabbi Avigdor Miller followed this route, going on to Yeshiva University and from there to the great European yeshivos.

In 1944, Rabbi Samson decided to open a yeshiva high school. Several years before, he had hired Rabbi Yaakov Bobrovsky and Rabbi Meir Katznelson, graduates of the Mir Yeshiva who had come to America before the Mir went to Shanghai. Both were first-class *talmidei chachamim* and had proven to be talented educators. He realized that with these two men as his nucleus, he could establish a fine yeshiva high school with a dormitory, and he moved forward with his idea. In 1944–1945, the two rebbeim taught the ninth and tenth grades, respectively, and the following year moved up with their pioneering classes to the tenth and eleventh grades.

Before the 1945–1946 school year began, Rabbi Samson decided to open a dormitory as well both in order to attract out-of-town students and allow serious local boys to dedicate themselves totally to Torah learning, without the distractions of home, on the model of Europe. The school would need a *mashgiach* who, Rabbi Samson assumed, should be an unmarried young rabbi who could live in the dormitory with the boys in his charge. Rabbi Samson therefore approached Rav Yitzchak Hutner, Rosh

Yeshiva of one of the few post-high-school yeshivas in America, Chaim Berlin, and asked him to provide an appropriate candidate for the position.

Rav Hutner sent him Rabbi Hirsch Diskind, a young man who had been studying directly under his guidance for nine years and whom he had just ordained the previous year. Moreover, during his rabbinical studies Rabbi Diskind had acted as "big brother" to several younger dormitory students in Chaim Berlin who were from Baltimore. Rabbi Diskind had been extremely impressed with the caliber and character of the Baltimoreans. In his own words, "They had displayed so much gentility and there was something so fine about them that I was just naturally attracted to Baltimore." He quickly accepted the position of live-in mashgiach at the newly inaugurated dormitory.

When I asked Rabbi Diskind why Rabbi Samson had specifically approached Rabbi Hutner for a *mashgiach*, he told me that Rav Hutner was "probably one of the greatest disciples of the *Alter* [Venerable Sage] of Slobodka," Rav Nosson Tzvi Finkel, the renowned *mashgiach* of the Slobodka yeshiva. As for Rav Finkel, Rabbi Diskind had this to say:

> The *Alter* of Slobodka was one of the wisest people in the whole world in understanding individuals. There were no two people from whom he expected the same thing. He expected to develop each person on the basis of his own strengths. What would have been a failure for one would make him jump for joy with another. When one person would leave the Slobodka yeshiva he would discuss with him the importance of *shemiras shabbos,* Sabbath observance. The Slobodka yeshiva – and yet he would talk about *shemiras shabbos*! That would be his greatest sense of achievement, if he felt that this boy would be committed all his life to keeping Shabbos. With others he expected them to become the *gedolei hador*, the luminaries of the generation, like Rav Aharon Kotler, Rav Yaakov Kamenetzky, Rav Ruderman, all these people who would not have become what they became if not for the *Alter* of Slobodka.

And Rav Hutner had that genius too. He was probably the genius of his own generation in that sense, treating each student with what he had to work with.

What Rabbi Diskind modestly did not and could not point out was that Rabbi Hutner probably thought that he, too, Rabbi Diskind, had successfully gleamed some of this tradition as well.

The Talmudical Academy at the time consisted of two buildings: an elementary-school building, where kindergarten through eighth-grade classes were held, and an attached structure which housed a huge auditorium on the first floor and classrooms on the second floor. The classrooms on the second floor were immediately set aside for the use of the high school. They included five rooms which were designated to be dormitory rooms, even if they were not really structurally made for sleeping. Four of the rooms were set aside, each for four boys, and the fifth was set aside for Rabbi Diskind.

By the second year, 1946–1947, the dormitory was filled to capacity with twenty pupils, more than half of whom were local Baltimore boys. The pioneering dormitory group included such future Torah luminaries as Rabbi Aharon Feldman of Jerusalem, who was a native of Baltimore. As time went on and the name of the school spread, the ratio in favor of out-of-town boys increased.

Rabbi Diskind had intense contact with the dormitory boys during all of their free hours both in the evenings, after classes, and during the mornings. He literally woke up with them and went with them to morning prayers and breakfast. During three of those years he taught tenth grade. On Shabbos, two personalities were a constant presence at all of the meals: himself and Rabbi Samson, who would be there without his family. Other school rebbeim would occasionally join as guests.

Rabbi Diskind remained at T.A. for four years, from the fall of 1945 until his marriage in early February 1949, two weeks before the marriage of Rabbi Milikowsky. By all accounts, Rabbi Diskind helped to mold the T.A. boy and to create an appropriate atmosphere in the new yeshiva. Immediately upon his marriage he left for Cincinnati, Ohio to become the principal of a growing Jewish elementary school. Suddenly he was gone! What was Rabbi Samson to do? Where would he find a suitable replacement?

As noted above, Rabbi Samson began with an assumption that the dormitory *mashgiach* should be unmarried. After all, how else could the person holding the position have the freedom to devote himself sufficiently to the boys? On that assumption, over the course of five months, Rabbi Samson successively hired two other unmarried rabbis for the position, yet neither of them proved a successful replacement for Rabbi Diskind.

Slowly another idea began to germinate in Rabbi Samson's mind. His new eighth-grade rebbe, Rabbi Boruch Milikowsky, was gaining a reputation for the warm rapport that he was developing with his students. Besides showing promise of becoming a fine rebbe, he seemed also to have the heart – and the instincts – of a first-class *mashgiach*, more than anyone else on the staff. True, he had not studied under Rav Hutner, but he had studied under and become close to Rav Yerucham Levovitz, who himself had been a student of the Alter of Slobodka. Furthermore, he had imbibed the atmosphere of the Chafetz Chaim's yeshiva in Radin for eight years and had taken a half year out of his life to have contact with Rav Elchonon Wasserman in Baranovitz, as well as with the famous *mashgiach* there, Ha-Rav Yisrael Yaakov Lubschansky, described previously.

In short, he was already starting to do much of the work of a *mashgiach* with enjoyment, without having the official post, and even without living in the dormitory. It was worth a try. If it did not work out, he could be removed from the position after a few months. Hadn't that just happened – twice – within six months?

Thus began Rabbi Milikowsky's career as *mashgiach* of the Talmudical Academy. More than anything else, it was his role as *mashgiach* that earned Rabbi Milikowsky the title "Rebbe."

Growth Years

The years 1949 to 1951 featured much joy and much positive growth for Rabbi Milikowsky and his wife Leah. In 1950, their first child, Malke, was born, followed in 1951 by their first son, Chaim.

Moreover, in September 1949, as Rabbi Milikowsky was taking up the post of *mashgiach* of the dormitory, he became the rebbe of the ninth grade. A year later he was moved into the tenth grade slot, where he would remain for twenty-five years.

During the early 1950s, Rabbi Milikowsky continued to develop as a teacher and rebbe. By this time, he was cultivating a classroom presence and getting beyond the problems of discipline that plagued new teachers. Some boys, in order to waste time, would try to trick him into talking about his war experiences during learning time, but he could not be distracted. A boy would call out, "Where were you born?" and he would answer, politely but firmly, "I come from a place not as good as here," and would continue the lesson.

He wouldn't put up with foolishness. Although he was humble and unassuming, he would not let anyone turn him into a rag. In those early years he sometimes had to raise his voice. If a boy acted up, he would let out a disappointed sigh, and he would say, "What did I tell you? *Vos vet zein mit dir*? What's going to be with you?" In extreme cases he would give "looks that could kill." Slowly he was gaining greater and greater control, so that the classroom could be devoted a hundred percent to teaching.

Yet as a thinking person, he began to ponder student motivation. He came to realize that boys who acted up needed and wanted attention, so he began to teach in ways that gave each boy individual recognition, reducing bad behavior. Some of this involved his experimenting with technical devices such as inviting various boys to spend a number of days sitting next to him at his desk. He would sit at the front of the classroom, often with his arm around the selected boy. His students craved the attention and loved to be chosen for this.

Yet he succeeded on a deeper level as well. Isaac Kinick ('53) said,

GROWTH YEARS

Rabbi and Mrs. Milikowsky with their
daughter Malke.

With their daughter Frady.

With sons, Chaim and Shaya.

"What I remember of Rabbi Milikowsky is that he showed an interest in all the students and he personally addressed each one, so that you thought that you were the most important kid in the class. He made you feel that way."

One way in which Rabbi Milikowsky always showed his students how much they meant to him was in his gift giving. For most T.A. boys, this made itself felt when they married, and one story later in this book relates to Rabbi Milikowsky's unique wedding presents. Since he was a tenth-grade rebbe for so many years, a pupil's wedding was the main life-cycle event to which Rabbi Milikowsky was invited.

Yet during his first few years at T.A., Rabbi Milikowsky also attended the bar mitzvahs of some of his younger students. Thus, Rabbi Dr. Yechezkel Babkoff recalls not a unique wedding present but a unique bar mitzvah present from his year as a precocious ninth grader in Rabbi Milikowsky's 1948–1949 class: It was a new set of Rabbi Akiva Eiger on Shas, printed in one of the pirate printing presses of Shanghai! Dr. Babkoff never heard the details about where the books came from. Could Rabbi Milikowsky have actually *shlepped* the books with him from Shanghai only to give them as a bar mitzvah present to a star pupil?

As Rabbi Milikowsky earned his students' respect, he had less of a need to resort to discipline. It was hard not to respect a teacher who showed such an active interest in his students. In the words of Warner Hirsch ('53), "He was not interested simply in giving a *shiur* and then going home. He had a kind of special relationship with the boys."

Mindful of the attrition rate affecting the weaker population in the upper grades, Rabbi Milikowsky began to place an emphasis on helping the weaker boys academically by tutoring them on his own time and offering moral support. In the words of Jack Pechter:

> He was just remarkable! He was a very caring individual, completely devoted to each individual student. If boys were having trouble, he would take the time to help them out, one on one. He made every student really feel comfortable. There were a lot of students who had difficulty with different parts of reading and studying and he

somehow managed to push them. He just went ahead and did his job by even staying after school. You know, he would hang around after class and kind of tell you what you should be doing. He was strict but in such an easy way that it was a piece of cake.

I loved the man and I like talking about him!

ॐ ॐ

Another way that Rabbi Milikowsky was improving was in his English language skills. He had not attended any adult-education evening courses to learn English – he did not feel he had the time – but his wife was doing just that, and it was she who helped him. Each evening she would drill him in his English until he had developed a functional use of that language.

It is true that all high-school Torah instruction was in Yiddish – in fact, all of the rebbeim had been told to use Yiddish exclusively. Even so, every year the number of students who could not function in that language on a satisfactory level was increasing, and it became more and more necessary for T.A.'s high school rebbes to be able to explain things in English, at least to some students.

Apart from the hard-and-fast curriculum focused on fostering Torah-learning skills, Rabbi Milikowsky also emphasized practical moral lessons and character improvement. As one boy put it, "Perhaps more than the learning itself, Rebbe wanted us to become *menschen.*" Moreover, he seemed to grasp quite quickly how to do this in a way that captivated the boys' hearts. Another boy recalled:

"He taught us a lot of good character traits, a lot of ways that the Jewish people should follow. He was a very inspiring teacher! When teachers are inspiring, you don't turn them off. Instead, you listen."

It was not easy to sidetrack Rabbi Milikowsky with irrelevant chatter. At the same time, during those years, the early 1950s, there was much confusion among some of the students regarding basic points of outlook. American non-Jewish society seemed much healthier and family-oriented than it is today. Paradoxically, non-Jewish attitudes were more enticing than they are now, and the result was the assimilation of non-Jewish attitudes to various aspects of life. Many boys whose families had already been in the United States for fifty or seventy years, and some who had been in the country for much shorter times, were confused. Rabbi Milikowsky thus found it occasionally worthwhile to engage in what is known today as "values clarification." As Isaac Kinick recalls:

> When he raised an idea that was new to us, we would think about it and sometimes discuss it. Rabbi Milikowsky encouraged discussion. Other rabbeim might say, *"Freg nicht kein kashas,"* Don't ask any questions. He, by contrast, would say, "Okay, let's talk about it," and we would. Sometimes even after school, we would discuss certain issues of the day. Religious issues. For example, should a boy belong to Young Israel? It had boys and girls. We, of course, always said you should, because it wasn't like today, when religious boys and girls constitute two different worlds. We were teenagers.
>
> We would ask, 'How about dating? Should dating only be for marriage?' We presented our concerns of that time. He would listen and we had a lot of good discussions. He wasn't an extremist. He was open-minded. He would listen to us, and he wouldn't always agree with us, but he would understand us. He understood that we were teenagers, and where we were coming from. And he would tell us what we could and what we couldn't do. We had frank discussions about that. That's besides the learning and discussing *Rashi.* We talked about life. That's why I liked him. He was a real mensch!

Thus, already in those early years, Rabbi Milikowsky was becoming a great and beloved rebbe. When boys would compliment him as a rebbe, sometimes even expressing the wish that some of their other rebbeim could be more like him, one of his famous responses went as follows:

"In Europe there were rabbis and bricklayers. After the war, some went to Israel and some went to America. The rabbis went to Israel and became bricklayers, and the bricklayers went to America and became rabbis..."

A moment arrived after several years when Rabbi Milikowsky had developed into an educator of some stature. Allow me to sum up the discussion with one final quotation from the class of 1953:

"We had one rebbe – we brought hundreds of grasshoppers into the classroom. The rebbe ran around trying to kill them. But we would *never* have done such a thing with Rabbi Milikowsky. We would never even have *thought* about it. Never!"

First Steps as *Mashgiach*

In September 1949, when Rabbi Milikowsky first became *mashgiach*, he was still a newlywed. In fact he had been married for only seven months. Thus, Rabbi Samson used a light touch in assigning him new tasks associated with the dormitory. Indeed, it was several years before Rabbi Milikowsky started eating his Shabbos meals with the T.A. dormitory boys. Until around 1954, that remained a mitzvah performed every Shabbos by Rabbi Samson himself, without his family.

Rabbi Milikowsky's main official task in those first years was to be in charge mornings and evenings, throughout the waking hours whenever classes were not in session. Thus, each morning he would get up a bit early, rush down the street to the school and wake up the boys. There he would go from room to room, calling out, *"Shteh uf! Shteh uf la'avoidas haBoireh!"* (Wake up! Wake up for the service of the Creator!) Years later he appointed students to do this – in fact he reserved this job as a perk to be rewarded for good behavior – but at first he did it himself. In the evenings he would be at the school, studying together with the dormitory boys at their night *seder* (nighttime Torah-study session) and answering their questions.

Of course, as *mashgiach*, he was in charge of crisis management. This included all the technical aspects of the health and physical needs of boys away from home, but it also included tending to the boys' emotional welfare.

During those early years of the T.A. high school and dormitory, Rabbi Milikowsky got to know all of the students, both the locals and out-of-towners. Thus, one city boy, although not a dorm resident, still had this to say about Rabbi Milikowsky the *mashgiach*:

> You felt that he was a teacher who was with you even if you were in trouble. You had difficult problems. Whatever it was in the school. You felt he was like an advocate for you. You could go to Rebbe, and you would say to him what was going on, and he would listen to you. And you felt that he really cared. He was really concerned. And he might give you some advice. One or two words. He didn't go into a shpiel.

Later on, Rabbi Milikowsky would become famous for his advocacy on behalf of students. That is, it was well known that he would often go to bat to keep boys in T.A. when they had committed infractions that in most yeshivos would earn a student expulsion.

The first serious case of this advocacy occurred sometime around 1951. A dormitory boy from a nonobservant family was caught smoking on Shabbos in the dormitory. The authorities, except for Rabbi Milikowsky, wanted to throw the boy out of the school. But Rabbi Milikowsky said, "Ein minuteleh! Don't be so hasty!" and earned the boy another chance.

It is true that Rabbi Milikowsky was eighteen years younger than Rabbi Samson, yet he too was a European *talmid chacham* and he knew how to make his point in a way that Rabbi Samson would accept. Equally important, by now he knew how to talk to American boys, however weak his English remained. He knew how to impress upon the boy himself that he was now on probation and must not squander this second chance to remain in the school.

In any event, the boy in question was allowed to remain at T.A. and later became genuinely Sabbath-observant. Like so many of Rabbi Milikowsky's "gambles" in which he placed his faith in his T.A. boys "against the odds," things turned out well in this case. Had Rabbi Milikowsky bet his money rather than just his reputation on more of these "gambles," he would have ended his career a very wealthy man indeed.

Chapter 11

"I'M STILL THERE!"

RABBI MILIKOWSKY HAD MANY *CHAVRUSOS* over the years with members of the Baltimore community, besides the learning contact he had with T.A. boys, morning, noon and night. Generally these *chavrusos* involved Rebbe-talmid relationships and reflected Rabbi Milikowsky's penchant for doing acts of *chessed*. Nevertheless, there was one man with whom he learned regularly, as an equal, for forty years: Rabbi Avraham Bayarsky, a friend from his youth. The saying goes that you can tell a man by his friends. Among Jews, you can surely tell a man by his *chavrusa*.

For forty years, Rabbi Boruch Milikowsky and Rabbi Avraham Bayarsky, *yibadel lechayim*, were learning partners and close friends, kindred spirits clinging to each other on a life raft floating in an ocean of change, refugees from a vanished world, two princes in exile from the European world of Torah. Both were from small towns in *Litvishe* White Russia and both achieved excellence in *Litvishe*, White Russian yeshivas. Both settled in Baltimore, Maryland, the one as a *shochet* [ritual slaughterer] and the other as a high school rebbe and *mashgiach*.

Rabbi Bayarsky was born and raised in Olshan, Belarus, not far from Vishnevo, Radin and the Mir. While Rabbi Milikowsky was in the *yeshiva ketana* of Radin, Rabbi Bayarsky was in *yeshiva ketanah* of Bielsk, which was a branch of the Novardok Yeshiva. The Rabbi of the city of Bielsk was Rabbi Arye Leib Yellin, the *Yefe Enayim*, who wrote a commentary that appears in the Talmud.

He and Rabbi Milikowsky met in 1930 when they were both seventeen and Rabbi Bayarsky had just moved to Radin to begin *yeshiva gedolah.* They became friends and were in the same *va'ad* together, although at Radin they never learned together as *chavrusos.*

When I asked Rabbi Bayarsky how many years he had spent at Radin, he answered me with just three words: "I'm still there." These three words sum up Rabbi Bayarsky's attitude toward life and yeshiva learning and tell us something about a true Litvak's use of language and deadpan humor. They also make clear how compatible a learning partner and friend he was for Rabbi Milikowsky.

Rabbi Bayarsky spent ten years at Radin and grew quite close to the two *Roshei Yeshiva,* Rabbis Zachs and Feivelovitz. Towards the end of that time, Rabbi Mendl Zachs was giving his weekly *shiurim* privately to Rabbi Bayarsky before he delivered them to the whole yeshiva. Often, Rabbi Bayarsky relates, Rabbi Zachs would say one set of *chiddushim* for him, and then, when he gave the *shiur* to the yeshiva, he would answer the same questions with different answers! When Rabbi Bayarsky would point this out to him afterwards, he would respond, "As I was talking, I thought of something better to say…"

When Rabbi Feivelovitz gave his *shiurim* to the yeshiva, he was transcribing them with the intent of having them published in book form, something which happened later on in Israel, after his premature death. Rabbi Bayarsky, knowing of his intentions, felt comfortable enough that he would sometimes approach him and point out where he had seen a *chiddush* from the *shiur* in another *sefer,* and Rabbi Feivelovitz would express his gratitude. Later, when the *sefer* appeared, Rabbi Bayarsky found many of these comments and references included.

In late September, 1939, when the Russians seized eastern Poland and so many yeshivas fled north to Vilna, Radin was among them. When the Lithuanians subsequently took over Vilna and the surrounding region, the yeshivas that had fled north spread out amongst the Lithuanian towns. Rabbi Milikowsky, with the Mir Yeshiva, went to Keidan and Rabbi Bayarsky, with Radin, went to Utian, where the famous Pis'chei Teshuva had lived during the nineteenth century. In early 1940, when the Russians recaptured Vilna, setting the stage for the Mir Yeshiva's move to Shanghai, Radin stayed put, remaining at Ochyan until 1941. Then late one night, the Russians suddenly arrested all the boys of the Radin Yeshiva and transported them to Siberia. Rabbi Bayarsky, who had learned for more than ten years in Radin, spent two years in a slave-labor detail on a starvation diet, chopping down trees in the forests of Siberia.

In 1943, the surviving Radin yeshiva boys were removed from Siberia and brought to Moscow, where they continued their forced labor under improved conditions. Unfortunately, many who had survived Siberia died in Moscow. The sudden move to a normal diet after years of starvation was more than their systems could bear.

In 1946, the Radin yeshiva boys were allowed to return to Poland. In the town of Lodz they met with the Va'ad Hatzoloh, the American Rescue Committee. The next step was France, after which they received visas to the United States. Rabbi Bayarsky traveled to the United States with his new wife, whom he had met in Russia and married in France.

Rabbi Bayarsky settled in Baltimore, where he had a brother, and was fortunate to find work as a *shochet*, a ritual slaughterer. Many of the Eastern European princes of Torah, primed for careers in Torah education, could find no work at all. During the early years, Rabbi Bayarsky lived in various homes on lower Park Heights near the old T.A. building, where he would daven. It was there in 1947, that he was reunited with his old friend and *landsleit* from Radin, whom he had not seen in thirteen years, ever since Rabbi Milikowsky's move to the Mir.

When Rabbi Milikowsky arrived in Baltimore and began teaching at T.A., he became a regular guest in the Bayarskys' home. Soon they formed a *chavrusa*. When Rabbi Milikowsky married, their wives became good friends as well. They too were *landsleit*, Galitzianers from southern Poland who had married Litvaks.

For forty years, Rabbis Milikowsky and Bayarsky learned Torah each week for an hour and a half, generally gemara with *Rishonim* and *Acharonim*, although they also learned *Minchas Chinuch* at various times. At first they learned in the old T.A. building. Later on, they learned in the basement of the Shearith Israel Synagogue. Both were busy all week long earning their living. Even if each, in his chosen livelihood, was still part of the Torah world – surely Rabbi Milikowsky was learning and teaching Torah countless hours each week – this *chavrusa* with an equal partner certainly must have been an opportunity for each to recharge his spiritual batteries.

Besides learning together, Rabbi Milikowsky and Rabbi Bayarsky shared each other's successes and challenges. The relationship between these two men was one of unspoken intimacy, of two men who each knew what the other was thinking, of true friends who shared the same background.

When educational challenges arose at T.A., when the boys in Rabbi Milikowsky's class or in the dormitory were undergoing crises that it was his job to deal with, Rabbi Milikowsky could share his troubles at the Bayarsky home. To Rabbi Bayarsky, who had himself undergone training that would have prepared him for a high-level career in Torah education, Rabbi Milikowsky would say, "Don't think I have things so easy. It's hard to be a rebbe and a *mashgiach!* It's a hard job because you have to worry. In the daytime when you're teaching you have problems with the boys, like *every* rebbe has problems. Then at night you have problems with the dormitory. Are they up late? Where are they? It's a hard job!"

For twenty years, the Bayarskys housed T.A. boys in their home, generally four boys each year. Rabbi Milikowsky always expended enormous energy on the dormitory boys, and he would regularly visit the Bayarskys to see how their four boys were doing. As Mrs. Bayarsky put it, "Rabbi Milikowsky was more than a father to the boys." If boys had permission to go to a movie at night, Rabbi Milikowsky wanted to know that the boys were accounted for when the agreed-upon curfew time arrived. Yet boys will be boys, and many were the times that Mrs. Bayarsky would call up Rabbi Milikowsky as the clock neared midnight to tell him that she was worried because the boys had not yet arrived home. Rabbi Milikowsky invariably knew where the boys were. Many were the times that he would run to the movie houses on North Avenue and go inside, pull out boys who had gone beyond their time limit and bring them home!

In Rabbi Bayarsky's words, "He knew the boys and he knew where they were and *what* they were. He knew them!"

Chapter 12

CLASSIC SCENES FROM THE EARLY YEARS

I REMEMBER COMING BACK FROM SUMMER VACATION, and Rebbe was there, and we ran out of the cab. A cab brought us from the train station, and when we got out of the cab we ran to see him. I'll never forget that. You know, we hadn't seen him over the summer. And we ran. He was like a father. Like a father! Mamash, just like a father. Me and Ronny Gray and Norman Rabb. We just burst out of the doors of the cab to run to see him.
    –Rabbi Yaakov Spivak, '62

In Hebrew, the word "chibah" means "affection." Rabbi Milikowsky once said that "chibah" is an obligation. The word "chibah," he said, comes from the same root as "chovah/mechuyav," obligation. The two ideas, obligation and love, are the same.
    –Joseph Friedman, '64

Shabbos at T.A.

As has been pointed out, until the mid-1950s, Rabbi Chaim Samson, the Rosh Yeshiva, ate all of his Shabbos meals with the T.A. boys, generally without his wife and children. Yet at some point around that time, Rabbi Samson passed this task on to Rabbi Milikowsky. For the next twenty years, Rabbi Milikowsky was with the T.A. boys for all of *his* Shabbos meals, apart from his own family. Even though he lived only a block away from the school, his wife and children generally did not join him. His aging mother-in-law, Mrs. Goldman, found it disorienting to eat outside the home on Shabbos, especially surrounded by a large crowd of boisterous youths. It was therefore decided that the family would eat at home.

This could not have been easy for Rabbi Milikowsky. He would rush home right after *davening*, Friday night and Shabbos morning, make kiddush, and then rush back to be with the boys.

On rare occasions, especially during the early years, his family would eat with him at T.A. all the same. Rabbi Milikowsky's daughter Malke thus recalls, as a young girl, befriending the daughters of the Grossman family, who were the caterers, and helping them to set up and to put the chopped liver on the tables. Yet as the 1960s progressed and Malke became a teenage girl, this ceased.

Rabbi Milikowsky elevated Shabbos to an art form. With him at the helm, every part of Shabbos for a T.A. dormitory boy became special. Former students waxed eloquent about all aspects of Shabbos at T.A.

To be sure, the food provided by the Grossmans was delicious, and the singing, aided by some very fine voices, was very special even by objective standards. Yet with institutional Shabbosim, there is no guarantee that everyone will have a rewarding experience. In fact, many adults go far out of their way to avoid such Shabbosim. All the same, every dorm student I spoke to from that period became emotional as he described Shabbos at T.A., and each of them named their beloved Rebbe as the magic ingredient in its success.

Shabbos at T.A. was a very special time. You really felt the atmosphere. And Rabbi Milikowsky played a very instrumental role, whether it was mussar shmuessim or shiurim or maaselach (stories) that he would tell us over lunch or dinner or shaleshudis. And he had a tremendous influence. I cannot imagine a Shabbos meal at TA without Rebbe. In fact, I cannot recall one Shabbos meal when he was absent, except when he wasn't feeling well."
–Dr. Chaim Botwinik '66

Rabbi Milikowsky ate his meals with the bochrim. He felt, again, as the mashgiach, 'Where are these children's parents? Would a parent want his children to eat somewhere on Shabbos and not have any input into the Shabbos meal with his children?' He said, 'I am the mashgiach. Therefore, I am the surrogate father. I am going to be with these boys during the meals!'

It wasn't only that. Many times we had a learning session after the Friday night meal. On such occasions, he never went home. He felt that his wife was there for his own children while the boys in the yeshiva had neither mother nor father.
–Henry Lazarus '59

Shabbos is something that every dormitory boy at TA remembers. After davening, everyone else would go home and Rebbe would be with the boys. We would all go down to the dining room on the bottom floor of T.A. on Cottage Avenue. And we would have Pepsi-Cola in a bottle, and chopped liver. The singing was incredible. Shabbos was so wonderful!
–Rabbi Yaakov Spivak

Occasionally *shaleshudis* would last for hours into Saturday night, with Rebbe giving long talks. These were special occasions which alumni remembered for many years. Here is Yaakov Taub's ('66) description of one such Shabbos.

At all the meals there would be *zemiros* – they were a big part of the meals. Of course, *shaleshudis* would go into Saturday night. No one would be checking the clock. Everything would be relaxed and easygoing. Very often *shaleshudis* would flow into a *melave malka*.

I remember one week at *shaleshudis*, it was already dark. Rav Aharon Kotler (founder and Rosh Yeshiva of the prominent Lakewood Yeshiva, in Lakewood, New Jersey), had just passed away two days before (2 Kislev, Thursday, November 29, 1963). Then, the next night, Friday night, there had been a total lunar eclipse. We were sitting there singing at *shaleshudis* when Rebbe told one of the boys to say *hamavdil ben kodesh le'chol* [an abbreviated formula for ending the Sabbath on Saturday Night] and to *turn off the lights*. Rebbe then started giving us a *mussar shmuess*.

I don't know how long it was. Boy, it was long! He was talking about his trepidations over what the future held for us. He was very worried! He was afraid because of the eclipse, and because Rav Aharon Kotler had passed away.

He told us that he remembered how so many *gedolim* had passed away before the war. These men, he said, were the people who were really supposed to strengthen the Jewish people, and they were no longer there! He was afraid that that was what was happening now.

I remember that evening very clearly. It was a very important experience in my life. The talk went on for a few hours. We didn't *daven ma'ariv* until very late.

There were a few other occasions like that. Every time it happened, you knew you were having a defining moment that you would long savor, an experience from which you were going to learn something of great importance.

Under the circumstances, one might have expected Rabbi Milikowsky to emphasize to his children the matter of his self-sacrifice on behalf of the T.A. boys.

Yet having spoken at length to each of Rabbi Milikowsky's children, I know that he never did anything of the sort. All of his four children denied ever having suffered from the situation, and each of them told me emphatically, in almost the same words, "What self-sacrifice? He had an *obligation*, a *duty*. My father felt he was simply fulfilling his obligation in being a rebbe for each *talmid*."

A rebbe. Nothing more, nothing less.

Always There

One way that the phenomenal level of Rabbi Milikowsky's commitment to the T.A. boys was made clear was by the enormous amounts of time he made himself available to them. Of course, we have already discussed Shabbos, but during the 1950s and 1960s Rabbi Milikowsky's commitment was superhuman, almost supernatural. In short, he made himself available round the clock, all week long.

For example, as in many yeshivah high schools, T.A. had an evening Torah-learning session called "night *seder*." To this day, night *seder* is attended by dormitory students and attendance is taken, but during the 1950s and 1960s, when T.A. and the Jewish community were both in the same place, night *seder* was also attended by some of the more serious city students who lived within walking distance of the school. At T.A. this session was held on Monday through Friday nights. During the week it lasted from 8:00 PM until 9:15 PM, followed by *ma'ariv*, and on Shabbos it took place after the Friday night meal.

For the vast majority of men, these were hours spent happily with one's wife and children in the warmth of one's home, but during all the years that he was associated with the dormitory – from 1949 to 1975 – Rabbi Milikowsky was a permanent fixture at night *seder*. Any time anyone looked toward the left front side of the *beis midrash*, they could see Rabbi Milikowsky there, sitting in his red upholstered chair, bent intently over a *sefer*, facing the boys (with an occasional covert peek in their direction).

Night *seder* usually consisted of learning with a *chavrusa*, and boys were encouraged to learn anything they wanted. Some newly religious boys from the small towns of Pennsylvania and Virginia or from the large cities of South America might learn *chumash*, while other boys learned *gemara* in preparation for the next day or reviewed what they had learned that morning. If anyone had questions, Rabbi Milikowsky was the address. The boys could ask him anything from their learning and he would answer them on their level. Everyone felt comfortable enough to ask him any question.

During the 1970s, T.A. would sometimes encourage older city boys to drive out to the new T.A. campus to attend night *seder* on Thursday nights. I fondly remember responding to this invitation on a number of occasions. One time I was studying *gemara* with a dormitory student from my class. When we got into a heated argument over the meaning of a particular phrase, we decided to take the question to Rabbi Milikowsky. Imagine our surprise when he pointed out that my understanding was based on one medieval commentator and my study partner's interpretation was based on another. Anyway, both interpretations were already in Rabbi Milikowsky's head, together with the relevant *gemara*. He did not have to look anything up for us.

Reach Out...

Throughout the years that Rabbi Milikowsky was connected to the T.A. dormitory, he always stressed to the dormitory boys the importance of staying in touch with their parents by letters and phone calls. Many boys went home only three or four times a year over a period of four years or more, so maintaining such contact was all the more important.

One way that he emphasized the importance of this mitzvah was by waiting until the boys were home on their visits to their parents, and then by calling the boys himself from Baltimore. By such means, Rabbi Milikowsky not only stressed the importance of staying in touch, but he had a valuable opportunity to touch base with the parents and families of many boys and to learn more about their backgrounds and problems. Many students shared with me the pleasure and surprise that they felt when they received such phone calls. Always one to teach by his own actions, he was also trying to teach the boys the importance of maintaining contact with one's family and one's rebbe at holiday time.

Such messages planted seeds that grew into large trees and bore much fruit. Thus, one student described the customs that developed in his own family from what he saw Rabbi Milikowsky do. First of all, after he graduated, he would call Rabbi Milikowsky before each holiday and receive his Rebbe's blessing. "Rebbe," he said, "was a *mevarech,*" a bestower of blessings. Second of all, starting when he was in the T.A. dormitory, and continuing onward after he married and moved to a different city from his parents, he would call his own parents every Friday. This practice carried on for forty years. Finally, he concludes, his own children, in turn, are now calling him every *yom tov* and *Erev Shabbos.*

Tending to the Sick

When it came to tending to the sick, Rabbi Boruch Milikowsky's approach went entirely beyond the simple fulfillment of the mitzvah of visiting the sick. He was a master at fulfilling the sick person's needs.

One student described the time a friend of his in the dormitory was sick in bed with a high fever, and Rabbi Milikowsky was up all night with him. Rabbi Milikowsky did not just come and visit the boy but literally nursed him. As soon as he came into the boy's room and felt his head, he took off his own jacket – there was work to do! Then he went and got a washcloth and wet it in the sink. Finally, he sat by the boy's bed, talking to the boy and pressing the cool washcloth against his forehead. After a few minutes, Rabbi Milikowsky rose and rinsed the washcloth until it was cool once more. He repeated this process over and over, talking to the boy, calming his fears, and encouraging him to drink liquids.

The Rabbis make a point of emphasizing the idea that when someone has a mitzvah to do, מצוה בו יותר משילוחו – it is best that one do that mitzvah oneself rather than asking someone else to do it on one's behalf (*Kiddushin* 41a). Abraham set an example in this regard when he rose early the morning he set out for Mount Moriah with Isaac and saddled his donkey by himself, even though he had many servants who could have done it for him. Just like Abraham, Rabbi Boruch Milikowsky liked to do mitzvos all by himself. When it came to ministering to the sick, nothing was beneath his dignity. The same student concluded:

"To see a *rosh yeshiva* or a *mashgiach* go to such lengths made a great impression on us and showed us just how much Rabbi Milikowsky really cared for us as if we were his own children. And what he did for my friend, I saw him do many, many times."

It was not just the intensity of Rabbi Milikowsky's efforts on behalf of the sick that made a great impression on T.A. students. It was his resourcefulness and the broad scope of those efforts as well:

"He was just unbelievable! I once even saw him take a splinter out of a boy's hand. He asked for somebody to sterilize the needle, and then he removed the splinter by himself."

Often Rabbi Milikowsky gave a novel interpretation to the idea of "fulfilling the needs of the sick." When it came to visiting the sick, Rabbi Milikowsky had a special custom for which he was justly famous – or notorious, depending on one's perspective. While other *mashgichim* visited sick boys and brought them words of comfort, fruit juice, or that evening's dinner, Rabbi Milikowsky would visit sick boys bringing with him two bottles of Coca-Cola! A student explained the phenomenon:

"For Rebbe, when you're sick, you drink. In fact you drink a lot. And what do you give a kid to help him drink a lot? You don't bring him healthy things like juice. You give him Coca-Cola! So I recall he would bring up bottles and bottles of Coca-Cola. Himself! He was just unbelievable."

Appendicitis, Take 1

It was twelve o'clock midnight in the home of Rabbi Chaim Samson, *Rosh Yeshiva* of the Talmudical Academy, and all was quiet. The Samsons prided themselves on running a tight and orderly ship. There was a curfew for all T.A. dormitory boys that applied in the Samson home as well for the boys who stayed with them each year. That year, as usual, there were two boys sleeping in one of the bedrooms on the second floor. One was an eleventh-grader from Atlanta and the other a ninth-grader from Washington.

Suddenly, the younger boy, Yaakov, began to awaken from his sleep. He was feeling severe stomach pains. At first, in a still dormant state, he wanted to go and wake up his parents. As his mind cleared, he realized that his parents were forty miles away and that this was not an option.

For a few minutes he lay in silence, trying to gauge just what it was he was experiencing. Finally, when he decided he could not deal with it alone, he woke up his older roommate, Gedalya.

"What's the matter?" asked Gedalya.

"My stomach hurts real bad!"

"Did you eat too many potato chips tonight or something like that?"

"It's not that kind of thing! *Aaiiggghhh!*"

"Oh, my God! That sounds awful! We've got to be careful, Yaakov. I've got a feeling this could be an appendicitis attack. Let's go downstairs and call Rebbe."

"Yeah! Good idea."

Two out-of-town boys, in the middle of the night, fourteen and sixteen years old, living in the home of the Rosh Yeshiva. The younger one was having an appendicitis attack. Whom did they call? Rabbi Milikowsky, obviously! It was just natural that they should call him. They couldn't bother Rabbi Samson, of course. They lived in his home, and boys had been told that in an emergency they should wake up their hosts, but Rabbi Samson was the *Rosh Yeshiva!* How could you bother the *Rosh Yeshiva?* And they didn't think of calling an ambulance either. Anyway, what ambulance would take a fourteen-year-old boy to the hospital without an adult supervising?

So they called Rabbi Milikowsky without hesitating for a single instant! Someone had to get Yaakov to a doctor, or to the hospital. Rabbi Milikowsky would handle it. He would do it!

Downstairs, mostly dressed, they called Rabbi Milikowsky.

"Shalom!" sang out Rebbe's voice, as if a call in the middle of the night was the most natural thing in the world.

"Hello, Rebbe? This is Gedalya Stanislovski."

"Gedalya! What can I do for you?"

"Well, my roommate, here, Yaakov, is having terrible stomach pains and they won't go away, you see."

"Gedalya, you and Yaakov get dressed! I'll be there in ten minutes!"

Very soon, Rabbi Milikowsky arrived in his beaten-up, old green Ford. In the meantime, Yaakov's pains had worsened. Rabbi Milikowsky and Gedalya helped Yaakov out to the car. Before Gedalya left the house, he made sure to bring along a garbage pail so that Yaakov, who was looking more and more like the original color of Rebbe's car, wouldn't ruin what remained of the Ford's upholstery.

Rabbi Milikowsky brought the boys to Sinai Hospital at one o'clock in the morning. Sure enough, Yaakov's appendix had almost burst. What would the boys have done without him? Half asleep, in the middle of the night, two teenage boys knew that in a pinch they could count on their Rebbe, and they felt comfortable enough to call him.

Appendicitis, Take 2

One year later, the same thing happened again. Here is Jay Pomrenze's oral narrative of what happened when he had an appendicitis attack at the end of tenth grade:

> I had appendicitis. It was the end of my sophomore year. It would have been 1964, and they had a thing where after school ended you could stay another two or three weeks for learning. Which I did. I had symptoms of an appendicitis attack. It came on very suddenly. My parents were in Washington D.C. It would have taken them a few hours to arrive. I don't even think they had a car. They would have had to call a taxi. It was a good hour away.
>
> Rebbe took me to the hospital. He stayed with me the whole night. He called my parents. He was there with me the whole time. It happened at 11 or 12 at night.
>
> It wasn't like he had to be convinced to come and do this. It was like, of course Rebbe will do it. There was no question about it. He took care of everything. One of the older guys, one of the seniors, went to get him, and he came and got me, and he called the doctor who came and checked, and he drove me to the hospital, and he stayed there. I think my parents came in and then went back. I had to be in the hospital for another two or three days. Rebbe came every day to visit me and to make sure that I was OK. He really took care! He sat with me all night in the hospital.

Jay Pomrenze is seven years older than I, a rabbi, a successful businessman and a wise, albeit a rather boyish, grandfather. At this point I asked him a question. I asked him how Rabbi Milikowsky spent that entire first night that he sat with Jay in the hospital. Had he brought a *sefer* with him? Did he spend the night learning Torah? Or did he sit and talk with Jay?

Jay's response, besides giving me some very appropriate *mussar*, shows the extent to which Jay was a close *talmid* of Rabbi Boruch Milikowsky:

> He talked with me. I can't say that I remember specifically what we talked about. I'm not saying that when you're on a bus you shouldn't have a *sefer*. You should have a *sefer*! Read a book, have a *sefer*, use the time productively.
>
> Being in the hospital with a kid who has appendicitis is not the time to sit there and be *shteiging* away so that you can get the *Tosafos* a little bit clearer. It's also a mitzvah to be taking care of a *choleh*. I was a *choleh sheyesh bo sakanah*, a patient whose life is in danger. I had a burst appendix. Rebbe didn't have to say, "Oy, maybe now's not the time to have a *sefer*." He knew. Those were the priorities at this time. Perhaps some young yeshiva graduate might have to call his rebbe and ask, "I'm taking a boy to the hospital. Should I take a *sefer* along?" – I'm being a bit extreme, but you get the point, right? – He didn't have to pretend that he needed the *sefer* there so that someone shouldn't say he was wasting time.

Postscript: Since the last two stories took place within a year of each other, in 1963 and 1964, I can only assume that there were plenty of other all-night hospital stories between 1949 and 1975. Later, I spoke to Rabbi Yaakov Spivak, who was a dorm student at T.A. between 1956 and 1962, and I asked him whether he also remembered such hospital stories. His response was as follows:

"Oh, yes! He always did that. When someone was sick he was responsible. It was just something that he did a lot. Remember, he was in charge. He was *in loco parentes*."

Remembrance of Things Past

During the 1950s, when Rabbi Milikowsky and his wife were starting to raise their family, they didn't talk much about their past. They preferred to keep things inside. "Why make the children sad and uncomfortable?" they thought to themselves.

Even if the Milikowsky children did not hear much about their paternal grandparents or about Rabbi Milikowsky's five deceased siblings, they always knew when the yahrzeit of the Vishnevo massacre, 17 Elul 5702, was approaching. In the preceding week, their mother would purchase seven glass yahrzeit candles, and as the evening began, Rabbi Milikowsky would light them. Then, when twenty-four hours had passed, the seven glass containers would be cleansed of the remaining wax and the labels removed, and they would join the drinking glasses in the kitchen cabinet. In a home where every penny counted, the addition of these glasses to the kitchen cabinet was a noteworthy event, even for young children who hadn't heard much about the precise events that had occasioned the arrival of those glasses.

Rebbe's Car

Anyone who has ever seen early Laurel and Hardy movies knows that the automobile was a common sight on the streets of large American cities as early as the 1920s. With each passing year, more and more people drove cars, although throughout the 1940s, most of Baltimore's Orthodox rabbis still did not own one.

Rabbi Milikowsky did not own a car during his first eight years in Baltimore, into the mid-1950s. During that time, he relied largely on the local trolley cars and the new bus lines, and on what some people in Israel call "the number eleven" – i.e., his own two feet. Yet as time passed and the responsibilities he bore as a yeshiva rebbe, *mashgiach*, kashrus supervisor and family man increased, so did his need for a car. Still, he could not afford one, and in the mid-1950s gasoline cost approximately twenty cents a gallon. (Let it be noted that in 1955, twenty cents could still buy you four large popsicles.)

Then suddenly, the yeshiva became eligible to place bids on government surplus items. Various items were available that the yeshiva needed. So the yeshiva went out and purchased two pick-up trucks. As part of this same arrangement, Rabbi Milikowsky bought his first car for twenty-five dollars. It was a big old Ford from about 1951, and it was in this car that Rabbi Milikowsky first learned to drive.

Rabbi Milikowsky saw God's hand in everything that happened, and his purchase of the car was no exception. He said, "Somewhere along the line there has to be a *bashert* here. That I should drive? Twenty-five dollars? I think this was a *siman*, a sign from Heaven that I was going to need this car somehow or other in my work, so I went out and bought that car."

Once Rabbi Milikowsky had the car, he realized how much he needed it. He had been losing a great deal of time leaving the yeshiva to go to Goldman's bakery, a trip that became much harder when the weather was cold and wet. Of course, Rabbi Milikowsky soon realized that in the United States, a car was not just a time-saver but a major means of performing acts of kindness for others.

Divine Ledger

One of the ways that modern secular society today differs from secular society a generation or two ago is in the extent to which young people are taught to take responsibility for their own actions. Nowadays, everything that anyone does wrong is assumed to be explainable and excusable. In short, it can be blamed on factors outside of the person himself. However much Judaism values the principle of giving the benefit of the doubt as an educational rule, nevertheless it rejects this approach. We are responsible for what we do. This is the whole message of reward and punishment. When we arrive in the World of Truth, our excuses will only go so far. Moreover, the Chafetz Chaim explains that even if our excuses do ward off punishment, we will still be left without reward.

Now it is well known from recent research that teenagers need much sleep, more than children or adults, or at least more than adults allow themselves. Even before this research was carried out, however, most parents of teenagers probably had some inkling of this characteristic. Nobody so fills up a living room with his presence as a teenage boy sprawled out on a couch for a two-hour summer afternoon nap. Even so, at the Talmudical Academy in the 1950s and 1960s, boys were held responsible for arriving at morning *davening* on time, and during those years, the man in charge of making certain that boys did not slip in this regard was Rabbi Boruch Milikowsky. Rabbi Milikowsky would come to *davening*, and besides the regular "equipment" carried by all married men – tallis, *tefillin* and *siddur* – he had still another tool, a small notepad. At morning *davening*, Rabbi Milikowsky would take attendance.

If you think that Rabbi Milikowsky's attendance taking was just *pro forma*, you are mistaken. There were fines for tardiness. If one came to morning *davening* after *Borchu* there was a ten cent fine. After *Kedushah*, the fine was twenty-five cents.

If there is one thing that boys remember now from those days, it is the fact that Rabbi Milikowsky collected those fines. Sometimes boys would try to skirt the issue. They would try to get away with it, but a lot of times he would come up to you with his little pad. All the boys' names were inscribed there, like God's ledger mentioned in Malachi 3:16. And he could tell you the exact dates when you had come late. He would say, "Moshe, you owe me a dollar twenty-five, and Chaim, you still owe me a dollar ten." Boys learned a very important lesson from this experience: you can't run away from responsibility.

The fines for *davening* were important because each boy's appearance at each day's *davening* was of earthshaking significance. Attendance at *davening* was something that Rebbe didn't even like to joke about. One time Moshe came to Rebbe on a motzaei Shabbos and said, "Rebbe, I'd like to give you something. I have here a dollar and a quarter." Rebbe answered with a smile, "What's that for, Moshe?" and Moshe replied, "That's for the coming week. I won't be coming to *minyan* this week." Moshe expected Rebbe to chuckle at this facetious comment, but instead Rebbe was suddenly very serious. Rebbe did not find Moshe's comment amusing. *Davening* was too important.

Rabbi Milikowsky didn't like to see boys miss *davening*, all of it or any part of it, period. During the early 1970s I once saw Rebbe get upset because a good boy from a small town was chronically starting to take off his *tefillin* during "*U-va le-Tzion*," five minutes before *davening* was over. Rabbi Milikowsky was annoyed, and he finally scolded the boy about this, emphasizing the importance of waiting until the end of *davening*. No doubt, the boy had seen this practiced in other places. Rebbe didn't like it one bit, and was no doubt afraid of bad habits developing right there in the T.A. *beis midrash*.

Even so, Rabbi Milikowsky was no slave to rules. T.A. had its share of rules, for example, about personal appearance (although T.A. certainly had fewer rules than in some of the large yeshivos in New York). But more important to Rabbi Milikowsky was the personal, emotional relationship between himself and each boy. For example, if he felt that a boy was doing everything correctly according to the rules but that he had serious character flaws or displayed irreverence, disrespect for authority or an improper attitude toward his fellow students, Rabbi Milikowsky would use rules to make his displeasure clear to the boy, to make it clear that some serious things had to change.

During the late 1960s, if Rabbi Milikowsky saw a boy with long hair and said to him, "What is that *chup* on your head? You look like a *sheigetz*," the problem usually was not that the boy wasn't following the rules about haircuts. More likely, the problem was that the boy's whole demeanor was lacking. The issue was much greater than the breaking of one rule.

On the other hand, if Rabbi Milikowsky felt that a boy was progressing spiritually in the ways that he wanted him to, then there was quite a long list of rules that he might ignore, because the spiritual side was what he was really interested in. What was going on with a particular student? Was he developing in the right way, with the right set of values and sensitivities, or was he not? These are the questions that Rabbi Milikowsky was constantly asking himself.

Chapter 13

FAILED EXPERIMENT
(A PROFILE FROM THE 1950S)

I ARRIVED FROM KIRYAT ARBA for my Friday morning interview
with Dr. Murray Kuhr (T.A. '57) in Jerusalem, and the first thing he
told me was that at 10:20, we would have to interrupt the interview
in order to go to an hour-long *shiur* by Rabbi Berel Wein in a nearby
synagogue. I thought to myself, "This is a successful T.A. graduate.
When it comes time for your *shiur*, everything else stops." The
following is the story of how that success story came to be.

Dr. Murray Kuhr was born in Dayton, Ohio. All four of his
grandparents had come to the U.S. just after the turn of the century. His
father was born in Dayton and his mother in Johnstown, Pennsylvania. By
the time Murray was a boy, there was not much left of the family's religious
commitment.

The turning point came in around 1950. That year, the family made
a sacrifice for the sake of one of the children. Murray had a brother with
asthma, and for the sake of that brother's health, the family moved to
Tucson, Arizona. There in Arizona, they met Rabbi Avraham Danzig, who
had been a student of Rabbi Avraham Yitzchak Kook in Eretz Yisrael. The
Tucson community had just built a mikveh, and Murray spent a short while
in the Tuscon day school. Over the course of a few years, the family began
to become religiously observant.

Back in 1950, the idea of a family in America becoming religious was
almost unheard of. Religiously, everyone was still moving in the other
direction. There was not yet any *ba'al teshuva* movement, and the Kuhrs

didn't know any other people who had become religious. Yet the Kuhrs, like Murray himself, were individualists and independent thinkers.

When the family returned to Ohio in 1951, Murray's father went into a business that allowed him to keep Shabbos. Back in Ohio, Murray was once more in public school. There was no day school. But the rabbi of Dayton, Rabbi Binyamin Lapidus, taught him privately and encouraged him to go out of town to yeshiva. Murray, who thirsted for Jewish growth, was very anxious to pursue his Torah education. Rabbi Lapidus personally took Murray to see Skokie in Chicago and T.A. in Baltimore. After seeing both, he chose T.A. Murray comments:

> It was a wild thing for me to become religious and a wild thing for me to go away. My parents had this faith, this wonderful faith. They had no experience with any of the religious world, but they were willing to let me do what I wanted to do. Going off to T.A. was considered an outlandish thing to do. Other people in Dayton thought I was crazy.

In September 1953, T.A. accepted Murray into the ninth grade. Rabbi Samson and Rabbi Milikowsky sensed that although Murray had no background, he would make an enthusiastic and capable student. Initially, T. A. put Murray into the seventh-grade Hebrew class. When Murray began, there were about twenty boys in the ninth grade, half of whom were dormitory boys. Although there were other boys who were in the same boat as Murray, few had as little background as he did.

Rabbi Milikowsky, the head of the dormitory, placed Murray in a dormitory room with older boys who could help him, and very quickly he learned the ropes. Murray took it all in. The whole experience was very exciting for him. Everything was new. He loved the atmosphere at T.A. There were some very spiritual, unforgettable moments, like Shabbos third meals that lasted into darkness, with slow, soulful songs that the boys would sing with all their hearts. Sometimes Rabbi Milikowsky would give haunting *divrei Torah* at the Shabbos meals.

As for the dormitory experience itself in those years (1953–1957), Murray has this to say:

> Rabbi Milikowsky was the primary influence. He was the *mashgiach* in the dormitory, the mother hen whom everybody came to with everything. He was a very caring, loving, reliable person, supportive, understanding of the stresses of adapting to the environment for a thirteen-year-old kid. He was very available and was there for them all the time. He knew that they were children without parents, and he was there to do as much as he could for them.

In 1954, Murray began tenth grade with Rabbi Milikowsky as his Rebbe. Murray comments:

> Tenth grade molded me more than any other. Rabbi Milikowsky was a really great teacher, the best teacher I ever had! He was very clear in what he wanted you to know. He had teaching techniques that compelled boys to come up with answers by themselves. Also, he had a terrific understanding of what a kid needed to know. He was very good at teaching the technique of how the *gemara* works – the nuts and bolts of how to learn. He was terrific. He taught me how to learn.

Murray recalls that when he was in the tenth grade he became "hyper-religious." Excited by his T.A. experience and by his contact with Rabbi Milikowsky, he would come home for vacations spouting notions of Judaism that were considered "really weird and extremist," at least in the spiritual backwaters of Dayton, Ohio in 1955. He wanted to wear his *tzitzis* outside his clothing and he wanted his home to have nothing but the highest standards of kashrus and Shabbos. It was a little bit scary for his parents, because to them it looked like he was going off the deep end. It reached a point at which Murray's parents called Baltimore and spoke with Rabbi

Milikowsky, whom they had come to respect, to see if he could offer any insight. Rabbi Milikowsky told Murray's father the following:

"When you make a cup of tea, first you bring the water to a boil. Obviously you're not going to drink it while it's boiling."

Unfortunately, Rabbi Milikowsky's class was Murray's last great learning experience for fifteen years. As often happens to teenage boys, following tenth grade Murray Kuhr began a rebellious period. Suddenly he felt the need to question everything, and he found it increasingly difficult to remain serious in his Torah studies. Based on the inertia of his previous efforts and reputation, he was moved up into the exclusive eleventh and twelfth grade *shiurim*, but he couldn't take those classes seriously. He wasn't interested in Torah learning any more at that time, so he did not take proper advantage of the experience.

When Murray had arrived in ninth grade, everything had been positive and rosy and exciting and new. Now he had become critical. Suddenly he found things to criticize. Suddenly he was disturbed by anything that conflicted with his secular upbringing. There was a period during which *Time Magazine* was discouraged in the dormitory. Some of the *rebbeim* were very much opposed to that magazine. For "the new Murray," this was heresy. "How could one live without *Time Magazine*?" he wondered.

Murray was rebelling against the European yeshiva model which had so attracted him three years before, and Rabbi Milikowsky certainly represented that. Even so, whatever resentment he might have felt during this period, he remained close to Rabbi Milikowsky:

Rabbi Milikowsky had a kind of humility about him that was very beautiful. He knew that as a *mashgiach* he had a great deal of responsibility. He went about his job – there wasn't any arrogance about it. He was just a loving, helping person who was doing the best he could. So that at the time that I was in a state of rebellion, I didn't have any negative feelings about him, because I knew that he was doing the best he could.

Murray himself realized what was happening to him. He knew that he needed help, but that it had to come from "outsiders." Rabbi Hirsch Diskind, Hebrew principal at Bais Yaakov of Baltimore, was someone he had been close to during the three years that Rabbi Diskind had been in Ohio. He played an important role at this difficult time. He and his wife were very kind to Murray. Murray is sure now that at the time he said challenging things to them, but they were able to handle it.

Also, Dr. Kranzler, the new English-studies principal who had only arrived in T.A. during the previous year, when Murray was in the eleventh grade, was like a bridge to the secular world for him.

When his high-school years were ending, Murray made it clear to his *rebbeim* that he would be going straight to college rather than to yeshiva. His impression at the time was that he was viewed by the yeshiva as a "failed experiment." The school had taken a chance on him and now, unfortunately, he was not going in the direction that they wished.

Yet his *rebbeim* could not know how much they had given him that would remain with him for the rest of his life. The seeds had been planted. Although Murray did not continue learning Torah in college and medical school, he kept up his mitzvah observance.

For many years, Murray had no contact with Rabbi Milikowsky. Then, eight years after he left T.A., he was looking around for internships, and he came back to Baltimore and looked up his old rebbe. Ultimately he chose to do his internship in Baltimore.

Although the internship involved a frenetic schedule that did not allow for much socializing, one time he had a Friday night rotation at Sinai Hospital, which made it impossible for him to get back to his room in east Baltimore. He therefore called Rabbi Milikowsky and was invited for Shabbos. On Shabbos afternoon, after resting from his long night's duty, he joined Rabbi Milikowsky at T.A. for *minchah* and *ma'ariv* and, at Rabbi Milikowsky's invitation, gave a guest *devar Torah* at the school *shaleshudes*. In preparing for the *devar Torah*, it felt strange to open books that he knew how to use but that he had neglected since high school.

Eventually, thirteen years after leaving T.A., at thirty years of age, Dr. Kuhr once more began to learn *gemara*, picking up where he had left off with Rabbi Milikowsky in the tenth grade.

Although Dr. Kuhr only learned a little bit each week at first, each year he made an increasing commitment. When he moved to Monsey, he became close with one of the *rebbeim* in his neighborhood, Rabbi Pessin, who gave a *daf yomi shiur* at 5:30 in the morning. He attended that *shiur* for several years and learned a great deal from it.

When the *daf yomi* reached *Yevamos*, he started finding it difficult to concentrate. It was then that he realized that he was very uncomfortable in a *shiur* in which someone else was saying the *gemara* the whole time. When he started with the *daf yomi*, he always had questions. After a while, however, the teacher answered the questions so well that Murray knew the answers before the teacher said them. At that point he became passive. Murray then realized that he had a great need to either be asking questions all the time or to be giving the *shiur* himself. Rabbi Pessin agreed that the *daf yomi shiur* was no longer the proper framework for him.

It was then, at the age of forty-six, that he began to teach *gemara* for the first time. He started teaching a simple tractate, *Ta'anis*, every morning in Rabbi Tendler's shul in Monsey at 7:15 AM. Dr. Kuhr's learning group developed into a respectable framework, and after thirteen years, they are now on their tenth tractate, with between four and eight people in attendance.

I asked Dr. Kuhr to what he would attribute his ultimate success in his learning, and he answered, "Rabbi Milikowsky was the beginning, and Rabbi Pessin in Monsey had a big influence on me, and a lot of it was on my own in between."

In the spring of 1979, Dr. and Mrs. Kuhr invited Rabbi Milikowsky to the bar mitzvah of their second son, Maimon, in Monsey, and Rabbi Milikowsky happily traveled from Baltimore to share in the joy of one of his "boys." In no small reflection of the spiritual growth that Dr. Kuhr had achieved during his lifetime, the array of speakers at the bar mitzvah was a star-studded one, including Rabbi Yaakov Kaminetzky, Rabbi Tendler,

Rabbi Pessin, Rabbi Berel Wein, and Rabbi Milikowsky. Naturally, Rabbi Milikowsky was asked to speak, and when he spoke, he touched the hearts of all by telling the story of Murray's father and the family's background, of the courage and faith he had had in sending Murray to T.A, and of the boy Murray had been in 1953. Rabbi Milikowsky spoke about these things as if they had occurred just the previous day rather than twenty-five years before. It was an object lesson for all present regarding how far one can come if one makes the effort.

Today, Dr. Kuhr, a respected physician in Monsey, gives a *gemara shiur* every morning. Recently, he has developed a new hobby: translating difficult Torah texts into English. At first this was very difficult for him, but considering his many successes, one should not be surprised to hear that he has begun to achieve the same sort of blessing in his new undertaking.

Chapter 14

BA'AL MUSSAR (MASTER PREACHER)

PEOPLE TALK ABOUT RABBI MILIKOWSKY, the "Mir *musmach* (ordained rabbi)," the European yeshiva student who spent thirteen years at the Mir Yeshiva and received his ordination there. Yet they forget that Rabbi Milikowsky spent his first eight years away from home in the Chafetz Chaim's yeshiva in Radin. As one who has learned in more than one yeshiva, I can attest to the fact that whatever effect one's later yeshivos have on one, the greatest emotional imprint comes from the earliest experience, when one is youngest and most impressionable.

Thus, besides the phenomenal relationship that Rabbi Milikowsky developed with so many boys on a one-to-one basis, he was also renowned among T.A. students as a *maggid* and a *mussar* preacher. Rabbi Milikowsky was a genius at conveying *mussar*. Yet, to paraphrase Rabbi Yosef Dov Soloveitchik, ז"ל, considering his background, his long-term exposure to the *mussar* giants, his eight years in Radin with the Chafetz Chaim, Rav Mendel Zachs and Rav Boruch Feivelovitz, his half-year in Baranovitz with Rav Elchanan Wasserman, and his thirteen years with all the great rabbis of the Mir Yeshiva, including two years as a student of the beloved *mashgiach* Rav Yerucham Levovitz, he would have had to be a genius *not* to emerge as a first class preacher and conveyer of *mussar*.

Rabbi Milikowsky was not just a brilliant conveyer of *mussar*. His relationship with *mussar* went deeper than that. Consider the following story:

When Malke Milikowsky was about nine or ten years old, her mother and grandmother decided that they would learn more English if there was a television in their home, so they bought one. One day, Malke was sitting and watching one of the old situation comedies, perhaps "Father

Knows Best." Her father, who had a bit of free time, sat watching it with her for fifteen or twenty minutes. When the program was over, Rabbi Milikowsky turned to his daughter and asked, "So, Malki, what do we see from this show? What do we *learn* from it?" It was a cute little sit-com, and Rabbi Milikowsky sat there, analyzing it with his daughter. *Mussar* was not just a tool to be used in educating his students. It was in his blood.

Although the topics of *mussar* that Rabbi Milikowsky mentioned in talks to his students were vast and varied, many students stressed that his emphasis was on a person's relationship to others, on proper speech and behavior. This was natural considering the age of the students, their not-fully-developed ability to deal with the abstract, and the fact that for most of the dormitory boys, the ninth grade at T.A. was their first experience away from home. Here were forty, fifty or sixty teenage boys from different homes and backgrounds living together for the first time! Now was the time for them to learn how to live together.

Within this field, Rabbi Milikowsky devoted himself to many different areas. Many students pointed to the centrality of *shemiras halashon*, guarding the tongue, in his talks. He would talk about the words that we use, about thoughtless, careless speech, even if unintentional, that results in our veering off in the wrong direction and offending our fellow man. And always he would bring the talk down to the teenager's level. One boy said:

I recall a very powerful *mussar shmuess* he gave about nonverbal communication and the way we gesture with our faces. What happens when a Rebbe asks a difficult question on the *gemara*, or a math teacher asks a question in calculus, and someone raises his hand and offers a wrong answer? Do we laugh out loud? Do we call out some insulting expression? And on the basketball court, when a boy shoots the ball and gets it in the hoop, we go crazy and jump up and down. But what do we do when the same boy shoots the ball and misses? He devoted a lot of time to talking about interpersonal relations in the context of physical and verbal expressions.

There were times, especially during the Ten Days of Penitence, when Rabbi Milikowsky even recommended a *"ta'anis dibbur,"* limiting talking altogether except for holy matters and Torah learning. He would explain how he had done the same thing when he was a yeshiva student in Europe, and he would describe how enriching and empowering an experience it could be.

Read the poignant words of an Atlanta boy as he describes what happened when he arrived in T.A in 1959:

> It had to be in about Elul, and Rebbe would *do* things. He would give schmuessim on Shabbos afternoon. It would be according to the way practiced in Novardok. The lights would be off in the dining room, or we would all go into a darkened room – you couldn't see a thing – and he would give a shmuess.
>
> You have to understand. I had never seen anything like this. I thought this was crazy! I was giggling so hard! I was a terrible person when I came!
>
> I look back at it and I laugh, but you want to know something? I never forgot that experience. Back then we would *do* things – I wish I had the frame of mind today to be as *frum* as I was then!
>
> We would have things like *ta'anis dibbur* in Elul on *Shabbos Shuva* (the Shabbos before Yom Kippur). How could a man who came from Poland, who couldn't speak English very well, succeed in such a thing? They had me in the fourth grade, in Rabbi Steinharter's class. I was in the ninth grade in English and in the fourth grade in Judaica. And I can sit here and I can remember having a *ta'anis dibbur*, and that I gained something from it! That I attached myself to it! Every time I think about it now I get so misty-eyed because there was something very powerful about that man that he could do that.

Kindness and compassion were other traits that Rabbi Milikowsky worked hard to instill in his boys, and once more he enlisted real-life experiences to demonstrate these principles. For example, one experience in his life in which both traits came into play was the boat trip taken by the Mir yeshiva from Vladivostok to Japan. On that boat trip, which lasted two days, there were plenty of opportunities to make use of both traits. There wasn't enough food, the boat was terribly overcrowded, and the students were exposed to the harsh elements. On that trip, Rabbi Milikowsky saw how the stronger and more fit students gave up their heavy clothing, coats and sweaters, and shared their food with the weaker, frailer students, and with those who could not bear the elements as well. He would allow the boys to make the analogy on their own to the somewhat smaller challenges of dormitory living.

No Subject Was Taboo

The fact that Rabbi Milikowsky's talks tended to deal more with people getting along together does not mean that other more philosophical and ethereal topics were avoided. Here follow the comments of Henry Lazarus, '59:

> There was many a Shabbos that R. Milikowsky did not even walk home, even though his home was only a block or a block and a half away. He constantly spoke to us no matter what meal it was. It was always a *mussar* shmuess, something that we should get out of the conversation.
>
> No subject was taboo. Whether it had to do with religion, whether it had to do with things that we should expect to encounter as we grow up, or with what's going on in the world around us. Environment-wise, how we were different from other people. All the way through explaining what man is, and analyzing his desires and his lusts. You will recall that he was addressing young boys between the ages of thirteen and seventeen. Everybody took *something* out of those speeches. Half of the time, you know, at that age, you thought he was talking to the fellow behind you or in front of you but never to you, but looking back in retrospect, I don't think that there was ever an area of life that he did not cover.

Rabbi Milikowsky had a knack for retelling Biblical stories in such a way that they presented relevant *mussar* for teenage boys. For example, when he wanted to teach about how important it is to try to realize one's potential for spiritual growth and how pitiful it is to waste that potential, he would teach about Esau. He would say, "Esau was such a good guy! Esau was such a good guy! Imagine what he could have accomplished if he had just gone in the right direction." At first, the students would look at Rebbe incredulously and a few brash ones would ask, "What's the matter, Rebbe? Did you have too much to drink?" Eventually, they would get the point, however.

Of course, Rabbi Milikowsky was not making up this idea out of his head. When all is said and done, the spiritual potential of Esau is dealt with in the Kabbalah, which teaches that Esau was born with the potential to be four hundred times greater than Jacob! Rebbe was expressing profound lessons even if the boys did not realize it at the time. All that mattered to them was that Rebbe's lessons were interesting.

In talking about "Esau's other side," Rabbi Milikowsky was teaching about the sin of squandered potential. In a more general sense, however, what he loved to do was to take Biblical figures and to show you the other side that you did not see or appreciate or understand. By such means he introduced his boys to the possibility of viewing Biblical figures – and life itself – in a more complex way.

Consider the following, from a *mussar shmuess* boys heard in the late 1950s, a week or two before Purim.

The Tragedy of Haman

RABBI MILIKOWSKY: Boys! You're always making fun of Haman! Purim is about *the tragedy of Haman!*

STUDENTS: What, Rebbe? What is this? Purim Torah?

RABBI MILIKOWSKY [banging on the table]: Boys! Quiet down! Quiet down! What's the matter, boys? You don't believe me?

Here's a man who was *sheni lamelech*, second to the king, the second most powerful man in the world. He's got everybody bowing down to him. *Nor ein yiddel dortn in a vinkel!* And there's only one Jew over there in the corner,

Mordechai, who refuses to bow down. So what's the big deal? What's wrong? You can't show that you're a democratic person? You can't allow a little protest? No! Haman couldn't! Haman said, וכל זה איננו שוה לי בכל עת אשר אני ראה את מרדכי היהודי – "All of this helps me nothing, as long as I see Mordechai the Jew sitting at the king's gate" (Esther 5:13). You don't see the Megillah as a tragedy about Haman? Haman had everything in the world! *Ein yiddel* shouldn't bother anybody.

As teenage boys approach adulthood, they have to learn how to get along with one another. They have to learn compromise. They have to learn how not to make an issue over small disagreements. They have to learn that often, happiness in life must be defined in terms of the larger picture. As represented in the above talk about Haman, Rebbe's *mussar* was always relevant to teenage boys, especially to dormitory students living in close quarters with one another.

Years after hearing Rebbe's *peshat* on Haman, Rabbi Yaakov Spivak, was inspired by it to create a new explanation of an enigmatic text from the Talmud. The Talmud asks, "What Torah verse alludes to Haman?" (*Hullin* 139b), and it responds, "Did you [Hebrew: "Ha-min"] eat from the tree of which I commanded you not to eat?" (Genesis 3:11).

Yet what does the Talmud mean? Is the whole point the phonetic similarity between *Haman* and *ha-min*? Rabbi Spivak points out that by applying Rabbi Milikowsky's explanation regarding Haman, we can understand the Talmud.

How were Haman and Adam exactly alike? Both had incredible power and control. Adam ran the world. Haman was the second most powerful man on earth.

So what was bothering Adam? *Ein boim!* One little tree that you couldn't touch. And Haman had everything in the world except for *ein yiddel in a vinkel.*

Haman min ha-torah minayin? What Biblical incident presages the tragedy of Haman? Adam and the one little tree. That one little thing God told Adam he could not have was a precursor to that one little Jew who would not go along with Haman.

Dealing with Adversity

Although Rabbi Milikowsky did not talk a great deal about his past, he occasionally allowed himself to mention various aspects of the adversity that he had had to deal with. By such means he hoped to teach the boys certain important points of *hashkafah*, the Torah outlook on life. For example, having himself lost most of his family in the Holocaust, he would tell stories of families who had suffered as his had and of the survivors who had been kept alive by the spark of Torah.

Although in the 1940s and 1950s he stopped short of sharing his own unpleasant memories with his classes, by the mid-1970s he would sometimes mention his own loss to his class as the most vivid illustration available to him. He hoped to teach the idea that everything is for the best even if it is hard for us to accept and that God has His own calculations which we often do not understand and are not necessarily meant to understand.

In the words of Rabbi Peretz Dinowitz, '74, "Rabbi Milikowsky knew how to increase everyone's trust in God. He just had a way with people. He knew what to say and how to say it. He had an incredible way of presenting his ideas, and he was a man of enormous faith."

Toot! Toot! Toot!

In 1960, the Mossad HaRav Kook Publishing House published the sefer *Menorat ha-Maor*, a midrashic collection gathered by Rabbenu Yitzchak Abuhav. In the sefer (page 587), we find a long parable about a ship that sails over the sea until it encounters an island famous for its delicious fruits and beautiful scenery. The captain allows the passengers to disembark with the proviso that they return when called, lest they miss the boat – literally. Five groups of travelers each relate with varying degrees of caution to the captain's warning. One group doesn't even leave the ship. At the other end is the group that ignores the call, remains on the island, and dies of overexposure when the seasons change. These five types of people, of course, are then likened to five approaches to repentance.

Rabbi Boruch Milikowsky came across this parable and, after simplifying it for his audience, turned it into his most famous *mussar* parable, known amongst his students as "The Boat Story" or "The Toot-Toot Story." Starting in September 1961, he would tell it each year during Elul, and older students who remember nothing else of their high school career tend to remember that story. Many students have written it down, while others continue to pass it on to their students each year, just as Rabbi Milikowsky did. The story has been performed in many settings, including a Hebrew version on Israeli television. Here follows Mr. Ely Schlossberg's tribute to Rabbi Milikowsky and his version of the Boat Story (1965).

Who can forget the beautiful, meaningful and moving delivery of Rabbi Boruch Milikowsky's holy words of *mussar*? It was a real *zechus* to have him as a rebbe. How I cherish his kind, soft words of encouragement. When he gave his *talmid mussar* the *talmid* went away with a good feeling. He made you feel very special, even when you did something wrong. He always gave positive reinforcement and spoke directly to the problem, speaking openly to you as a *talmid* and also as his friend. He had a very special relationship, especially, with every dorm boy, acting as a father in many a way. While I was a Baltimore resident, I knew rebbe as both a *talmid* and as a neighbor. His experiences in Europe, the Holocaust and Shanghai were transmitted to us, his *talmidim*, with his deep roots of his past Torah life, with his beautiful and unforgettable *mussar* words, and his very warm friendship.

The 1960s was a difficult era for teenagers in America, but Rebbe understood and listened to each *talmid* and was very much in tune with the contemporary, turbulent, topsy-turvy hippie culture. With his thick accent and with his style of speech, he spoke our language and we listened. He spoke with love and care. His talks and his listening to his T.A. boys and his Torah and *mussar* were absorbed by his hundreds and hundreds of students. His advice and counsel have guided us all, in all of our different walks of life.

Much of what I have accomplished in my own life I attribute to what my wonderful parents, our Rav, Rabbi Mendel Feldman, my elementary school rebbe Mr. Kurt Flamm, zt"l, Rabbi Milikowsky, my high-school rebbe zt"l, and my very special principal and mentor and dear friend, Dr. Gershon Kranzler zt"l gave over to me. It is interesting that each of these *mechanchim* (educators) taught at T.A. during the 1960s. Each gave me an important perspective on respect for Torah, love of Torah, God and Israel, and respect for all of mankind.

Rabbi Milikowsky was part of an old, rich Judaic world, a world destroyed by horror, and he survived, b"h, to give over to us the rich European Jewish culture. He so meticulously bridged his life to us in the modern world with his love and charm and keen intuition. He reached his boys with a warm smile and a very special "chen" (Jewish charm) that endeared him to all. Most memorable was his most ingenious way of giving over his masterful words of *mussar*.

My most favorite *mussar* was the "Toot, Toot, Toot" story, which I have repeated time and time again to *Pirchei* groups, Camp Agudah and Camp Munk groups, NCSY kids, my own children and, iy"h, to my grandchildren in the very near future. The story will always be the same, but the delivery... no; only Rebbe could do it the way he did, so simple, so sweet and so perfect! Singing it in his rich warm voice, eyes rolling back, where only the white of his eyes was visible, swaying back and forth. We were entranced, completely fixated and nobody could deliver *mussar* in a more beautiful and meaningful way. So here is Rebbe's story of "Toot, Toot, Toot."

Rebbe entered the classroom and turned off the lights. He then closed the door and told us to close our *sefer* for now, for today our learning would begin a little differently. Today Rebbe had a story to tell us. He sat at his desk with his head in his hands and he began to chant a sweet, sad melody of old. "Ay-yay-yay, ay-yay-yay," over and over again. He chanted:

"My dear *talmidim*, I have a story to tell you all. Listen, listen carefully to the story because there is so much we can learn from this beautiful story.

"There was a captain who had a ship, and he went to the town people to make them a proposition. 'I know of a place, I know of a very beautiful place, an island where all the sand and stones on the island are made from diamonds. You are free to gather up all the stones you can carry and load them on my ship to take home to your families. This wonderful place I can take you to, but there is one important thing you must each remember. When I say it is time to leave, I will sound the ship's horn on three occasions. First time is a warning toot-toot, and a little later the second toot-toot means that you had better come aboard at once, and the third toot-toot is my final call. And once that final toot-toot sounds, moments later the ship will leave the port and return you to your town and your home. So remember the rules and take heed of the horn.' The town's people were excited and all agreed to the rules. The ship left port on the way to the beautiful island. Ay-yay-yay, ay-yay-yay," over and over, Rebbe sang and swayed…. And we were absolutely transfixed. Each *talmid* was on that ship. We were going to wherever Rebbe would take us.

"From the ship, after many weeks of travel, a lookout perched high in the rafters and sails of the ship saw a sparkle far, far away. He called out to the people, 'Land ahoy, I see the sparkle of the diamonds,' which were getting brighter and brighter as the ship approached the shore. Excitement was building and the captain called together all the crew and passengers to repeat the rules one more time so all clearly understood:

"'Remember the three toot-toots and never forget the rules and our agreement.' As the ship docked everyone excitedly ran onto the diamond-covered island. They could not believe their eyes. It was just as the captain had told them… diamonds, diamonds everywhere. The people scattered across the island, each gathering diamonds wherever they could.

"After many days the captain knew the time had come to go back to sea and return to home. As he blew the first horn, toot-toot, the people took heed. The cautious ones took their diamonds and, satisfied with their lot, boarded the ship.

"But you know, but you know," Rebbe would say, "many people would say: 'There are so many diamonds left. We can wait for the second toot-toot and there is still plenty of time.' And so it was a day later the captain sounded the second horn, toot-toot. By now the anxious crowd streamed in haste to the ship. After all, the instructions were quite clear, and there would be just one more warning. But you know, but you know," Rebbe would say, "There were those people who could not leave a single diamond on the ground. They said, 'How can we leave these precious stones here? We will wait to the very last minute and run back, just before the ship leaves port.'" And so it was, hours went by and the captain realizing foolish people were still on the island gave the final toot-toot. Minutes later the captain raised anchor and the ship began to leave the port. Frantically some stragglers jumped into the waters to board the ship. With the help of those on board they climbed aboard, cold, wet and frightened from a near-disaster. "But you know, but you know, my precious *talmidim*, that there were those very foolish people whom greed kept away from even the final toot-toot. Gazing down to the ocean, they finally realized the ship had set sail, and as they helplessly ran to the shore, it was of course much too late. Soon after, a severe winter set in and they all perished. Ay-yay-yay… ay-yay-yay! What good were their diamonds to them now?"

By now, Rebbe had us completely entranced. He continued his melodious chant: "And who, my *talmidim*, is the captain? Why, of course, my dear boys, the captain is Hakadosh Baruch Hu. And who are the passengers? Of course it is we, we, His dear children. Hashem takes us to a world of *gashmius* (materialism), filled with sparkling, tempting diamonds. But we have an agreement and the agreement, it is our Torah. Hashem allows us to gather much physical wealth, the abundant diamonds, but he never wants us to forget our agreement, and to always live by the rules. And he gives us warnings so many, many times, we have the opportunity to return to the Torah and not to get caught up into our greed. Some do *teshuvah* (repent) at the first toot-toot, but not all return. Some of us need a second chance to return to the Torah, and we only return at the second toot-toot. Ay-yay-yay, but you know how very foolish some of us are. We can't, oh, we can't pull ourselves out of greed. We *mamash* wait till the very last second and then only with help from others we are finally pulled aboard the ship. Our *teshuvah* is late, very late, yet Hashem accepts our last-minute *teshuvah*. But *nebech* (alas), oh, *nebech,* some either don't hear, or just don't want to hear, the final toot-toot. They will have to meet with Hashem empty-handed in both *gashmius* and in *ruchnius* (spirituality). They never, never do return.

"My dear boys, you, my wonderful *talmidim*! Please! Please! Always respond to the toot-toot. It's Hashem's way of telling us that He loves us, and we must all eventually one day return home. You see, the real home is the *olam ha'emes*, the World of Truth. Don't get caught up your whole life looking for the diamonds. Always take heed of our Torah and the agreement we have with Hashem. Listen carefully to each toot-toot. Hashem is waiting for us all to come home. Please listen for the toot-toot!"

The room was totally still and a hush was upon the entire class. Rebbe finally opened his eyes, and with a glimmer of a smile, and a reassuring nod, that day, we learned very, very well, and we davened with a great deal of concentration. That concentration and special learning didn't always last too long, but ever since then, all twenty-five of those *talmidim* have been listening very carefully to the toot-toot of Hashem.

Chapter 15

CLOSE CALLS

You Have Incurred Guilt, You Have Betrayed...

THE TALMUDICAL ACADEMY HAS ALWAYS been blessed with fine students who went on afterwards to bring the school both secular and spiritual fame and glory. The names of renowned *roshei yeshiva* and prominent pulpit rabbis who have graduated from T.A. are far too many to list individually. During T.A.'s early years, this was particularly the case. T.A.'s student body represented the cream of the crop. Anybody who wished to send his sons to day school but, for whatever reason, did not want the boys to study in New York City, sent them to T.A. There was nowhere else.

Saadya Tzaddikman* was one such source of pride to the school. During his last years in T.A. in the early 1950s, he excelled in Rabbi Bobrovsky's *shiur* and subsequently went straight into the Lakewood Yeshiva at age eighteen. Let it be noted that at the time, there were quite a few other such occurrences thanks to the newness of Lakewood, the quality of Rabbi Bobrovsky's *shiur*, and the excellence of the students in that *shiur*.

Saadya was a boy who was one hundred percent Torah. For him there was nothing else. He was an enormous *talmid chacham* even before he left T.A., and by the time he came back from Lakewood to spend a Shabbos at T.A. five years later, he had become a *kanai*, a zealot, whose gaze, like that of Rabbi Shimon bar Yochai, seared like fire.

In honor of Saadya's visit, Rabbi Milikowsky asked the boy scheduled to say a *devar Torah* at *shalashudes* to accept a postponement, and then he invited Saadya Tzaddikman to deliver a *devar Torah* in the boy's place. Saadya accepted.

Saadya's *devar Torah* began well enough. Saadya had chosen to speak about the importance of total devotion to Torah learning, devoid of distraction. Certainly a fine topic and one for which he was eminently qualified to hold forth.

And then it happened. Saadya suddenly said, "And I understand there are boys who are going out with girls here!" Immediately, without missing a beat, Rabbi Milikowsky started to sing *"Shir Hama'alos..."* in the loudest voice he could muster. The meal was over. Saadya Tzaddikman's *devar Torah* was over. Rebbe had cut him off.

After a few days, boys began to ask Rabbi Milikowsky why he had done such a thing, cutting off Rabbi Saadya Tzaddikman, and Rebbe chose to quote from Rambam, Hilchos Teshuvah 2:7. There, Rambam teaches that while it is praiseworthy to publicly specify one's sins against one's neighbor as part of repentance, it is considered insolent and unbeneficial to publicly specify one's sins against God.

Rabbi Milikowsky knew that some of the boys at T.A. had a social life and went out on dates with girls. Certainly the yeshiva frowned on this. Yet Rabbi Milikowsky had his own ideas about how to raise the spiritual level of his boys, a project to which he was lovingly devoted day and night, and he wished to protect them from sudden and unbidden "shock treatments" administered by outside visitors. He feared that more harm than good would result. Rabbi Milikowsky related to each boy individually. Sometimes he would confront a boy and strongly forbid him to have contact with girls. With other boys he would look the other way, or chide them gently. It depended on the boy.

In Accordance with His Own Way...

King Solomon taught, "Train the child in accordance with his own way" (Proverbs 22:6). Rabbi Boruch Milikowsky was one educator who truly put these words to practice. The advice he gave always varied with the student receiving it.

Rabbi Milikowsky was not a robot and his advice did not sound pre-recorded. You could never guess what he was going to say. He would tell one boy, "Get out of the *beis midrash* and go play ball." He would tell another one, "Spend more time in the *beis midrash*." He told one boy, "Go home for Shabbos, you need it." He told another, "Stay another three Shabbosim. It will be good for you and you can handle it."

One dormitory student described the matter as follows:

> He understood that the Washington guys had a different experience than the Baltimore guys. The Washington guys were coming from a town without a yeshiva. Thus, for example, he knew that a bunch of us would see girls in Baltimore. We thought, of course, that we were fooling him and that he never had an idea of what was going on. But he knew the whole time what we were doing. This became clear to me.

By the same token, Rabbi Milikowsky did not push all boys to go on to become *kollelniks*. This was especially so during the first decade in which he was connected to the Talmudical Academy. During those years, the percentage of students from non-observant homes was higher than it was later on, as was the percentage of students whose parents were first-generation refugees from the war. The religious standards of the religious families themselves were lower, the standard of living was lower, and just surviving and striking sound economic roots on American soil was still the central issue for many families. Thus, in advising students, Rabbi Milikowsky would take into account the student's background, where that student's parents were situated religiously, and, as much as possible, he would take into account what he thought those parents might want for their child.

For example, if the parents were academics, Rabbi Milikowsky might encourage the boy to explore that direction as a career. This seemed most natural to Rabbi Milikowsky, and if it worked out, it would certainly make it easier for the boy to get his parents' moral and material support.

If someone's parents were part of the business world, Rabbi Milikowsky would take that into account as well. He would size up students and give advice suited to that student. One student from the 1950s, the son of a businessman, recalled Rabbi Milikowsky always using the phrase, "Listen, Tzvi, later on when you're in business..."

Of course, if someone came from a rabbinic family, then even during the 1950s Rabbi Milikowsky would "let his hair down," so to speak, and if the boy seemed suited to continue in that direction, Rabbi Milikowsky would encourage him. One student from the 1950s reported:

> There was one person I have in mind, a classmate of mine, whose father was a rebbe. Rabbi Milikowsky continuously gave that person advice to learn in yeshiva and *kollel*, to remain in the four cubits of Torah learning, and to become a yeshiva rebbe. He did not advise him that he should necessarily enroll in college, because, after all, that boy's own father had not gone to college. Rather, he kept repeating to that boy to continue in Jewish education. Today, that person's efforts have met with much success.

Back in the 1950s, many students came from non-religious backgrounds as well. Many students, especially in the dormitory, came from non-observant homes, but the rabbis of their communities had recommended T.A. for them, knowing full well that the parents were not even Sabbath-observant. Such students came to T.A. during the 1950s and lived Orthodox Jewish lives there. Although many became religious Jews, that was not always the case. Sometimes a boy who had fit in at T.A. for four years would return to his hometown or go to the university campus and stray. Rabbi Milikowsky had an excellent sense of which direction a boy was moving, and he often seemed able to tell in what direction a boy was headed in the future. Often, his advice to boys was, "You go to college. You get your degree. Try and be an outstanding Sabbath-observant person in your community." The human conscience is a complex mechanism. Different boys would hear such advice and interpret it in different ways:

– Hank, you look spooked!

– Boy! Am I!

– What happened?

– Rebbe just had a talk with me about next year.

– Yeah? What did he say?

– Listen, he took my hand and smiled at me with his special smile, and then he started asking me about the University of Georgia. I told him how big the Hillel was and everything. And then he looked me in the eye and said, "Try to be conscientious in college. Don't forget the yeshiva. And try – *try*, he said – to keep Shabbos." *Try*, he said. For crying out loud, *how does he know what's going on in my head??*

One boy who heard such advice did not, in fact, remain Sabbath-observant, but he always remembered Rabbi Milikowsky. Many years later, when he was a very successful businessman and Rabbi Milikowsky was old and retired, that person – we'll call him George – suddenly contacted Rabbi Milikowsky and came to visit. After a warm greeting and a few minutes of exchanging memories of old times, the visitor came to the point:

"Rebbe, I have been a successful businessman now for many years, and have put away quite a sum in stocks and savings. I feel that I owe a great debt of gratitude to you, Rebbe, and I know that you have never been wealthy, so let me ask you: What do you need? I know you have four married children, all of them with large families. You are my Rebbe and I want to send you a big present!"

Rabbi Milikowsky chuckled quietly for a moment and answered, "What do I need? George, George... Why, I don't need anything! But thank you for thinking of me!"

George insisted, "But Rebbe! I want to do something for you!"

Now at the time, the Talmudical Academy was in need of financial help – what day school ever isn't? – so Rabbi Milikowsky said, "Listen, George, if you want you can make out a nice donation to the Talmudical Academy, and you can give it in my honor," and George responded, "If that's what your desire is, that's what I'll do." He gave a substantial contribution to the Talmudical Academy, amounting to tens of thousands of dollars.

చ్ఛ ళ్ళ

Rabbi Milikowsky believed in "training the child in accordance with his own way," not just as far as guidance in life, but as far as the nuts and bolts of Torah learning as well. He was against the idea that success in a gemara *shiur* was the be-all and end-all of a yeshiva student's spiritual essence. He described to his students that when he was a student of Rav Elchonon Wasserman, if a hundred students out of the three hundred present understood the *shiur*, that was considered a great success.

He said that you can't force a boy to be what he's not. Better that each boy should be good in what he's naturally good at. One boy can be great at *Chumash*. Another can be great at *bekius* (basic non-analytical Talmud study with the purpose of covering much ground). As Rabbi Yaakov Spivak put it, "That's why they loved him. He found out what was your good point and he said, 'Work on that point.'"

చ్ఛ ళ్ళ

Spare the Rod?
During the 1950s, some aspects of education were different from today. For example, not only parents and educators, but students themselves, had a different attitude to corporal punishment than they have now. Back then, certain behaviors by parents and teachers that would never be condoned today were not only condoned but expected. The following story exemplifies this.

Harvey Jacobs* and his roommate Melvin slept on the second floor of Rabbi Milikowsky's house. It was a Saturday night and they had gone to the movies with permission from Rabbi Milikowsky. However, they had stayed out beyond curfew to have an ice cream and to do some other things. Now these two giggly boys, drunk on good ice cream and camaraderie, came back to Rebbe's house, and it was past pumpkin hour. Everyone in the house was asleep. The question was this: Could they make it inside and up the stairs to their bedroom without waking anyone and without arousing the wrath of Rabbi Milikowsky? Could their entry into Rebbe's house be as smooth as the ice cream that they had so recently and so illicitly enjoyed?

Harvey turned the knob of the front door, and the door opened. It wasn't locked. A good omen! The two boys came inside and shut the door. Silence! Even better. They moved stealthily towards the back steps which would lead them up to the second floor, and they began to ascend the stairs.

Harvey had a problem, however. Creaking up the back steps of Rabbi Milikowsky's old wooden house without making noise was almost impossible. Knowing this made Harvey nervous, and that, in turn, made him giggle. Of course, this was the very worst thing he could have done at that moment, worse than any noise that the stairs might have made.

It wasn't any good. Harvey woke up the entire house with his giggling, and Rabbi Milikowsky came running out of his bedroom and ran down the stairs, grabbing a broom. Harvey was fast and he managed to flee the house, but Rabbi Milikowsky was faster, and he chased Harvey down the alley behind the house, occasionally whacking him from behind with the straw end of the broom. Some of those whacks hurt!

Harvey was so incensed that when they came back inside, he ran to the phone and called his father and told him what had happened. Harvey's father and mother lived forty miles away in Silver Spring, and Mr. Jacobs came up to T.A. the next day. Harvey thought to himself, "Now Rebbe's really in for it!"

In even tones, Mr. Jacobs asked to be told what had happened. When he heard the story, he took off his belt and gave it to Rebbe, saying, "If you ever need to do this again, don't use a broom. This is what you use. A belt!" Mr. Jacobs then got up and drove home to Silver Spring.

Harvey Jacobs sat there with mouth agape. He had gotten the message. Henceforth, his efforts to honor the curfew showed marked improvement!

A different era, different parents, and Rebbe.

First Son of the South

Rabbi Yaakov Spivak grew up in a religious home in Atlanta, Georgia. The problem was that when Yaakov was a boy, during the early 1950s, there was no Jewish day school in Atlanta, so he went to the Orthodox afternoon Hebrew school founded and run by Rabbi Emanuel Feldman. Yaakov's father, who had learned in Torah Va-Da'as as a boy, gave him such a good education at home that he was more advanced than most of the kids in the Hebrew school. Mornings he would go to public school, and there were long periods of time when he would wear a yarmulka there. For an elementary school boy to wear a yarmulka in an Atlanta public school fifteen years before the Six Day War took the courage displayed by the Patriarch Abraham when he smashed the idols in his father's store. It tells us something about his home, about the influence exerted by Rabbi Feldman, and about Yaakov's own strong will.

As Yaakov approached the end of elementary school, his father began to see that the time was right for him to go somewhere to yeshiva. In the meantime, Yaakov was becoming a discipline problem in Rabbi Feldman's class because he "knew everything" and was bored. Rabbi Feldman said, "I'm tired of putting you outside the class! We've got to send you away to yeshiva." So in 1956 Yaakov was sent to the Talmudical Academy, where Rabbi Feldman and his two brothers, born and raised in Baltimore, had themselves studied. Yaakov suddenly went from being the most advanced student to being the kid who knew nothing. He was the first of many boys to be sent to T.A. by Rabbi Feldman.

When Yaakov came to T.A., he was twelve years old. He had a southern drawl. He was the tallest boy in the seventh-grade class of T.A, and due to his low level, they could only put him in the fifth-grade Hebrew class. Imagine how embarrassing it must have been for Yaakov to be in this situation! He walked into the fifth-grade Hebrew class, and when his "fellow classmates" saw him they laughed their little heads off. He felt terrible. He phoned his father and then he went to Rabbi Milikowsky, who was responsible for him.

"Rebbe!" said Yaakov, almost in tears. "I can't stay here!"

"Why not, Yankele?"

"I open up the *chumash*, and Moshe speaks in Hebrew and I don't understand him. And I open up the *gemara*, and Abaye speaks in Aramaic and I don't understand him. And then in the class, the rebbe speaks in Yiddish and I don't understand him. And then in the dormitory, my roommate is from Brooklyn, and he speaks in English, and I don't understand him either!"

Rabbi Milikowsky sat there, puffing on a cigarette, sizing up the boy before him. He had done his homework, and he knew that this Yaakov was a tough cookie.

He said, "Yankev! Yankele! *Zos haTorah. Adam ki yamus ba'ohel.* [Such is the Torah: When a man dies in a tent… (Numbers 19:14)] The Rabbis said that one cannot acquire Torah learning unless one first *kills himself* over it! You'll see! You'll go back to the fifth grade and *you will be better!* You will understand and you will learn the Torah portion of *Shemos*. O.K.?"

Yaakov cried and cried.

The next day he walked into the fifth grade class and again the kids were laughing. He turned to them and said, "The day will come when you will not laugh."

Rabbi Yaakov Spivak, today a Rosh Kollel in Monsey, New York, and a popular Jewish writer and radio personality, concludes this story as follows:

"Rabbi Milikowsky saw me through it all. That's how I came to T.A. I was one month in the fifth grade and one month in the sixth grade, and after that I was in the seventh grade.

"When I graduated T.A., I won the award for the best student in *Tanach* (Bible) and Hebrew at the school. And even though I have *Yoreh Yoreh, Yodin Yodin* from some of the top *roshei yeshivos*, the top diploma in my office is the Zushi and Bessie Cohen Memorial Award for excellence in *Tanach* and Hebrew. And I have that above *Yodin Yodin*. Because that was the one that hurt the most, and that was the sweetest of all victories."

In 1985, Rabbi Spivak was asked to deliver the keynote address at the T.A. dinner in Rabbi Milikowsky's honor. More on that later.

Succos in the Desert

Rabbi Boruch Milikowsky always viewed it as his duty to protect his boys from negative influences. The list of what "negative influences" included was a topic for good-natured debate between him and some of the more spirited dormitory boys. For example, Atlanta, Georgia during the late 1950s was, for Rabbi Milikowsky, the seat of the Devil himself. He used to joke, "Atlanta, Georgia? You come from *Atlanta, Georgia*? Who knows what's there!"

Sometimes the Atlanta boys would serve as willing participants in "the burning of Atlanta." One boy would say, "Rebbe, the *Soton* (Satan) dances in the street in Atlanta. We dance with the *Soton*!" Or, Rebbe, himself, would ask, "What do you do when you come home for Pesach, boys?" and the boys would answer, "We dance with the *Soton*, Rebbe!"

Of course, such conversations tended to occur most often when holidays were approaching, and the Atlanta boys really did want to go home to see their families. If the boys slandered their town, it was at least partly to persuade Rebbe, through the use of ironic exaggeration, to let them go home.

Sometimes Rebbe was convinced and sometimes he held his ground. One time, a fourteen-year-old boy from a non-observant home in Atlanta asked him for permission to go home for Succos. Rabbi Milikowsky knew all about the boy's background. There would certainly be no succah for him at his home in Atlanta. Also, during the late 1950s, Jewishly, Atlanta was not the same town that it is today. In short, there was no certainty that if the boy went home for Succos, he would have a spiritually uplifting experience, let alone a kosher experience. Often Rabbi Milikowsky let boys make decisions by themselves, sounding them out and letting them come to their own conclusions. In this case, however, he looked at the boy and said decisively, "Don't go to the desert for Succos!" The boy was upset. Succos was late that year; he had been in school a few months already since the start of September, and he had been looking forward to seeing his family.

Still, even though the boy had been counting on going home, Rabbi Milikowsky managed to talk him into staying and arranged for him to be with a religious family in Baltimore. The boy ended up having a wonderful Succos in Baltimore, and he later told Rabbi Milikowsky how much he had appreciated it. Indeed, there was a Pesach a few years later when he again did not go home, but preferred instead, on his own initiative, to spend the holiday with a religious classmate.

It would have been much easier for Rabbi Milikowsky to tell the boy that he could go home. Certainly he would have had much less explaining to do the next time he saw the boy's family. Yet, because he really cared about his boys, he persuaded the boy to stay in Baltimore and went to the trouble of arranging suitable housing for him. Religious dormitory boys from Brooklyn, and some from Atlanta as well, went home for Pesach and Succos without any problem. Yet for many years Rabbi Milikowsky personally undertook the task of persuading boys from non-observant homes in Jewishly weak towns to spend the holidays with religious families, and he found hosts for each boy by himself.

Enveloped in a Mitzvah

Nobody who visited Rabbi Milikowsky in his succah could fail to be moved. The man who had seen so much suffering in his lifetime sat in his succah in total joy, enveloped in the mitzvah that of all mitzvos most symbolizes the Jew's total trust in God and reliance on Divine Providence. Rabbi Milikowsky would sigh, with his eyes half closed and that angelic smile by which all knew him, and he would tell his students, with renewed astonishment each time, "Succah is a mitzvah that *the whole body* goes into! One's body actually goes inside the mitzvah! It is *surrounded* by it!"

In 1954, Meyer Weinstock was an eleventh grade dormitory student in T.A. That year, he decided in agreement with Rabbi Milikowsky that rather than make the long trip back to Toronto for Succos, he would spend the holiday right there in Baltimore, and that is what he did, staying with the Milikowskys.

As part of his preparations for the holiday, he helped Rabbi Milikowsky to build his succah. When the succah was complete, Meyer looked at it and wondered whether what they had just built would be able to remain standing until the end of the holiday. It looked flimsy to him. That year, however, Hurricane Hazel, one of the worst hurricanes of the 1950s, struck the Eastern seaboard, destroying many of the succahs built in Baltimore that year. Yet Rabbi Milikowsky's succah remained standing until the end. After that, whenever Meyer Weinstock thought about the storm winds Rabbi Milikowsky had weathered during his lifetime, the tribulations that he had suffered, Rebbe's succah and the storm winds of Hurricane Hazel would always come to mind.

Chapter 16

RECURRING THEMES

Four Surprise Visits

A COMMON THEME of our rabbinic literature is God's humility. Rabbi Yochanan said (*Megillah* 31a): "Wherever you find God's greatness, there you find His humility." The Chafetz Chaim, in *Chomas HaDas*, Chapter 12, quotes the Midrash as saying that God did ten things beneath His stature for the sake of Israel, including descending to Mount Sinai to give Israel the Torah (*Yalkut Shimoni*).

Rabbi Milikowsky was no guru sitting on a mountaintop, awaiting pilgrimages from his disciples. He was a flesh-and-blood rebbe, concerned over his students' spiritual and physical welfare and ready to travel far to keep in contact. For many years he traveled across America – and Israel – during his vacations, as far as California and the American South, seeking out his students. Very often he just wished to derive contentment from their success and spiritual growth. On the other hand, if a student had decreased his level of observance, Rabbi Milikowsky felt some measure of responsibility, as though he himself had done something wrong. He thus hoped during his visit to be able to put in one final word, one last bit of input, that might ignite a spark. At times he succeeded in this, but he was always making the effort.

Here follow four "surprise visits," a mere fraction of what was.

I. Surprise Wedding Gift

Chaim Botwinick '67 walked into shul the Friday afternoon before his wedding. He was getting married on Sunday night, and he looked forward to having his beloved Rebbe, Rabbi Boruch Milikowsky, come up on Sunday from Baltimore to Philadelphia to officiate. On his right sat his brother Moshe, three years younger than he, but on his left sat no one. Unfortunately, his father had passed away two years before.

He started *davening minchah*. All of a sudden he felt as though someone was on his left. It was a feeling of comfort, of familiarity, of someone he was close to, as if his own father were there. Finally he turned to his left and saw it was Rebbe! Rabbi Milikowsky had decided to show up for the *aufruf*. Of course, Chaim's mother knew that Rebbe was coming early. He had called ahead of time so that the family could find a place for him to stay for Shabbos. But he had told Mrs. Botwinick, "Don't tell Chaim!"

Imagine the effect of such a visit on a young *chassan* about to be married. Chaim's reaction after thirty years bears out the great impression that this experience left upon him, and the great lift that it gave him: "Rebbe showed up! As a matter of fact, he didn't even say 'Shalom aleichem.' He just walked into shul, sat down next to me and started *davening*! Very, very special! Very special! He made the whole Shabbos very special."

II: It Is Not Good for Man to Be Alone

Alan Messer's* parents liked Rabbi Milikowsky very much, and Rebbe liked them in return. Impressed by the conscientious way that he had taken care of their son during his years at T.A., they became personal friends of the rabbi and stayed in touch after Alan graduated. Of course, Rabbi Milikowsky attended Alan's wedding, and to this very day, Alan's parents visit Rabbi Milikowsky's daughter, Malke Bina, whenever they come to Israel. Anyway, this story relates what happened the week after Alan and his classmates graduated from T.A.

The years of yeshiva high school were over and the graduating dormitory boys were heading back to their hometowns. Naturally, Rabbi

VISITS FAR AND WIDE

In Toronto for a wedding of Meir Weinstock's daughter.
Meir is to the left.

Officiating at Ben Froelich's Vineland, New Jersey Wedding.

On Israel's Coast with Ivan Lerner and Eli Schmell.

155

Boruch Milikowsky, who knew everything there was to know about his boys, also knew that Alan Messer was going back to his parents' home in Washington and that he was going to be working for the government during the summer. Somehow, Rabbi Milikowsky also knew that Alan's parents were going to be away from home during that first week following graduation. Alan had not mentioned this little fact to Rebbe, but perhaps Alan's parents had.

Picture the scene. Alan was going to be home, alone. He was a high-school graduate. He was not a baby. He had all his friends in Washington. And he was looking forward to it. His parents were gone, he had the car, and he thought to himself, "You know, maybe now would be a good time to sow some wild oats..."

Two days after he arrived home from T.A., he was standing in his living room. It was five or six in the afternoon and he had just come home from work, when all of a sudden there was a knock at the door. It was Rebbe!

"Rebbe! Rebbe! What are you doing here?"

"Oh, I know your parents aren't here! I thought you might be feeling lonely. I've come to keep you company!"

Alan wasn't fooled. He knew very well that Rabbi Milikowsky was not afraid of his being lonely! Quite the opposite was the case.

Rebbe came for three days and stayed with Alan in his home. At night, Alan had all the guys over, and they sat around and *shmuessed* and sang and ate and went visiting. In short, they had a ball! The way things worked out, Alan had no time to do anything he might later be ashamed of. And shortly after Rebbe's departure, Alan's parents returned.

III. Voice from the Past

Here is George Stanislavski, describing Rabbi Milikowsky's surprise visit in the early 1980s:

> I had already been out of T.A. for seventeen, eighteen years. I was already married with children. One day, I get a phone call. And the

person on the other end says, "Reb Gedalya?" I recognized his voice right away. I cried out, "Rebbe!" He says, "I'm here in Israel visiting my children." There's Chaim, and Malke Bina, his daughter, lives in the Old City. "I'm visiting with my children and I'd like to see you." This is seventeen, eighteen years after I had already graduated T.A. He had made a point to look me up. I had come to Baltimore once or twice and I had just briefly seen him. I had come for simchas, something like that, and I had just briefly seen him. I had occasionally corresponded but after I moved to Israel in '72, I had sort of lost contact with him. This was like ten, twelve years after I came to Israel. And he just called me. What I did was, that afternoon, I gathered together all of my kids and my wife. We went to Bayit Vegan. He was staying in an apartment in Bayit Vegan and I went to visit him there. I showed him my children. *And I introduced them to my rebbe.* It was absolutely fantastic!

IV. Experiencing Yaakov Neufeld

In 1984, when Rabbi Milikowsky was seventy-one years old, he traveled with his wife Leah down to Florida to visit the several alumni who had settled there. When he was in the Miami area, he spent Shabbos with one student, ate dinner with several others, and visited the homes of still more.

The following is one story, as recalled by Rabbi Yaakov Neufeld, '72. After Yaakov graduated T.A., he learned in yeshiva and in kollel and made a personal commitment to Jewish education. By 1984, at age twenty-nine, he had become the principal of a Jewish day school in Miami and the happy father of three children. Yaakov fondly recalls the telephone ringing that Wednesday night, and the playful words, "Hello, Yaakov? Do you know who this is?"

Yaakov's heart skipped a beat. It sounded like his old Rebbe, Rabbi Boruch Milikowsky, although he hadn't heard his voice in five years. Yet he wasn't sure. More likely it was one of his old friends playing a trick on him. That would be just like them! They knew his feelings for Rabbi Milikowsky.

157

Flustered, he answered, "I *think* I know who it is, but I'm not really sure it's who I think it is."

"Well, what do you mean?" the voice continued. "Who do you think it is?"

"Now I'm *really* not sure," he answered. Finally, at the risk of being the target of a practical joke, he asked, breathlessly, "Is it Rebbe Milikowsky?" and, of course, Rabbi Milikowsky responded, "Of course it's me!"

After overcoming his surprise, Yaakov suggested that he take Rabbi Milikowsky and his wife to lunch at one of the local restaurants. Yet Rabbi Milikowsky would not hear of it. He said, "No! I want to come and see your house. I want to see your wife. I want to see your children. I want to see the school where you are a principal." Rabbi Milikowsky didn't just want to *see* Yaakov Neufeld. He wanted to *experience* him.

So on Sunday afternoon, Yaakov went and picked up the rabbi and rebbetzin, showed them his school, introduced them to his family and took him on a tour of his home. His oldest son even got to learn with Rebbe for a short while.

Not only did Rabbi Milikowsky and his wife truly experience Yaakov Neufeld, but Yaakov himself had an unforgettable experience in a Rebbe's love for his *talmid*. At the end of the visit, still another student came and picked up Rabbi Milikowsky and his wife and took them to visit with *him*.

Three Helping Hands

In 1863, at age twenty-five, the Chafetz Chaim left Radin for a year to immerse himself in Torah learning in the city of Minsk. So much did he overwork himself in his studies that he became seriously ill and had to cease Torah learning for an entire year at his physicians' insistence.

Henceforth, he always advised his students on the importance of taking care of themselves. He said they should maintain a regular schedule with fixed times for eating and sleeping so as to avoid overworking themselves and ultimately losing learning time.

(from *Tenuat HaMussar*)

I. Yom Kippur, 1958

During the month of Elul, the *rebbeim* at the Talmudical Academy have always gone to great lengths to prepare the boys spiritually and psychologically to take full advantage of Rosh Hashanah and Yom Kippur. It is no surprise then that during the 1950s, when T.A. was located in the middle of Orthodox Jewish Baltimore, the Yom Kippur afternoon break before *minchah* would find large numbers of boys from both the city and dormitory spending their last free moments of the Days of Awe in Torah learning.

One year, Morris Landau,* a serious ninth-grader, was sitting in the *beis midrash* on such a Yom Kippur afternoon. He had the flu and had lost much fluid over the course of the day. He felt chilly and weak. In fact, he felt terrible and he looked it too, but it was Yom Kippur, and he reasoned that this was not the time to worry about such things. Had anyone suggested to him that he was very sick and should drink something, he would have responded, "I'd rather die first!"

For a half hour he had been staring at the same page of *Chumash*, and the words were running together, but he did not want to leave the *beis midrash* to rest. The gravity of these moments had been impressed upon him. But Morris was about to get a lesson in priorities.

Suddenly Morris felt a gentle and familiar hand touching his forehead. Rabbi Boruch Milikowsky, sitting in the front of the *beis midrash*, had sensed that something was wrong.

"Moshe, you're burning up! Why, you must have a 103 temperature, and you look like you're about to faint. I've been watching you and you haven't learned a thing in twenty minutes. You're in a fog! Let's go up to your room. I'm going to get you a drink before something terrible happens to you!"

"Rebbe!" Morris replied. "Are you forgetting what today is? It's Yom Kippur!"

"God forbid! I'm not forgetting at all. That's why I'm coming up with you to see that you drink something!"

"But I don't want to drink anything!"

"Then I'm going to stand here until you come with me. I want you to know that you're transgressing a tremendous *lav* (Torah prohibition)!"

"What is that?" Morris answered, surprised.

Rabbi Milikowsky pulled himself up straight and looked sternly at Morris. Then he said slowly, "*Venishmartem me'od lenafshoseichem* – Guard yourselves very carefully" (Devarim 4:15). I am the father here! I am telling you that you must drink!"

Morris was stubborn and for a long time continued to refuse. Finally, Rabbi Milikowsky sighed and said, "Look, Moshe, I'll show you how to drink little bits of water in a shot glass every several minutes so that you avoid the Torah prohibition. All right?"

Morris relented. "Well... all right."

Together they went up to Morris's room.

II: Purim 1963

Purim for the dormitory boys during the early 1960s was a happy time. The Baltimore winter was beginning to thaw. The trees were in early bloom. You could often run across Cottage Avenue from the dorm to the main school building without a coat without having to hope that your mother wouldn't see you. After long winter months of serious study, curfews and attendance-taking, the school let the boys run loose a bit on this day. There were the regular Megillah readings, of course, and, in the morning, the ritual exchange of breakfast plates to fulfill the mitzvah of *shalach monos*, but both at night and during the day there were also long hours of singing and dancing and merrymaking. Moreover, alcoholic beverages were available to the older boys.

One Purim night, Shlomo* had had a bit too much to drink. If normally, Shlomo was a pensive, reserved and philosophical sort with an occasional tendency towards melancholy, the drink that he had imbibed only accentuated these traits. All around him, he saw his friends carousing, wearing silly hats, doing imitations of various personalities and public figures, and he felt a certain awkwardness at being part of this.

"I'm going to go upstairs to the *beis midrash* to learn," he said to himself firmly. He let the thought roll around in his brain for a few moments, and he was pleased with the way it sounded. He slowly walked upstairs, occasionally steadying himself on the wooden banister.

The beis midrash was empty. "Everybody is downstairs dancing and singing and reciting *gramen* (humorous poems improvised on Purim). There's no one up here but me, holding down the fort," he thought, and he was happy that he had come. He went to his regular spot in the *beis midrash*, and he opened a *gemara* to where his class was learning that week. His head hurt a bit and the words were slightly blurry.

"Who knows?" he asked, pursuing his thought a bit further. "Perhaps all the Jews in the United States are celebrating Purim right now, and only I am learning. Perhaps at this very moment millions of Jews owe their very existence to my study."

Rebbe often quoted the Chafetz Chaim, who said that a mitzvah abandoned by the masses is worth all that much more for the few who fulfill it. Who could fathom the great reward that would belong to Shlomo in return for his choosing these moments to learn? He put his head down to find the place and begin his review.

Suddenly he felt a hand on his shoulder.

"Shleimeleh!"

It was Rebbe. He had noticed that a boy was missing from the festivities.

"Shleimeleh! Go join the others. It was a good thought! A great *machshavah*! But you're separating yourself from the *klal*. You're cutting yourself off! There's a time to learn and there's a time to dance. Go dance!"

Forty year later, Shlomo sums up his feelings: "For Rebbe, learning was the greatest thing, the most important thing. For him to react the way he did made it clear to me just how great a man he was."

III: Winter, 1979

The following is a story that I received from Rabbi Benyamin Fleishman, '81, of Baltimore.

I remember one day when I was about fifteen years old. I was attending the Talmudical Academy in Baltimore, Maryland. I used to take the city bus daily to go to T.A.'s *minyan* each morning. There were not many other city boys in my class who did that. In order for me to catch the bus, I had to walk two very long blocks to wait for the bus, which never ran on time.

One day, it was particularly brutal outside. It was very cold with a freezing rain, precisely the type of day I would rather have spent at home.

I had walked the two blocks to the bus. The bus was, of course, running behind schedule. My clothes were soaked, I was cold, tired, and frustrated. I would have preferred that school be closed for the day. When I finally arrived at school, there was still time left for me to sit in the *beis midrash* for a few minutes before *minyan* started.

While I was sitting there, with my back to the door of the *beis midrash*, I suddenly felt a hand on my shoulder. I looked up to see Rebbe standing to my left. He had just walked in, and had not even seen my face.

Rebbe told me that I should imagine all the cement of my entire walk and my journey on the bus to get to *minyan* daily, piled high on my scales in the Final Accounting.

This was the exact encouragement that I needed at that moment. He said that although I go through a hard time every day getting to *minyan*, it is well worth the effort. He told me that when I arrive in Heaven, all the cement from my walk, and the time and effort to get to *minyan* daily, will be taken into great consideration.

Rebbe had not even seen my face. When he walked in he sensed that something was bothering me. With his typical caring approach, so far beyond the norm, Rebbe had understood what was bothering me. Instantly he had come up with the exact words to give me the encouragement that would help me get through the day.

The lesson that Rebbe taught me in those few moments is something that I have tried to teach to my own children and students.

Friend of the Family

Solly Gordon (all names and places in the next two stories have been changed) met his wife while he was at T.A. He was a tenth-grade dormitory student at T.A. during the early 1960s. The summer before tenth grade, his mother had given him the name and telephone number of a good friend of hers, Mrs. Baumel, a Baltimore matron, in the hope that Solly could enjoy some home hospitality during the long months that he would not see his own family.

Late in the fall, Solly finally called Mrs. Baumel. He obtained permission from Rabbi Milikowsky to be absent from supper on a particular Sunday night so that he could instead go over to the Baumel home for supper. Solly enjoyed his dinner at the Baumels. Mrs. Baumel was active in the T.A. Ladies' Auxiliary, and at the end of the evening, Solly volunteered to help her with various activities connected with that, stuffing envelopes or whatever else she needed.

Solly continued to call the Baumels and to spend occasional Sunday evenings with their family. He would always help Mrs. Baumel with her Ladies' Auxiliary affairs and perhaps talk a bit with their children, including their daughter, Ellen, who was about his own age. As time went on, however, the boy's main reason for visiting the Baumels began to change, as he became increasingly smitten with Ellen.

Mrs. Baumel had eyes in her head and could see what was happening. At some point she phoned her friend, Solly's mother, in Virginia. Mrs. Gordon, in turn, called Rabbi Milikowsky in Baltimore, described the situation to him and expressed her approval. (Who knows if the two mothers had not in fact plotted the whole thing in advance?)

In any event, Solly continued to ask Rabbi Milikowsky for permission to visit the Baumels "to help Mrs. Baumel with her Ladies' Auxiliary Affairs," and Rabbi Milikowsky continued to give him permission.

Solly had two reasons for going to the Baumels, but he was only telling Rabbi Milikowsky one. Rabbi Milikowsky, of course, knew the other reason, but Solly did not know that he knew.

During the four years that the couple knew each other before they married, they went out formally on a total of just four dates. A few times they took some long walks. The rest of the time, they would just sit on the front porch talking.

It was a different era, the early 1960s. Solly's mother had said it was all right with her, Solly was asking permission, and he was always where he was supposed to be when he was supposed to be there. He would ask Rabbi Milikowsky, "Is it all right for me to go over to Mrs. Baumel's for supper on Sunday night?" and he would receive permission to go. If Rabbi Milikowsky said, "Please be back for Sunday night *seder*," he was back for *seder*. If Solly said, "I'm not sure I can be back in time for *seder*," and Rabbi Milikowsky acknowledged it, he then came back in time for *ma'ariv*. But he was always where he said he was going to be.

The whole time that this was going on, Rabbi Milikowsky knew about it, but he just kept quiet.

The man who told me this story about himself, and who is today a rabbi who runs a family business, had the following to add:

"I always said, 'Rabbi Milikowsky was a European-trained rabbi who knew the American boy's mind better than the American boy knew his own mind.'"

Two years after he graduated, Solly and Ellen were married, but the end of the story really takes place twenty-five years later.

Solly's son Meir was himself in the tenth grade at T.A. when he met a girl named Leah, whom he was interested in dating. However, Leah's father rejected the idea, so Meir put it out of his mind. A few years later he ran into Leah once more. By now, he and Leah were both in the twelfth grade. Once more he expressed interest in dating her, but once more, Leah's father said no.

For their part, Solly and his wife had no problem with the couple going out, considering that this was precisely how they themselves had met.

164

Leah's father, Rabbi Moshe Liber, like Rabbi Solly Gordon and his son Meir, had himself gone to T.A., and Solly phoned him to discuss the matter. Rabbi Liber's response was short and to the point: "The day she finishes high school, she can become a *kallah*, but as long as she's in high school, no dating." Ultimately a compromise was worked out such that the two couples approached Rabbi Milikowsky, who knew all the parties concerned, for him to decide whether the couple could date. First, Rabbi Liber called Rabbi Milikowsky and they talked, and then Rabbi Gordon and his son went over to Rabbi Milikowsky's house and they talked.

At the end of the second conversation, Rabbi Milikowsky said no. Meir Gordon turned to Rabbi Milikowsky and asked, "But Rebbe! Why not? After all, my own father did the same thing for two years, didn't he?"

Rabbi Milikowsky answered, "Fine! What are you going to do after high school?" Meir shrugged his shoulders. He didn't yet have any specific plans. Rabbi Milikowsky looked him in the eye and said, "Your father already knew what he was going to do for college and for his livelihood before he even graduated high school." That was the truth. By tenth grade, Solly Gordon knew that first he would learn in yeshiva and study engineering, and then he would join the family business. Rabbi Milikowsky continued, "Your father already had his life planned out. He was ready to settle down."

Despite this setback, three years later Meir and Leah met each other in New York once again, and this time, by all accounts, they were ready. They dated and were married.

ಹ ೯

The following story, told by Rabbi Eliyahu Rabovsky, is from the early 1970s:

Love for a Talmid

My parents did not drive, so I often hitched a ride with Rebbe. Once another boy, who was on the quieter side, was in the car. That boy happened to live still in the old Lower Park Heights neighborhood, a bit removed from most of the Jewish community. Rebbe asked where the boy wanted to go and he mentioned I think a certain corner, somewhat closer than his home. The student must have felt awkward and embarrassed to ask Rebbe to drive so far down into the city, out of his way. Rebbe sensed the situation, and said with a voice that defined the love of a rebbe to a talmid, "Tell me where you really want to go! If you needed to go to Washington [forty miles away], I would gladly take you! Don't you realize that I would do anything for you?"

Were these idle words? Compare the preceding story to the following story, about an event that occurred nine years later, four years after Rabbi Milikowsky's official "retirement":

In 1979, Rabbi Avraham Leventhal, a rebbe in T.A., was thirteen years old and had just arrived in the dormitory. It was around Succos time, and he became very ill. Avraham needed to go to the doctor for a throat culture, and this had to happen quickly. He had just been examined in the school office when Rabbi Milikowsky happened to come by on his way out of the building, ready to go home. Hearing what had happened, he said to the school secretary without batting an eyelash, "Mrs. Gold, I'll take him to the doctor."

Rabbi Milikowsky took Avraham to the doctor in his car, then waited with Avraham at the doctor's office until his turn came. Then he brought Avraham back to the dormitory. What did all of this mean?

First, Rabbi Milikowsky took Avraham to the doctor, which involved driving six miles into Baltimore City, two miles past his own home, to the hospital. Then, after waiting with Avraham at the doctor's office for an hour, he drove Avraham the six miles back to T.A. When the mission was accomplished and Avraham was safely back at T.A., Rabbi Milikowsky actually apologized to Avraham that he had to leave, since he was expected home to baby-sit for his granddaughter.

 る ⤳

The very short story that immediately follows refers to an event that occurred during the 1950s. The longer story that follows it happens to come from the son of the man who told the first story. The similarity in endings is striking.

The author of the second story has requested anonymity. I have seen fit to let him tell his story in his own words since the story, as he tells it, not only describes a particular event but also attests to the powerful relationship that continued to exist between Rabbi Milikowsky and T.A. students years after his "retirement" years began.

I

One time I was walking down the hall, and I was thinking about doing something naughty. I hadn't talked to anybody about what I was planning to do. And suddenly Rabbi Milikowsky was standing there, and he said, "Please don't do it."

II

It was during the days between Rosh Hashanah and Yom Kippur one year. It was in the late 1970s. I was sitting in *chumash* class with Rebbe teaching in his usual way – making the stories of the *chumash* come alive for the class.

Rebbe had immeasurable patience with everyone, and his love and caring for every student shone through with every word that he said to every student.

I was sitting on the side of the room, and for some reason, I had a large box sitting on my desk at the time. If memory serves, I had used the box as a *stender* (lectern) to prop up my *siddur* for the *davening* of Rosh Hashanah. The reason that I did this is because I used to try to stand for as much of the services as possible. I had learned this from Rebbe. He seemed always to be standing for the *davening* on these special days. In order to assist me with holding a *siddur*, I used a box to hold the *siddur* up to an easier level.

I had brought the box into class and had it on the desk for class. For some reason, Rebbe was the only one who did not ask me to take it off my desk. As will be noticed in this true story, there was no need for Rebbe to ask me to take it off the desk.

Of course, I had my *chumash* open and was "listening" to what Rebbe had to say. At the same time, I had decided that I wanted to have some fun with another classmate of mine. He was sitting about five feet away from me, and would be a perfect target for a spitball.

I took my Bic pen out of my pocket and removed both ends and the ink cartridge. Then I took a piece of paper, balled it in my mouth, and now I had a spitball ready to shoot at my classmate. I sat there for several minutes poised at my peer. My friend saw what was going to happen and would not betray me, as it would be beneath his dignity to tattle on me. Because of the box on my desk, there was no way at all that Rebbe could see what I was planning to do with my pen.

My classmate was not happy with what he knew was about to happen, and I was enjoying the suspense that I was adding to what I was doing since I was not shooting him right away.

After several minutes of this, I was finally ready to shoot. I took a deep breath in order to shoot the spitball. Rebbe, who was about seven or eight feet from me and could not hear me take a breath, called my name.

I looked up, and there was Rebbe looking at me with his warm smile. Then he said just two words: "Please don't." I was in such shock that all I could do was to put the spitball away and I never did anything like that again.

Chapter 17

SOMETIME DURING THE PAST SIXTY YEARS...

Ladder Day Saints

DAVID*, AN ELEVENTH-GRADE out-of-towner at the Talmudical Academy, lived with his roommate, Marvin*, a twelfth-grader, in the second-story back bedroom of Rabbi Milikowsky's house. Most families hosting T.A. boys in this manner maintained a curfew hour beyond which they felt free to lock the door. Rabbi Milikowsky's home was no exception. Apart from any wish to train the boys in discipline, there were security considerations as well. No one wished to leave his front or back door unlocked all night long, night after night.

While David had no problem coming home on time, his older roommate Marvin liked to come in after curfew. This was a pesky business because while sometimes he would find the door open, at other times he would find it locked, leaving an exceedingly small number of unsavory options. David, a helpful sort, wanted very much to help his roommate, so what did he do? He carefully crafted a rope ladder for him. Ostensibly, he and Marvin were the only ones who knew about it. Rabbi and Mrs. Milikowsky slept in the front room downstairs, and all the happenings with the ladder took place in the back of the house.

Rabbi Milikowsky would lock the door after a certain hour each night, and Marvin used to come in at two or three o'clock in the morning. The ladder sat neatly rolled up on a window sill, and to the ladder was attached a thin string leading down to a key which the boys kept hidden behind a drainpipe in the back of the house. During the daytime, one couldn't really see the ladder or the string. When Marvin wanted to climb the ladder, he would simply remove the key from behind the drainpipe and pull on the string, and – voilà! – the ladder would fall like Rapunzel's hair. The window above was always kept unlocked. Marvin would climb up the ladder and pull himself into the bedroom. Of course, he would pull the ladder back up as well. The next morning, one of the boys would make sure to be out of the house very early to put things back the way they had to be in order for the little scheme to remain a secret.

If nothing else, David was fulfilling the Rabbis' words, "Let your house remain open to the wise men." A greater weisenheimer than Marvin who could find?

One night, Marvin pulled the ladder down just as Rabbi Milikowsky was going into the powder room in the back of the house, which offered a view of where the ladder came down. Rabbi Milikowsky heard this noise and looked outside, but the boy pulled the ladder aside, far enough against the wall that Rabbi Milikowsky didn't see him.

The year passed and Marvin graduated. About two days after graduation, with the rest of the high school still in session, Rabbi Milikowsky approached David in the hall of the school and asked him, "So who has the ladder?" David's eyes bulged and he lost his breath. He couldn't talk. Rebbe waited for David to regain his composure, and then he told David that not only was he aware of the ladder, but that he had been aware of it from the day that David made it. In fact, he told David the precise date on which David had produced the ladder. He had known about it the entire time but for his own reasons had chosen to say nothing.

An Almost Perfect Crime

One year there was a group of boys who got into some serious trouble by anybody's definition. Late one night they sneaked into the old T.A. school building and climbed up onto the roof. Once there, they hung a boy over the side of the building, and lowered him down by ropes to the window of Dr. Kranzler's office. Although the door was locked, the window was slightly ajar. Hanging in mid-air, the boy pried open the window, climbed into the office and advanced to the filing cabinet where the permanent student records were held. He took out those records and changed many of his own grades and those of his three partners who were waiting up above. No doubt, the boys standing on the roof whispered the prayer, "Let salvation come from below." When he was finished, he restored everything to look as it had been before he arrived. He then returned to the window, retied himself and tugged on the rope so that the boys would know that it was time to pull him back up onto the roof. The boys then hurriedly left the building and made it back to their dormitory rooms without having been seen. The perfect crime? Well, almost.

What they didn't realize was that a second copy of all the records had been sent to a different office, and somewhere along the way someone in the office noticed the discrepancy. Somebody had been tampering with the grades! Often it involves much detective work to uncover who has committed a crime. In this case, however, exactly four boys had been involved, and exactly four sets of grades had been changed, so the perfect crime had an even more perfect solution.

Rabbi Milikowsky often went to bat for boys who had been expelled, winning them "last chances." But in this case, even Rebbe's efforts could not succeed given the seriousness of the crime, and the four boys were expelled for good.

But what do you do when a sixteen- or seventeen-year-old boy is thrown out of yeshiva for a terrible crime such as this? I am not a school principal, so I cannot answer that question. I can only report what Rabbi Boruch Milikowsky did. He boarded a train with the four boys and took them up to the Mir Yeshiva in Brooklyn, New York, and was successful in getting them all enrolled there!

The person who told me this story, who today *is* a school principal, concludes it as follows:

"I throw guys out of school. I do try to get them into other schools, but I'm not ready to get on a train and go to another city and plead with another school to take the boys in. Rebbe did it, though. That's who he was!"

Demonstrating Commitment

If one were to make a list of activities that one should not perform in jest, getting married would be high on the list, just ahead of divorce and just behind bullfighting. Even so, whoever peruses the *Iggros Moshe* of Rabbi Moshe Feinstein, *zt"l*, will find at least four responsa dealing with teenagers doing precisely that: marrying in jest. In each case, Rav Moshe had to determine based on the details of the case as presented to him whether the transaction could indeed be considered just a joke or whether, God forbid, the young woman in the story might need to receive a *get* (writ of divorce) in order to remove any doubt about her status.

What follows is one such story involving a T.A. boy, sent to Rabbi Moshe Feinstein for his opinion, although this specific case does not appear in *Igaros Moshe* as far as I can tell. Of course, the reason the story is included here is the way that it demonstrates Rabbi Milikowsky's conscientious concern for his boys' welfare.

One other point before I begin. While most of the other "naughty behavior" stories in this book indicate that boys are far ahead of girls in this sphere, this is one story where by definition a girl will always be an equal participant.

George* was at the end of eleventh grade, his third year at T.A. To put it mildly, George represented one of the greater challenges that Rabbi Milikowsky faced during the four years that George spent at T.A.

George's heart was in the right place, however. Often he would cry on his rebbe's shoulder about how hard things were for him and Rabbi Milikowsky would try to give him encouragement, doing or saying whatever was necessary to get George to stick it out until the end of twelfth grade.

One time, George decided to go to the yearly carnival of the Bais Yaakov Girls' High School of Baltimore. He went with a few other *bochrim* and they spent some money. With one thing and other, George's money ran out, playing games and doing whatever one does at a carnival. So he began chatting with the Bais Yaakov girls, some of whom he knew.

Now George was not a terribly great student, but had you asked him at 3:00 in the morning what Talmudic tractate he was learning in school, he would have known the answer right away. Many years have passed, however, since this story took place. Here is George's description of what happened next:

> And we had just learned in the *gemara* – I don't know if it was *Gittin* or what – about how to get married. And I said to one of the girls – I was wearing my class ring, see – "All I have to do is to take this ring off and hand it to you and say, '*Harei at mekudeshes li be-taba'as zu.*'" The girl said, "What do you mean?" And I said, "Here! Let me show you." And there were a few people around there with us. I took off my ring and put it on the girl's finger and said the line.

In most cases, this would have been the end of the story and nothing that follows would have occurred. No one in authority would have heard what happened. Here, however, we are talking about Rabbi Boruch Milikowsky, who somehow knew *everything* that happened to his boys, during school and on their free time.

The next day, when George got back to yeshiva, Rabbi Milikowsky came over to him and drew him into a side room. He seemed very agitated, and the following conversation took place:

– George! Oh, George! What have you done this time?

– What do you mean?

– You went to the Bais Yaakov carnival?

– Yeah! I went with some people. I wanted to give some *tzedakah* (charity)! You know?

– What else did you do?

– Nothing!

– What about your ring?

– I taught some *Torah* there! We'd just learned in the *gemara* about how to get married. I was just showing them. Also, I was out of money. That's why I was talking to the girls. I don't usually talk to girls.

Rabbi Milikowsky suddenly looked immensely sad, not so much because of the fib he had just heard but because of the possible implications of what had occurred. He looked George in the eye and put his hands on his shoulders and said to him very slowly, "Tell me exactly what happened." George told him the entire story, and when Rebbe heard it, he rocked back and forth, with his eyes closed and his hands on his beard, chanting, "Oy-yoy-yoy! Oy-yoy-yoy!"

George still did not understand what the problem was, but he was alarmed to see his Rebbe looking so sad. "Rebbe! Rebbe! What's wrong! What's the matter?" he asked.

Rabbi Milikowsky gently explained to George about the serious *halachic* complication that might exist, and he arranged for George to go with him to meet with the Rosh Yeshiva, Rabbi Chaim Samson. Once more, George told his story, if perhaps in a slightly more circumspect manner. Rabbi Samson and Rabbi Milikowsky explained to George the gravity of what he had done. The two men then consulted together and decided that George should have a hearing before a group of Baltimore's greatest Torah scholars.

A few days later, George went with Rabbi Milikowsky to the home of Rabbi Nathan Drazan and answered the very serious questions of a group of ten Torah scholars who were assembled there. George did not know it at the time, but hidden behind the curtains on the side of the room were the girl in the story and her very nervous father.

At the end of the session, the unspoken mood was one of relief. It seemed unlikely that a *get* would be required. Still, just to be safe, HaRav Moshe Feinstein was also contacted once all the details were clear. Fortunately, the end result was that George and the girl were not considered to be married.

This was not the end of the ordeal for George, however. Before he was fully aware of the possible consequences of his deed, he had boasted to his classmates of the trouble he was in. The news then spread quickly that George was "married," and whenever George arrived in class, all of his classmates would jump on tables and sing lively wedding songs. Since it was the last week of school and all the testing was completed, Rabbi Milikowsky decided to send George home to his family a week early.

Forty years later, George, now a grandfather, met the girl, now a grandmother, at the wedding of the son of a mutual close friend. It was she who told him that Rabbi Moshe Feinstein had issued the final ruling that no get was required.

Swinger: Part I

Rabbi Milikowsky had a great deal of experience with the emotional and spiritual vicissitudes so common to teenage boys. There was very little that could surprise him, however much it might distress him. Witness the following.

One time, when Yissachar* was at the beginning of his senior year, he was involved in a physical fight with twenty guys. It started out when he decided one day that it was up to him to rebuke all his classmates at once to get them to repent their evil ways. He was going to save the whole world, starting with his own class.

When he saw a couple of fellows, mischief-makers and less serious learners than himself, he said to them, "You guys are on the wrong path. You're running around, doing the wrong things!" Perhaps he expected them to break down in tears and run off to the *beis midrash*, but they only snarled at him, "Oh, yeah? Wanna make something of it?"

Since this answer was not the one Yissachar was expecting, he was caught off guard and put on the defensive, and he had to defend his honor. He said to them, "Bring any twenty guys you want to bring, and I'll lick them all. Whoever wins is right. OK?"

The two fellows said to themselves, "We're gonna bring twenty guys. We're gonna show him," and then they ran off. Yissachar thought the whole thing was over. But soon afterwards, they came back with a large crowd of hooting boys intent on teaching Yissachar a lesson about arrogance. Almost at once he was surrounded by a crowd slowly closing in on him. Yissachar was not very tall, but he was very powerfully built, and for a while he held his own. But then he started getting stomped. It was the kind of fight that takes place only rarely in American yeshiva high schools, but that does happen occasionally, all the same.

And then, as always seemed to happen when there was trouble, Rebbe showed up, and as the only neutral, universally beloved party there, he walked straight into the midst of the fray and pulled Yissachar out of it before anything worse could happen.

As Yissachar told me when I interviewed him, "It was a stupid thing. Teenage boys! They're *meshuga*, you know! And Rebbe physically came in there and saved my life."

Swinger, Part II

This same Yissachar, whose zealousness had led to a free-for-all early in his senior year, himself suffered a spiritual crisis later that year. Since the day that he arrived at T.A., he had been one of the strongest learners of his class, so it was all the more surprising when he went straight to college after high school rather than to Yeshiva University or one of the full-time yeshiva programs.

Rabbi Milikowsky did not forget him, however. He stayed in touch over the phone, calling him at his college and counseling him at length regarding his spiritual doubts and worries until Yissachar decided, after one year of college, to enter a full-time yeshiva program as he had originally intended. Rabbi Milikowsky helped him select the program best suited to him, and he went on to become a great *talmid chacham* and a prominent rabbi in the Jewish world.

As Yissachar put it, "Rebbe didn't just save my life physically. He saved my life spiritually as well."

Works of Faith

Jack Sitrin's* earliest memories of T.A. were of his sitting in class not knowing what was going on. He spent his twelve years at T.A. in a fog. He never seemed to be listening to what the teacher said. He didn't disturb the class, but it was as though he wasn't there. His father, who had learned for many years in post-high school yeshiva, was at a loss as to why his son was so much less successful. Mr. Sitrin's strong sense of humor, together with a philosophical approach to life acquired while in yeshiva, helped him to maintain his sanity. When Jack was sent to psychologists they could do little for him, although he seemed to enjoy the attention. He seemed to have normal, even above-average intelligence, but in class and particularly in his Torah studies, he seemed totally uninterested.

After many years of this, accompanied by occasional sympathy from understanding teachers and occasional bouts of frustration when the teachers were less patient, Jack spent his last two years of T.A., tenth and eleventh grades, in Rabbi Milikowsky's class. If you are expecting me to describe some miraculous turnaround, you are going to be disappointed. Jack's uninspired school career continued during those years despite Rabbi Milikowsky's efforts, although Jack has a fond memory of the two times he heard Rebbe's "Toot-Toot Story" retold above.

Actually, Rabbi Milikowsky, based on experience, sized up Jack right from the start as having a unique sort of problem that had to be treated delicately, and he more or less decided that it was best to leave Jack alone. Thus, Jack sat in the back of the room, unintruded upon by what was happening in the front of the room, observing what he wanted to observe, coming and leaving as he pleased.

The year ended, and it was mutually agreed upon by Jack, his parents and the school administration that Jack should be allowed to finish school a year early by enrolling in summer school and evening programs. Although many students asked for this, it was not always granted. Here it was approved without delay not because Jack was the best student, but because he was the worst. Jack thus finished high school a year early. He then set off for Israel to spend a year doing agricultural work on kibbutz. He had just turned seventeen. When he flew to Israel, he did not know a word of Hebrew.

Well, he did know one word. Before leaving for Israel, Rabbi Milikowsky had asked him if he knew how to say "towel" in Hebrew, and when he answered in the negative, Rabbi Milikowsky told him that it was called a *magevet*, from the same root as *negev*, meaning "dry." Rabbi Milikowsky also gave Jack some advice: "When you visit Tel Aviv, before you leave the men's room in the Tel Aviv bus station, look up to the right and you will see a sign in Hebrew that says: 'Please close your buttons before going out to the street.'" Jack remembered this advice and when he was in Tel Aviv, he followed it. He looked up, and there was the sign! This made a huge impression on Jack, who had never seen trousers with buttons instead of a zipper.

After about three months of living on the kibbutz, Jack suddenly noticed that he had become relatively fluent in Hebrew and had even developed a credible Israeli accent. After years of gaining nothing from his Hebrew classes, this was quite a surprise. He decided to write a letter in Hebrew to Rabbi Milikowsky.

When Rabbi Milikowsky received the letter, he became very excited. For once he, the master of surprise letters and surprise visits, had been outdone! He ran over to Mr. Sitrin in shul with the letter and gave it to him to read. Mr. Sitrin wept as he read the letter. He never imagined that Jack would reach the point of being able to write a letter in Hebrew, and after only three months in Israel!

At the end of the year, Jack came back to Baltimore with a much improved attitude toward himself. He realized that if he could master Hebrew in little time, he could learn other things as well. His father had arranged that all that summer, while he took courses at a local college, he would also learn *Gemara Succah* with Rebbe in the basement of the Shearith Israel Synagogue, perhaps three afternoons a week. At first, it was very slow going. Even with Jack's much improved knowledge of Hebrew and his improved attitude, he still became dreamy as soon as the *sefarim* were opened. Yet he did enjoy some success that summer, and the reason for it is this: After a few weeks of unsatisfactory results, Rabbi Milikowsky decided to try a different approach. He turned to him one day and said, "You know what? *Gemara* is not for everyone. Some people don't have a head for it. And that's OK. If you do you do, and if you don't you don't. That's fine!"

For Jack, it was a moment of truth. He felt frustrated over the fact that he could not focus his attention sufficiently to grasp what Rebbe was saying as he explained the *gemara*. His mind was wandering all over the place. He was thinking of other things. At the same time, he felt certain that he was smart enough to learn *gemara*. "Any fool can do this," he thought to himself (although that isn't quite so). "I should be able to at least have a basic idea of what is going on." From that moment on, he worked and toiled very hard to grasp the *gemara* that Rabbi Milikowsky was trying to push into his head. It was the first time he had ever really learned *gemara*. He worked with Rabbi Milikowsky for two summers. It was a very good experience.

In the fall, Jack went off to university out of town. At this point, Rabbi Milikowsky was no longer spending Shabbos in T.A. but rather in the Jewish neighborhood. Whenever Jack was home from school, he would sit and have long talks with Rebbe on Friday nights and Shabbos afternoons. They were no longer learning together – indeed, at this point, Jack was not learning at all – but there was this connection, sort of a friendship, that transcended the normal bounds of the teacher-student relationship.

The relationship continued. By sheer willpower, Jack got himself accepted into professional school, and soon after he began that program, he became engaged to be married. Rebbe's wedding present to him was a miniature set of Talmud, a little green Shas, a very special gift and rather expensive for a yeshiva rebbe of little means. Why did Rabbi Milikowsky buy such an extraordinary gift for one of the weakest students he had ever had, a person who at that time was not learning any Torah and showed little prospect of ever learning it?

Jack struggled through law school despite his difficulties – difficulties that he still did not understand – and managed to graduate successfully. He had children and started a successful practice somewhere on the East Coast. All this time, he kept up his relationship with Rabbi Milikowsky, but since he was married and living out of town, he returned to Baltimore less frequently.

Late in 1990, when Jack was in Baltimore with his growing family, he brought his oldest son to Rebbe's house. Rabbi Milikowsky was now older. For the first time in his life, he was walking with a cane. He had survived a bout with kidney cancer and sometimes needed oxygen to help him breathe. Jack and Rebbe talked and *shmuessed* as always, catching up on old times. And then Rebbe did something out of the ordinary. He called Jack over to him

179

and placed his hands on his head and gave him a *berachah* (blessing). Then he did the same with Jack's young son. When he was done, he said to Jack, "Make a *misheberach* (prayer) for me! Here is my name. This is the last time that we'll be seeing each other. Don't forget me! Don't forget that you had a Rabbi Milikowsky!" And then they both wept and embraced. Soon after, Rabbi Milikowsky passed on to the World of Truth.

Jack never forgot Rabbi Milikowsky. Five years after Rabbi Milikowsky's passing, he made a new commitment to study Torah. Soon he was maintaining brief, weekly sessions. Slowly he increased the frequency and duration of these sessions, and a few years ago, he tried *daf yomi* for the first time. It was very hard for him to follow, but he found that with enormous effort he could concentrate enough to benefit from it.

A few years ago, one of his clients, a psychiatrist and close friend, recommended that he have himself tested for ADD, Attention Deficit Disorder. Jack did so and the results were positive. The psychiatrist friend then prescribed certain drugs for Jack to take every day, and suddenly Jack discovered that after thirty years of suffering, he could now concentrate on his *daf yomi* classes with much less effort. A forty-year-old riddle was solved. Today, twenty years after receiving the miniature set of Talmud from Rabbi Milikowsky, Jack has started to use it. Surely one can picture Rabbi Milikowsky triumphantly smiling down from heaven each time Jack opens one of those books, as one more student he had faith in proves him right.

We would like to wish you, the young couple, that you should simultaneously merit Torah and greatness, and that your love should last forever and ever. Your marriage represents the blessed "mingling together of fine grapes." God will certainly send you His blessing that you should succeed in all you do, and may your precious, worthy parents derive much nachas from you. And may the sound of joy be heard in your home!
With love and friendship,
Rabbi Boruch Milikowsky and his wife Leah
P.S. And you will certainly have time… or you will make time, to learn each day from the little Shas.

Rebbe's wedding note that accompanied the little Shas he gave to "Jack Sitrin."

Chapter 18

STORIES AND VIGNETTES FROM THE 1960S

"Rabbi Milikowsky was the only rebbe whom we called "Rebbe." You ask ANY T.A. boy from my time. 'Rebbe said...' 'Rebbe told...' It's always Rebbe. No one else. It was always him."

(a 1964 graduate of T.A.)

Dateline: 1964

* Wearing a suit and a hat is now called "dressing conservatively."

* Television has become the common pastime of most Americans during the evening, and its influence on the American home is increasing.

* Yiddish is disappearing from American homes.

* If in 1947 many Jewish Americans were struggling immigrants, many more have become affluent.

* A group of Yemenite folk dancers from Israel are refused permission to enter a non-kosher Baltimore restaurant due to their skin color. While the liberal faction of Jewish Baltimore adopts this discrimination as a cause celebre, the more conservative faction of Orthodox Jewry responds that the dancers had no business going to the restaurant in the first place.

In 1960, after only thirteen years at T.A., Rabbi Milikowsky was already honored with a full-page dedication in the Talmudical Academy Twelfth Grade Yearbook. It was but the first of many honors that he would receive. What is especially revealing is that the honor was generated by his students.

Similarly, in 1963, when Rabbi Milikowsky had been teaching for only sixteen years, the parents of the T.A. boys felt so beholden to him that they raised money to send him and his wife on a trip to Israel, a luxury that he could not have afforded himself at the time. In this, his first of many trips to Israel, Rabbi Milikowsky had an opportunity to visit with his maternal grandfather, whom he had not seen for many years. He also visited Rabbi Weinstein, the rabbi of Vishnevo, who had retired to Safed. Rabbi Weinstein had certainly had an influence on him when he was a teenage boy. No less significant was the time he spent at the Jerusalem branch of the Mir Yeshiva, the yeshiva he loved so much.

So it happened that Rabbi Milikowsky was walking down the street one day towards the Mir Yeshiva, accompanied by Rav Eliezer Yehuda Finkel. Rabbi Finkel, son of the Alter of Slobodka, was the long-time Mir Rosh Yeshiva who had made sure that his yeshiva had a way out of Europe before taking advantage of his certificate to Palestine.

As one approaches the Mir Yeshiva, one goes down past a bunch of what seem to be garages, and when the garages are open, one sees that they are carpenters' workshops. As Rabbi Milikowsky and Rav Finkel were walking along, Rav Finkel remarked to Rabbi Milikowsky, "These carpenters are making my life miserable!"

"What do you mean?" asked Rabbi Milikowsky. At first, he assumed that what was bothering the old man were the noise and the dust and the wood chips.

Rav Leizer Yudel answered, "Every morning I get up. I get up! Yeshiva *davening* starts at seven, I get up at five-thirty or at six and start learning. Yet *they* always get up before me. No matter how early I get up, they get up before me! It's making my life miserable! *How can it be that they're getting up before me?...*"

God's Agent

The social upheaval in the United States and in South America during the 1960s and 1970s brought many boys to the Talmudical Academy, boys whose parents had a variety of reasons for sending them there besides "to get a Torah education." Sometimes their agenda was different from that of the school itself.

I came from Atlanta, Georgia. I didn't know which end was up in terms of Yiddishkeit. There was nothing in Atlanta. Probably the only reason I came to Baltimore was that the fear of integration was coming to the South, and my folks weren't even sure that they would be able to send me back to my public school the following year. So my father was convinced by the local rabbi, Rabbi Emanuel Feldman, to let me be one of the boys who came from Atlanta. We had ten boys who came from Atlanta, and so I joined them.

So I came to the yeshiva. I was a nice little Southern boy. I had a southern drawl. I didn't know where I was headed. As far as I was concerned, I was going to a Northern Jewish Prep School. But when I got here, I said to myself, "Hey! I'm back in Europe!"

...My mother sort of had an ulterior motive. She wanted me to be the best performer for my bar mitzvah. Not just the same *haftara* and stuff like that. She wanted me to spend a year in yeshiva, you know, so she could say, "My son went to yeshiva!" Then, I would know more and I would have a more impressive bar mitzvah.

I learned how to *lain* (chant the Torah portion). I think I was the first kid in our shul who *lained* the *parasha*. She thought I was only going to go there for a year and that after my bar mitzvah I'd come back and go to public school in Florida, but I got hooked on T.A. and I stayed until twelfth grade....

ॐ ॐ

So many of the good things that happen to us occur without our understanding precisely what is taking place. We need God's blessing and assistance to make everything work out for the best. God does expect us, however, to try to take steps in the right direction. Thus the Talmud says: בדרך שאדם רוצה לילך בה מוליכין אותו – "God leads us in the direction that we ourselves wish to go" (*Makkos* 10b). Obviously, this source is referring both to positive and to negative intent. If someone wants to steal, God will eventually let him steal. If he wants to improve his spiritual life, God will help him with that too.

At the Talmudical Academy, God had a full time agent doing God's work to help people from spiritually weak backgrounds to move in the right direction, and the name of that agent was Rabbi Boruch Milikowsky.

The two boys from Atlanta and Florida described above never returned to public school. Both remained in T.A., became close to Rabbi Milikowsky and grew in learning, going on to learn in yeshiva after high school as well. In fact, one became a rabbi and is presently a yeshiva day-school principal.

Typical as well was the experience of the many South American boys who came to T.A. during this period. Some were fleeing revolutions, anti-Semitism, dictatorships and other phenomena associated with untimely death. Others were being sent by their parents to Americanize their English and assure themselves a brighter future. If they arrived at T.A. with "soccer on the brain," many of them left, four years later, with a great deal more relevance – timeless relevance – to occupy their thoughts.

It is not surprising that the Talmudical Academy successfully achieved a situation in which boys from South America kept Jewish law, Shabbos and kashrus to the best of their ability from the first day of their arrival. These were the terms and conditions upon which their acceptance into the school was based, and if they wished to find a safe haven from the phenomena that threatened them south of the border, they would have to comply.

Yet how did so many nonobservant boys from South America come to T.A. and become observant *in their hearts*? How is it that after a year, when their parents offered these boys safe but secular alternatives to T.A. to enable them to come home, the boys insisted on staying? Certainly, a major factor in the equation was the subtle, sensitive, behind-the-scenes efforts of Rabbi Milikowsky. When a new boy arrived from South America, Rabbi Milikowsky was exceedingly careful in the way he handled the dynamics of the social relations that developed between the newly arriving South American students and their classmates from the city and the dormitory.

With Rabbi Milikowsky, the accent was not on rules and regulations, although the school expected that they be obeyed. Rather, what he tried to do was to develop a whole system of big-brother relationships between older and younger students. He would work in the best tradition of the great *mashgichim*, pairing up personalities. Rather than leaving all the work for himself to have an influence on a particular boy, he would pair that boy up with other, older and more mature boys who could have a positive influence on him. Ostensibly, the purpose of these matches was never "so that Reuven can have an influence on you." Instead, it was always presented as a means of an older boy, familiar with the school, with the English language and with American culture, "showing the younger boy the ropes," and the need for such a relationship in that sense was totally legitimate. Yet a by-product of these relationships was that the older boys were very influential in helping to shape and mold the thinking of the younger boys. Because these were relationships between peers, the younger students were able to accept changes naturally, over time, without feeling threatened or overwhelmed as they might have if the efforts had originated with authority figures.

One student told me:

> I can vividly recall seeing kids who didn't come from Sabbath-observant backgrounds walking around with kids with *peyos* and *tzitzis*. The kids with *peyos* and *tzitzis* showed great sensitivity to their "little brothers," and I witnessed some tremendous success stories. Kids who came from non-*frum* backgrounds, non-Sabbath-observant backgrounds, ultimately became towering figures in the Torah community.

For many Americans, 1964 was "the year of the Beatles and the year of the Stones." For T.A. boys, however, especially those in the dormitory, it was nothing of the sort. Rather, it was the year of the fire. One night, shortly after Purim, the main building of the Talmudical Academy burnt down.

The morning after the T.A. fire, Rabbi Peretz Dinowitz, who was in third grade at the time, witnessed the following:

Dr. Kranzler came out to inspect the damage, and the devastation he saw shocked him to the core. Standing there amidst the ashes and the debris, he began to weep. Suddenly he felt an arm around his shoulder. It was Rabbi Milikowsky.

"Why are you crying?" Rebbe asked, and Dr. Kranzler answered, "What do you mean? The yeshiva burnt down and you're asking me why I'm crying?"

Rabbi Milikowsky looked at him and said, "That's not the yeshiva! The *bochrim* and the *rebbeim* are the yeshiva. This is just the building. There's no reason for crying! Baruch Hashem, the yeshiva is still standing strong!"

Rabbi Milikowsky's words made such an impression on Peretz Dinowitz, who was only in third grade, that he remembered them for thirty years and was able to tell me the story.

Tzitzis: The Difference Between Life and Death

When the Mir Yeshiva first arrived in Japan by boat from Vladivostok, late that night they were brought before a high-ranking Japanese military officer. That officer announced to the yeshiva administration that they had agreed to allow the yeshiva students into Japan, but would accept no riffraff trying to pass themselves off as Jews. They therefore asked the heads of the yeshiva what test could be performed to prove that all of the students were really Jewish yeshiva men. The rabbis conferred and their response to the officer was this: Anyone who is wearing *tzitzis* is one of us. Anyone who is not is an impostor. The officer therefore ordered that all of the students line up and reveal their *tzitzis* beneath their shirts, and they did so. The Japanese officer, like a seventh-grade yeshiva rebbe, then proceeded to check the *tzitzis* of each *talmid*. Needless to say, they were all wearing *tzitzis*, and all were accepted.

From this story Rabbi Milikowsky learned two things: First, *tzitzis* can make the difference between a Jew and a non-Jew. Second, even though all of their paperwork had been completed before they left Vilna, including legitimate transit passes through Japan and visas to Curaçao, it was the students' *tzitzis* that had made the difference between life and death.

Joseph Friedman, '64, who heard this story from Rabbi Milikowsky and passed it on to me, concluded by saying, "For this reason, I wear *tzitzis* at night."

Going to Bat, I

CRASH!

— Hey, what was that?

— Dunno. I was asleep, but it wasn't in this room. I'm going back to shluffy land. Hey! Why'd you turn on the light, Little Sam?

— I want to see better outside.

— Dummy! You can't see better outside when you turn on the light. Stick to your fancy vocabulary, Little Sam. Your physics is lousy. What time is it, anyway?

— It's 10:30.

— Cripes! We seniors have a big math test tomorrow, so if you ninth-graders could kindly arrange for there to be no loud noises anywhere in the dormitory or in the city of Baltimore, for that matter, it would be greatly appreciated. And turn off that light!

— Sorry. Look, I'm leaving anyway. I see *bochrim* running down the hall. I'm gonna go see what's going on... Hey, Marco! What happened?

— Don't look now, but there's some local kids across the street standing there and staring over here, and one of them just threw a rock into the dormitory.

— Did he break anything?

— Sure looks like it. See that little window? And watch where you're walking. There's broken glass on the floor.

— Jeepers. I'm gonna go get a broom to sweep this mess out of the way.

REBBE WITH HIS BOYS

With Joel Greene.

With Joseph Abrams (left)
and Joseph Friedman, 1964.

With Larry Hirsch and son.

– Great idea! I'll help. In the meantime, there's some beefy eleventh-graders looking for baseball bats to go outside and wallop those kids out there.

– Oh, brother! There's gonna be trouble. Wait till Rebbe hears about this.

– But Rebbe's asleep now at home, a block away.

– Don't be so sure! He always shows up somehow. Remember that fight in the dorm between Pinky and Sherman?

– I guess I do. He came at a good time, too – just when it was turning into World War III. Nipped it in the bud, he did. What were they fighting about, anyway?

– Who can possibly remember? Probably fighting over a pencil eraser – that's the kind of thing we fight over. But the thing is that Rebbe was there. He showed up at the right time.

– Come to think of it, you're right. He always shows up at the right moment. Although I don't know how he does it.

– And remember last week with the water fight?

– Well, yeah.... That was kind of a surprise. I didn't really expect him to show up at the exact moment that he did...

– He caught you, all right!

– Yes, he did.

– Right when you were about to dump two *negel vasser* cups on Harry Gelbart's head!

– Just a second there! I was only thinking about it.

– That's a moot point.

– A what?

– Never mind. Gosh! Here come the eleventh-graders!

– Rumble! Rumble! Gonna be a rumble!

– And there they go! They're running outside. But they're not crossing the street. They're thinking about it. There's about five local kids and five *bochrim*, and the *bochrim* have bats!

– Yeah, but who knows what the local boys have!

– Now they're yelling something.

– Can you hear anything?

– Not really, but the words "punk" and "drape" seem to figure prominently in the dialogue.

– You got a mouth on you, Little Sam!

– Hey! Look over there!

– Who is it? Clark Kent?

– Nope, it's Rebbe! And boy, is he walking fast!

– I can't believe it!

– What'd I tell you? He's going to give those *bochrim* one of his kicks! No! he's crossing the street! He's walking towards the local kids! Oh, my God. I don't believe it! He's going to beat up the local kids!

– Nooo! Can't be!

– Hmmm, you're right. He stopping…. He's… he's *talking* to them! They're staring at him… They don't know what to do with him!… He's been talking for a long time! What's he saying?… Hey, I don't know what he said, but the local kids are packing up and moving out. And the eleventh-graders are coming back inside.

– Little Sam, Little Sam! You're friends with Big Marv. When he comes back in here, ask him if he could hear what Rebbe was saying from across the street.

– All right! Here's Big Marv. Hey, Marv! Marv! Wait a second, Marv! Pleeeease, Marv! Tell us what Rebbe was saying to those kids outside, pretty please?

– Well, Little Sam, I didn't hear everything, but I saw Rebbe flash his big smile, and he said, "How are you guys doing? It's awfully late, isn't it? Why don't you guys go home? You've got to wake up early tomorrow morning for school. Your folks are probably looking for you. And anyway, there's probably a good show on television!"

He caught them *totally* off guard! They just stood there, staring at him with their jaws hanging down to the floor, and then they just sort of turned around and walked away. They went home!

– Thank God that's over!

– I'm not sure it is, Little Sam. I'm not sure. I've got this funny feeling, you know? I don't think Rebbe has said the last word.

– Why? Where is he now?

– Oh, he's gone back home all right, but I think we're going to hear from him.

– Marv, we missed you at recess. Where'd you go?

– It was Rebbe. He called together all of us who had been out on the street with the local kids two nights ago.

– Oh, yeah! I remember that. What happened?

– So he called us all together just after lunch…

– Yeah?

– And I thought, "Uh-oh. Now we're done for." He brought us into his classroom and closed the door. It was recess time, and everyone else was outside. We all just sort of sat there, kind of nervous, you know, looking down at our sneakers. And he let us stew for a while.

Finally he looked at us, mostly at me, I think, because he could tell that I was the one who pushed the others to go out there. And he said, "OK! So they threw stones! They threw stones…. So you call the police! Or you call me! *You don't run out with a bat!* I am responsible for you, and something *very bad* could have happened. Do you all understand?" And that was all he said. We all nodded our heads very quietly.

We all knew how fortunate we were that Rebbe took care of us and made sure the local boys went home before trouble began.

Going to Bat, II

The following story is a personal narrative by Rabbi Shlomo Schwartz:

When I was a teenager in high school I was a wild kid. My parents lived four hours away in Atlantic City, New Jersey, and I felt after being in T.A. for one year that it was time to *party!*

191

At the end of my junior year I was pretty much out of control. I was playing basketball much more than going to any classes, whether Jewish or secular.

Just before I was to come back to T.A. for my senior year, after an entire summer of non-stop partying, the Rosh Yeshiva, Rabbi Samson, called my father and told him that T.A. would not be accepting me back for my senior year (they figured – correctly – that there would be no stopping me). I called Rebbe and cried to him that I didn't want to go to public school for my last year of high school after four years as a yeshiva *bachur* (even though I was not so religiously observant at that time).

He interceded on my behalf with Rabbi Samson. Rabbi Samson told him that under no circumstances would he allow me to corrupt the other boys in the dorm. (He didn't believe any promises from me anymore.)

Then Rebbe proposed, "How about if he lives in my house for the year and I take full responsibility for all his actions?" Rabbi Samson finally agreed on condition that whenever I did anything wrong, Rabbi Samson would come looking for Rebbe – not me.
And that's what happened. I lived for one year in Rebbe's home.
And as the saying goes, "The rest is history."

Rabbi Shlomo Schwartz ultimately became a Lubavitcher rabbi and has been active in conventional and unconventional religious outreach on the American West Coast for thirty-four years. At first he operated within the framework of Lubavitch, but more recently he has gone out on his own, creating the Chai Center. He is today one of the foremost rabbinical outreach professionals on the West Coast. He concludes as follows:

"I have one of the *largest* attended High Holiday outreach services in the USA, with almost *two thousand* coming for FREE Yom Kippur services. Thanks, Rebbe!"

൙   ൏

Big Game

When Mr. Emanuel Friedman was a sixteen-year-old T.A. dormitory student, two things that he particularly loved were football and Rabbi Boruch Milikowsky. Most of the time he didn't have to choose between them, but the following story clearly illustrates how he chose when push came to shove:

One time, on the day before Yom Kippur, T.A. boys were playing a game of touch football against Ner Israel in a field a few blocks away from the school. It was perhaps twelve noon, and Yom Kippur was fast approaching. Yet because the game was so close, the boys just kept on playing.

Suddenly, Rabbi Milikowsky came running up to the football field, and he was in a panic. "Boys!" he cried out, "This is ridiculous! It's almost Yom Kippur! What are you doing? You're sitting here and playing football! That's crazy!"

"Manny" Friedman, with all the youthful brashness of a sixteen-year-old, went up to Rabbi Milikowsky and objected, saying that there was plenty of time. Rabbi Milikowsky therefore turned to him and asked, "I don't understand. If you were getting ready to meet the President of the United States in two hours, would you be playing football? No! You'd be home. You'd be showering. You'd be putting on your nicest suit. You'd be making sure that everything was perfect, down to the last detail, to make the proper impression."

At the time, Manny didn't think too deeply about what Rebbe was saying. Perhaps he said to himself, "Come on! The President of the United States? Who meets the President of the United States?" He and everyone else left the field and went to get ready.

Thirty years passed. Emanuel Friedman grew into an important captain of the business world. The day arrived when he was going to go for the first time as part of a delegation of fifteen people to meet with President Clinton. As he saw the people in the delegation preparing themselves, fretting over ever detail, making sure that their appearances were fitting to meet a head of state, he thought about what Rebbe had said. Rabbi

Milikowsky's message, obviously about Yom Kippur, but also about responsibility and advance planning, hit home. More important, Emanuel experienced Rebbe's figurative analogy and realized that God is infinitely greater than the President of the United States.

❧ ❦

Vision of Elijah

The following story from Eli Schlossberg is not so much about Rabbi Milikowsky as it is about the effect that he had on some of his students, even city boys…

We lived on Jonquil Avenue, and I was getting older, maybe sixteen or seventeen. It was Pesach, the second Seder night. When I was little I truly believed that one day when I opened the door for Elijah, he would miraculously appear, and on eagles' wings he would take us right to Yerushalayim for the final Redemption. I would gaze at the wine in Elijah's cup the next morning, and even though he failed to show up, the glass was always less full.

As I passed bar mitzvah and was a bit disappointed that he still had failed to show up, my faith in that action was a bit diminished, and when I opened the door it became more of a ritual ceremony. That night as I opened the door, I was shocked to see a dark figure in a pure white *kittel* walking down the street. The wind was blowing the *kittel* and the figure looked angelic. Could it be? Was this the year? Why was he passing my home? "Come back!" I cried. "Come back! My family is here." As I ran to get a closer view, the figure was with his back to me. I ran with excitement to catch up and all of a sudden he turned to me, for over his shoulder he heard me running up. With a warm, familiar, angelic smile, that of my beloved rebbe, he looked me in the eye. It was Rebbe Milikowsky and his smile and demeanor always lifted your spirit and faith. While it wasn't *Mashiach*, it was Rebbe, and once again I regained the faith

Rebbe always instilled in his *talmidim*. Now at fifty years of age when I open the door for Elijah I again believe that this could be the year!

Looking beyond the Details

The following is a story that took place forty years ago. Perhaps what follows could occur today, and perhaps not.

Jay Pomrenze and Howard Spitzer* were best friends from Washington D.C. Jay came from a Sabbath-observant home, while Howard did not. The two boys had gone to the Jewish coed day school in Washington until the end of eighth grade. Then Jay moved to the Talmudical Academy of Baltimore, while Howard continued through the last year of the local day school.

At the end of ninth grade, a large group of boys from the day school decided to continue in T.A, and Howie, even though he was neither from a Sabbath-observant home nor Sabbath observant himself, had an interest to continue with his friends, and especially to be reunited with his best friend Jay.

This posed a dilemma. How do you take a non–Sabbath-observant boy from a non–Sabbath-observant home into a yeshiva when the boy has no interest at the moment in becoming Sabbath-observant? Nowadays, how many yeshivos would be willing to do this?

When Howie came to T.A. for his interview, Jay had already been at T.A. for a year, so as a fourteen-year-old "man of experience," he broached the subject first with Rabbi Milikowsky. What Rabbi Milikowsky came up with was the following:

Howie would come to the yeshiva, and he would have to keep Shabbos while on campus. But what about going home for Shabbos? The Washington boys used to go home for Shabbos once every three or four weeks. Rebbe said, "He won't go home for Shabbos. He'll go home, once every three or four weeks, on a Sunday or Monday." This way, Howie could be in the yeshiva and he could go home without violating the Sabbath on his visits home.

This is indeed what happened. Howie came to T.A. He learned *gemara* like everybody else, and he graduated with everyone else at the end of twelfth grade.

Today, Howie is not Sabbath-observant, but there is no doubt that he was influenced by this experience and that in turn, he, a very fine person with much to offer, had a positive influence on those around him. In this case, as in so many others, Rabbi Milikowsky looked beyond the details of the case, getting to the essence. He had the flexibility to know how to approach a problem of this sort in a way that would prove acceptable and beneficial to all.

Howie's stay at T.A. was not a "success story" in the sense of our being able to conclude, "He became Sabbath-observant and today he's sitting and learning in Lakewood." None of that happened. Despite that, it was a positive experience for him and for the people with whom he interacted during those three years.

There was never a psychiatrist in the world who could relate to someone the way he could. He knew a boy, and he would know everything about that boy. I mean, this man was a psychologist like nobody. He understood what made you tick. The man understood kids. We've got guys in their fifties now like I am who can't imagine how Rebbe knew us so well. Rebbe was a psychiatrist! And he would joke about it and say, "I am a psychologist." And he was! You know the complexities of what would go on there?
– Rabbi Yaakov Spivak

On Blowing Up

Jack Milkins* was always a bit on the wild side. Whether it was a matter of missing curfews, cutting classes or just seeking out unauthorized adventures, you always knew that he would have a hand in it.

One afternoon he decided that things were too quiet in the hallways of T.A., so he took a whole roll of children's blasting caps and emptied the gun powder into a small plastic receptacle. This took a lot of skill and determination, because the black circle on each red cap had to be carefully perforated so that the bit of gun powder underneath could be freed to fall into the container. When he had what he considered enough for whatever injurious little plan he had conceived, he put the receptacle in his pocket and went to class.

It is unclear just what Jack's plans were, but the plastic container decided on its own to explode just as Jack was walking down the hall, creating a loud noise. The chemical reaction that led to this explosion, inaugurated a further chain of events. The first thing that happened was that Jack, who suddenly felt sharp pain in the area of his body nearest his right pocket, lowered his trousers to see if he had actually hurt himself seriously. Jack performed this immodest act on the assumption that as he was enrolled in a boys' school, only boys might see him. Now at the time of this incident's occurrence, there was in T.A. an elderly and somewhat squeamish woman teacher, who was teaching in the classroom closest to where the explosion occurred. When she heard something explode out in the hall, she very quickly ran to the door of her room to survey the scene and decide whether there might be anything outside that could threaten the welfare of her students. Imagine her surprise when she looked out into the hallway and found a seventeen-year-old boy standing unclad before her! She of course let out a loud shriek, and Jack immediately ran into the school restroom.

Next came involvement from higher up. The principal at the time was Dr. Kranzler who, hearing the explosion and the shriek, rushed to the scene, where several passersby told him what had occurred and who was involved. Dr. Kranzler thus proceeded into the restroom, found Jack Milkins and suspended him for the day. As Jack was an out-of-towner and a resident of Rabbi Milikowsky's home, that was where he headed.

As Jack walked home he had much to think about. His academic situation was precarious enough, and now he might have to explain to Rabbi Milikowsky why he was coming home in the middle of the day. As head of the dormitory, Rabbi Milikowsky was most directly responsible for his welfare.

When he arrived at Rabbi Milikowsky's house, which was a block away from the school, he found Rabbi Milikowsky waiting for him at the back door. Apparently Rebbe had already heard what had happened, perhaps by phone from Dr. Kranzler. Anyway, Rabbi Milikowsky now invited him in and wanted to hear from Jack, in his own words, exactly what had happened. After explaining, he prepared himself to receive some kind of rebuke.

Instead, Rabbi Milikowsky said only, "The right side of your pants are all black. Go upstairs and change, and when you get changed, come back down." Jack shrugged his shoulders and went upstairs to change. When he came back down, Rabbi Milikowsky handed him money, and said simply, "Go to the movies." For a moment Jack hesitated, rather surprised, but soon enough he took the money, turned around and left.

When Jack returned, seven hours later, it was about 11:00 P.M. Rabbi Milikowsky had waited up for him. Jack had missed supper, he had missed night *seder* and he had missed *Ma'ariv*. And Rabbi Milikowsky was sitting in the kitchen waiting for him. When he heard him come in, he invited him into the kitchen. He made Jack a cup of tea, and invited him to sit down. They began to talk.

Three hours later, a very excited young man went up to bed. Jack was floating on Cloud Nine, soaring in a spiritual high such as he had not known in many years. Sleep was out of the question. He woke up his roommate and tried to express his feelings to him. Rabbi Milikowsky had turned him around!

The roommate, who told me this story, never found out precisely what Jack and Rabbi Milikowsky had discussed during those three hours, but when he finished telling me this story, he concluded as follows:

"Rebbe gave love! His trademark was love! And we were *his* boys! *His boys!*"

Bare-Bones Approach

Jay Pomerenze had been in the T.A. dormitory for all of three days. He had just come from Washington D.C. and was spending his first Shabbos at T.A. He was a precocious thirteen-year-old boy starting ninth grade in a place where he had never been. He was disoriented, and literally did not have the lay of the land. The only boys he knew were a small group who had come with him from Washington. After Shabbos, a bunch of fellows set out for a pizza shop, asking if he wanted to come along, and he said yes. It turned out that it was a non-kosher pizza shop.

It was the fall of 1962. The issue of pizza having to be kosher was a relatively new idea among American Orthodox Jews, but kosher cheese and kosher pizza were now available. Great rabbis who ten years before had ruled leniently about cheese made with rennet were no longer ruling that way. By now, yeshiva students were expected to understand that they could not eat pizza in a restaurant without kashrus supervision.

The boys went inside and sat down. Some ordered pizza, while others ordered soft drinks. Jay ordered a soft drink.

It turned out afterwards Rabbi Milikowsky had managed to find out exactly who had been at that pizza shop, who had eaten pizza and who had just sat there. As Jay later found out, Rebbe always knew everything that happened, although Jay never found out how Rebbe did this.

Anyway, a few days later, Rabbi Milikowsky summoned Jay into his office, and Jay thought, "Uh-oh! I'm going to be expelled, and I got here a week ago!"

Wide-eyed with fear, he entered Rabbi Milikowsky's office and sat down.

Forty years later, Jay Pomrenze recalls fondly that despite his own expectations, Rabbi Milikowsky did not focus on the technical halachic question of pizza consumption in a non-kosher restaurant. That wasn't the point. Instead, passionately but without anger, Rabbi Milikowsky brought up larger issues: How should a yeshiva student conduct himself? How should he spend his time? How should he choose his friends? What kind of places should he go to during his free time? Jay, rather than hearing a lecture on the evils of rennet, instead learned an important lesson in how to conduct himself during the next three years, and during the rest of his life as well.

"Refresh Me with Apples" (Song of Songs)

One way that Rabbi Boruch Milikowsky helped to prepare T.A. boys for Jewish adulthood was by having them say *divrei Torah* at the Shabbos meals. The talks did not have to be long – five minutes or so. Besides serving as good training in public speaking, this forced the boys to look up Torah sources on their own, to think independently about them, and to teach what they had learned to others. Helping a teenage boy to realize that he was indeed capable of this constituted a many-faceted act of kindness.

Twelfth-graders would talk three or four times a year, eleventh-graders would speak twice, and tenth-graders once. You always knew who was going to be speaking next. In fact, lists were put up on the bulletin board, making it clear two or three weeks in advance who the speakers were going to be. Rabbi Milikowsky always made sure that everyone would have plenty of time to prepare – except for one time.

There was one boy, a nervous twelfth-grader named Yitzy, who used to fiddle with his fingers when he said his *devar Torah*. Now it just so happened that one week, at Friday night dinner, when Yitzy was the scheduled speaker, he was sitting next to Mark, a classmate of his. Mark was a good learner. That was well-known, but he was also known for being spirited. All through the meal, Yitzy seemed to be talking to himself, as, over and over, he went though the points he wished to make in his *devar Torah*. He touched little of the food, and when the dessert was brought out, apple sauce, it sat at his place, unnoticed – at least by Yitzy.

The time came for Yitzy's talk. He scraped his chair back and stood up. Everyone in the room leaned forward slightly, gazing at him in anticipation. Rabbi Milikowsky looked at him with a big smile of encouragement. Abruptly, after a few moments of silence, Yitzy lunged into his *devar Torah* like a large refrigerator truck changing gears on Interstate 70 outside Indianapolis at 2:00 AM. All in all, Yitzy was well prepared, and despite his nervousness he made his points clearly, even if he twiddled and twaddled his fingers up and down as he talked. He quoted a verse, twiddled, asked a question, twaddled, and quoted a Rashi that answered the question. Things were going well, even if his hands were soaring and dive-bombing over the table surface.

Now just as Yitzy was about to raise an objection to the Rashi that he had quoted, Mark, seated to Yitzy's right, noticed the little bowl of apple sauce sitting untouched at Yitzy's setting. A brilliant idea occurred to him.

He took the little bowl of apple sauce and held it up so that the next time Yitzy's fingers took a dive, they would land in the apple sauce, and this in fact is what happened. Yitzy distractedly plunged his fingers into the applesauce, too preoccupied with his *devar Torah* to even notice what he had done. Rabbi Milikowsky, of course, noticed the whole thing, but he kept his silence. But as soon as the meal was over, he did two things. First, he approached the boy who was scheduled for lunch the next day and apologized to him that his talk was being postponed for another week. Next, he went over to Mark. He did not yell about what had occurred. He said only this: "Mark, it wasn't nice. You're speaking at the next meal."

Mark, who told me this story, added that on this occasion, he did succeed in coming up with a talk on short notice, but that henceforth he tried to avoid such pranks. After all, you shouldn't press your luck.

૎ ૏

Things You Wouldn't Tell Your Own Mother

Although many of the students I spoke to used the expression "surrogate parent" to describe Rabbi Milikowsky, he also filled certain roles not normally filled by parents. Things that you "wouldn't tell your own mother," boys would tell Rabbi Milikowsky.

> Of all the people in TA, Rabbi Milikowsky probably had the most profound influence on me. And it's interesting why. I mean, as far as improving in my Torah-study methodology I was interested, but it was more on the personal level, because of his warmth and his understanding. It's also interesting because I came from a family of Holocaust survivors. And you know, however much I cared for my parents, there was always this generation gap between myself and them. First of all, this is because all children have a generation gap with their parents. Also, however, I always had this thing about them being much older than I, you know, like being grandparents. But with Rabbi Milikowsky, for some reason or another, I was able to – let's say – share and discuss certain things with him, as the *mashgiach*

201

ruchani, which I couldn't do with my parents. With my parents, I could discuss things up to a certain level. But with deeper things, like being a confused teenager and stuff like that, I felt that Rabbi Milikowsky had a greater understanding. I was able to share with him.

જ ભ

Auto-Motives

Bert Horowitz* came to T.A. from a weak religious background. His parents were non-observant, and he himself was not fully committed to observance when he came to T.A. Bert's parents had given him a car, and he brought the car up to T.A. He and his roommate did not live in the dorm across the street from the school. There weren't enough rooms. Instead, they lived in a second-story home owned by the elderly resident of the first story, a Mrs. Wasser, whom they did not see very often.

Now Bert had a car, and as far as he and his roommate were concerned, this was a great thing. They could travel around, cut classes and visit girls. It was Paradise! Of course, they didn't want most of the guys to know that they had a car. First of all, they didn't want the information to get around, and second of all, they didn't want Rabbi Milikowsky to find out. So the number of people who knew was a very small group, really only three or four other students.

Only months later in the middle of the year did they find out that one other person knew about the car as well: Rebbe! Somehow he brought it up, and the following conversation took place:

– Oh! You know about the car?
– What do you mean? I've known about the car all year already.
– In that case, could you do us a favor?
– Yeah, sure. What would you like?
– Don't tell the other guys, all right?
– Of course not! I don't want them to know!

Bert's roommate, who told me this story, concluded it as follows:

"The point is that I think Rebbe made an assessment that us having a car was not a negative. He didn't simply say, 'The rule is that no one can have a car.' He probably felt that for Bert to have a car would probably keep him in T.A. another year. Rebbe knew that we were seeing girls, using the car. But I think he made an assessment that since we were both continuing to function well as students, growing in our learning, etc., it was worth it for Bert's sake not to mention it."

Putting His Foot Down

Despite the many stories of what appeared to be Rabbi Milikowsky's leniency in the face of adolescent frivolity, he was not a yes-man. There were times when he put his foot down.

One time some boys decided to open up a food canteen. The partners in this enterprise were two tenth-graders and one twelfth-grader. The idea was that at night they would sell hamburgers, hot dogs and French fries in the school. They were all excited and they actually began to do it. Their purpose was to make some extra money.

Melvin, one of the two tenth-graders, was in Rabbi Milikowsky's *shiur.* One day soon after the canteen opened, Rebbe started talking about it during class, and he said: "And there are boys who are coming from other towns and they are sitting and learning, and there are boys who are coming and think they want to be a business! And they are not learning any more." Rebbe then made it clear that the canteen was to close immediately.

At the time, Melvin said, "What's the big deal?" But he now realizes that Rebbe was right. It was too draining. The boys were getting too involved with it. Melvin concludes:

"Rabbi Milikowsky just said, 'You can't do it.' He wasn't afraid of us. He put his foot down, and said, 'That's it. You're not going to do it,' and he stopped it."

Cut Out to Work

In addition to the many students who "majored" in Rabbi Milikowsky while they were at T.A., a small number also had "strong minors" in Rabbi Milikowsky's wife, Leah. She could often be counted on as a source of down-to-earth advice, or to get one out of a tight spot.

Moe Wolner* was a lively and outgoing fellow who spent a year living in the home of Rabbi Milikowsky's mother-in-law, Mrs. Goldman, before moving into another home. By such means, in addition to getting very close to Rabbi Milikowsky like so many others, he also got to know some of Rabbi Milikowsky's family, including Rebbetzin Leah.

Although Moe was a good student and a good worker, he had a mischievous side. He liked to find ways to earn a little bit of extra spending money. One way he did this was by working for Schleider's Caterers. Moe worked for them as a dishwasher and did all the other unskilled labor in the kitchen. They generally hired him on Sundays when there were late luncheons. Moe could learn Torah with his class on Sunday mornings, when classes ended at noon, and run over to Schleider's to work. His industriousness did not go unnoticed. Finally they asked him one time, "Can you work any more? Can you work days?" and without thinking he said, "Sure."

On Monday morning, Moe starting working days, and he cut classes in order to do it. He simply didn't go to school. He had his roommate Yaakov tell Rabbi Milikowsky that he was ill, and that roommate kept bringing dinner back to their room.

As described elsewhere in this work, a dorm boy at T.A. couldn't be sick for more than a few days without expecting a visit from Rabbi Milikowsky. Rebbe was Rebbe, after all. So after three days Rebbe approached Moe's roommate and said, "Take me to Moe. He's sick." Yaakov replied, "Nah! I think maybe he's too sick. He doesn't want to see anybody."

When Rabbi Milikowsky heard that, he immediately knew that something was rotten. He went with Yaakov to the house where they lived, and of course Moe wasn't there. Rabbi Milikowsky was angry. He said to

Yaakov, "Get Moe on the phone within five minutes or he's out of school!" So Yaakov called up Moe at the caterer and whispered into the receiver, "Moe! You're in big trouble! Here's Rebbe."

Rabbi Milikowsky did not try to hide his emotions. He let Moe have it, threatening to have him thrown out of the school. Here was an intelligent boy who did well in school, and now look what he had done – the lies, the lost study – this story was almost too much even for the practiced ear of Rabbi Milikowsky!

But Moe kept yelling, "Wait, Rebbe! No! I'm coming back! I'm coming back!" Somehow he got Rabbi Milikowsky to calm down a bit, and then after he hung up, he used his secret weapon – he called Rabbi Milikowsky's wife. When she answered he described what he had done, how he had been discovered and what his present situation was, and he said, "First of all, I want you to make sure that he doesn't call my father. Second, tell him to calm down and I'll be back later."

The next day, Moe found out that Mrs. Milikowsky had done everything Moe had asked. She had gotten Rebbe to calm down. She had persuaded him not to call Moe's parents, and she had averted threats of expulsion – at least this time.

The previous story demonstrates how much power is possessed by a worthy rebbetzin. The story that follows, told by Rabbi Pinchas Fleishman in his own words, demonstrates the kinds of things that worthy rebbetzins do to earn that power:

One time a young student from the dormitory came down with severe stomach cramps and was taken to the hospital. The surgeon decided that it was appendicitis and that they were going to operate in the morning. The rebbetzin, Mrs. Milikowsky, stayed overnight in the hospital with the boy, as she sometimes did. The boy was young and scared, and his parents were out of town.

Somewhere around one or two in the morning, Rabbi Milikowsky called the hospital and asked to speak with his wife. The nurses said that she was sleeping. Rabbi Milikowsky was exceedingly agitated and insisted on speaking to his wife, so they woke her up. When he heard her voice he said, "Do not let them operate! Under no conditions must they operate!" Now can you imagine the next morning: Here's this European woman, quoting her European husband, saying that the operation is off, but she managed to stop the surgeon from going through with it. It turned out to be something that the boy had eaten.

I don't know how or what he knew. You have to understand. People on his level, of his caliber, operate on a different level from ours.

❧   ❧

The nights she spent in hospitals are just one example of how Leah Milikowsky proved her worthiness for the very public role of rebbetzin. In a home where there were always teenage male boarders, she was ever the gracious hostess. She would implore the boys under her care to feel comfortable to take fruit and snacks. She would tell them to view the refrigerator as their own and to feel free to make themselves a drink or just to come downstairs and visit the family. Moreover, she would offer help with homework as well – she was, after all, an educated, cultured woman. She would also call the boys' mothers to ask if there was something special she could provide for their sons. In short, in the tradition of our mother Sarah, she did everything in her power to make her young guests feel comfortable.

Also, in the words of King Solomon, "she looked after the ways of her household." Together with her husband, she was a full partner in educating her children to develop good traits and fine character. At report-card time, she would tell her children, "The most important grade is 'Behavior.' I don't want to see any bad marks on that score. You'll be a professor one day later." The Milikowskys may have wanted their children to achieve scholastically, but becoming a good and moral person came first.

On a more mundane level, however, Rebbetzin Leah took care to ensure that the Milikowskys could make ends meet. They were never wealthy people, but thanks to the rebbetzin, they managed to save money. Mrs. Milikowsky was always looking for ways to be frugal. If anyone in the family wished to spend money, it had to pass her scrutiny.

One result of this approach was that she sent her four children to Camp Milldale, the general day camp of the Jewish Community Center of Baltimore. Considering that the family enjoyed a discount, it was an inexpensive way for the children to have pleasant activities during summer vacation. Yet, there were other virtues as well, as pointed out by her daughter, Rabbanit Malke Bina:

> My mother always felt that the whole community had to work together, and that if there was a community camp that was kosher you could go to it, even if you were more religious than the other children. She said, "You shouldn't keep your head up so high! It's a fine camp. The community is organizing it and they'll give us a discount. So, you should go and you should mix with the other kids as well. You should be strong enough in your yiddishkeit that it shouldn't bother you to go there. You should see other parts of the Jewish community."

Rabbanit Malke Bina, a Jerusalemite, concludes her comments by pointing out that when her own Israeli children reached age ten or eleven, she sent them to be with their grandparents in Baltimore for the summer, and Mrs. Milikowsky sent them to Camp Milldale as well!

Rebbe's Personality

Rabbi Edward Davis, '64:
Rebbe was terrific! He was a warm, real person. He never, ever hid his personality or played games with us. We saw him laugh. We see him cry. We

saw him get angry. We saw him show the gentle warmth of a mother to her children. All of that – in the course of one *day* you could have seen all of these emotions. He was very strong, as we all knew. But he was a real person. I think that's the key as you reminisce about it.

The Assassination of John F. Kennedy

On Friday, November 22, 1963, rumors began to circulate that the President of the United States, John F. Kennedy, had been shot. Yanky Taub, who had been in T.A. for three months, remembers that before it became clear precisely what had occurred, the entire high school assembled in the *beis midrash* to recite *Tehillim* (Psalms).

When the truth came out that the President had been assassinated, Rabbi Milikowsky was devastated. On Friday night he gave a talk in which he spoke with dignity about how good America had been to the Jews and how terrible it was that the president had been murdered. Jay Pomrenze remembers that Rabbi Milikowsky spoke from the heart. He was not just paying politically-correct lip service. Rabbi Milikowsky related to people as people, Jewish or not. That Shabbos he was very upset, and everyone could see it. As in so many other instances, Rabbi Milikowsky wore his emotions on his sleeve.

Rebbe as a Rebbe

Jay Pomrenze, '66:

Rabbi Milikowsky was a phenomenal rebbe, and I really developed a love of learning because of him. In tenth grade I got there, and we learned *Gittin*. I have to say he had a tremendous influence on me. I'm giving you all the things about how we fooled around a lot, but I really loved learning. I had extra night *seders* at night. And I was in the *beis midrash* fairly late. I'm trying to remember…. There was a short period of time when I had an extra night *seder* with Calman Weinreb, who is a rebbe at Ner Israel now. And I think a few times I had an opportunity to learn with Yisrael Neuman, who is now the Rosh Yeshiva at Lakewood. He was older.

He was a phenomenal rebbe. I really enjoyed him as a rebbe. Because of Rebbe, I was selected to go into Rabbi Bobrovsky's twelfth-grade *shiur*. He had to pick you for you to get in. He used to come in and *farher* us, test us, in tenth grade. Rabbi Bobrovsky would come in and then decide whom he was going to take from tenth grade into twelfth grade. I was jumped. That was because of Rebbe's influence on my learning. The shiur was a mixture, whoever he picked from tenth, eleventh and twelfth. So I don't want to give the impression that Rebbe was all fun and games. There was a real learning relationship as well.

Justice Once

One night Rabbi Milikowsky summoned a T.A. boy to his house for a talk. The boy had been causing a lot of trouble in T.A., and there was pressure to expel him. Rabbi Milikowsky told the boy, "Look, we have to find a way for you to succeed here in yeshiva. How about this: let's say we give you a trial period of a month. A month! Let's see if for this period you can pull through. And then, you'll go home and rest a bit. OK? Let's try a month." The boy agreed and left to go back to the dormitory.

Rebbe's daughter, Malke, who heard this conversation, later approached her father and asked, "So, he's good for a month. So what? How has that accomplished anything? Afterwards won't he just behave badly again? And then he'll have to leave the school."

Rabbi Milikowsky shook his head and gently answered his daughter as follows: "Maybe he'll be good this month and he'll decide it's the right thing to do! With him I have to take it slowly. I can't burden him with too much. Let him try it for a little while. A month!"

Three Tragedies

Henry David Thoreau said, "Most men lead lives of quiet desperation." Besides the Vishnevo massacre that took most of his family, Rabbi Boruch Milikowsky also suffered from three other tragedies.

The first tragedy, the disappearance of his younger brother Avraham Elya and the sense of guilt and loss that it left with him, were described in Chapter 7 above.

The second was a fire that struck his home during the night, three days after Purim in 1966, in which two fourteen-year-old T.A. boys died. Shmuel and Meyer Leib Katz, z"l, first cousins from the New York area, were living in the Milikowsky home. When the fire broke out, they were trapped on the second floor in the back of the house and there was no way for anyone to reach them.

In the third tragedy, on the 18th of Tishrei in 1969, Rabbi Milikowsky was driving his daughter's car pool. He let one of the girls off at a particular corner in accordance with her parents' instructions. However, she never arrived home alive, but was abducted and killed by a child molester.

Glen Avenue, a new Jewish neighborhood at the time, was considered totally safe. Most families had moved there during the preceding decade. The incident sent shock waves through the Jewish community. The family of the murdered girl moved to Israel soon after the tragedy. Even if the parents later described their long-time friend Rabbi Milikowsky as "an outstanding tower of strength who held their hand" during that tragedy, it was still a very hard time for him.

Each of these three incidents affected Rabbi Milikowsky deeply, and although there was no question of guilt regarding any of them, his enormous sense of responsibility was such that he bore the burden of these incidents for the rest of his life.

Eli Schlossberg, '68, was a tenth-grader in Rabbi Milikowsky's class the year that the fire struck his home. He shares with us the following memory:

It was four or five days after the very tragic house fire where the two Katz cousins, a"h, perished. The Milikowsky home burned and in the tragic fire the two boys died. Only a week before, I had played knock-hockey with one of the boys. We were all stunned and in shock and finally Rebbe returned to his class. He was so very despondent and broken! I remember he came back without his false teeth, which were lost in the fire. He was so sad and it was difficult for him to speak. You could see how deeply he was affected and his eyes were bloodshot from tears of grief.

We were learning *Chumash* and we were being especially careful to be quiet and on our best behavior. I was not the most attentive student and Rebbe sat me right next to his desk on the left side. It was a warm day and the window was open, and as we learned two white pigeons appeared on the windowsill. Rebbe looked up and, seeing the two pigeons, he muttered under his breath, "The souls have come to learn!" I don't think anybody else heard him, but I will never forget his words.

Word spread among Rabbi Milikowsky's students about what had occurred and how terribly shaken it had left their rebbe. A large group of T.A. alumni studying in New York, students of Rabbi Milikowsky, decided that they would not leave their rebbe alone over Shabbos when he was in such a state. Starting immediately after the fire, a list was made up and a pair of alumni traveled down from New York each week for over a year to spend Shabbos at T.A. with their rebbe as he slowly healed from his trauma. Although alumni poured in money, linens and other necessities for starting life anew, Rebbe particularly cherished the new Shas that was purchased for him.

Students close to Rabbi Milikowsky during the 1960s refer to how much Rabbi Milikowsky suffered as a result of these tragedies. It is a tribute to his resilience, however, that he continued to function at a high level and maintained his cheerful demeanor, whatever he may have felt inside. Certainly the man who was my tenth-grade rebbe in 1970–1971 could only have been described as cheerful.

Part III of this work, "The Later Years," will show that Rabbi Milikowsky's energetic commitment to his students, his family, and the Talmudical Academy did not suffer in the wake of personal tragedy.

Part III

BALTIMORE – THE LATER YEARS

Chapter 19

CHANGING DEMOGRAPHICS

UNTIL 1967, RABBI MILIKOWSKY LIVED a block away from the Talmudical Academy and was physically at the school much of Shabbos and much of the week. Then, in the wake of changing demographics and the fire that destroyed a building, T.A. moved to the Jewish suburbs.

At this point, Rabbi and Rebbetzin Milikowsky had to make a decision: Should they move out to the suburbs in order to be near the school, or should they move to Upper Park Heights, the Orthodox Jewish neighborhood? In order for Rabbi Milikowsky to continue the type of twenty-four-hour-a-day contact with the T.A. boys that he had maintained until then, they would have to move to a house in the suburbs within walking distance from the school.

There were two problems with this, one surmountable and the other not. The first problem was that the school's new location was not in an Orthodox Jewish neighborhood. If they moved into a house in this neighborhood, they would cut themselves off from Orthodox Jewish Baltimore. However, this was a problem that Rabbi Milikowsky was willing to overlook. After all, he had made greater sacrifices in the past for the sake of making himself available to the T.A. boys twenty-four hours a day.

The second problem, however, was more serious. Suburban houses of the sort available in the area of the new campus were beyond the Milikowskys' means. Now in his mid-fifties, Rabbi Milikowsky did not savor taking on a large new mortgage that he could not afford. Thus, the final decision was that the family would move to Upper Park Heights.

However, being Rabbi Milikowsky, he made a decision that even if he could no longer be available to the T.A. boys twenty-four hours a day as he had been, he would still spend every Shabbos away from his family, sleeping in a dormitory room, in order to give the T.A. dormitory boys a taste of Shabbos. This he did from 1967 until 1975, when the dormitory closed down for four years.

Read the following to learn about the fruits of Rabbi Milikowsky's sacrifice during those years.

Rabbi Yisrael Beller attended the Talmudical Academy for only one year, 1971–1972. Even though he was in the ninth grade that year and therefore not in Rabbi Milikowsky's *shiur*, he still had a great deal of contact with Rebbe since he was an out-of-town resident of the dormitory. Like Yisrael, many of the *bochrim* in the dormitory came from a public-school background and Rabbi Boruch Milikowsky made great sacrifices on their behalf. Three years after the dormitory had moved from the older Jewish neighborhood to the suburbs, Rabbi Milikowsky was still spending every Shabbos with the dormitory boys, but now he was totally there, sleeping in the dormitory with the boys, without his family. Yisrael commented, "Because of him, we felt Shabbos."

Some of Yisrael's memories are recorded elsewhere in this book. Here are a few more that relate specifically to his year with Rabbi Milikowsky:

It was Erev Yom Kippur 5732, a half-hour before *Kol Nidrei*. About a half-dozen boys were sitting together with Rebbe, listening to him explain some of the laws of the day, particularly regarding the five ways that we afflict ourselves on Yom Kippur, and Rebbe chose this moment to tell the boys a parable:

There was a musician known far and wide for his great talent and expertise. He used to play sweet music for the king, and the king would derive great enjoyment from it.

One day, however, the musician committed a grievous crime against the king. Ordinarily, the king would have had someone hanged for perpetrating such a terrible act against him. Yet since he enjoyed listening to the man's sweet music, he had pity on him and did not condemn him to death. He did, however, have him thrown into a deep, dark dungeon.

After a while the king began to miss hearing the music, so he descended into the dungeon to speak with the musician. The king gave the musician his violin. He told him that he could have had him killed for such a rebellious crime, but because of the sweet music that he so enjoyed, he had decided to spare his life.

Rebbe said that the king in the parable represented the Supreme King of Kings, and that we are like the rebellious musician. Yet when we recite the Shema every day, that is like the sweet music.

ह॰   ॰ह

Every now and then Rebbe would speak to us in the T.A. *beis midrash*. He would sometimes have to admonish us for something we did wrong or neglected to do properly. He would tell us that after 120 years they would call him before the Celestial Tribunal and ask him to see what he could do to save some of his students. Almost with tears in his eyes, Rebbe asked us, "What will I say? What can I answer?"

ह॰   ॰ह

After that year in T.A., Yisrael left the Baltimore area to finish high school in a public school elsewhere. Then, for one year, he went to a community college in a small town in New Jersey. Yisrael was the only boy there who wore a yarmulka. He still didn't know how to "make a *laining*," to decipher a page of *gemara* by himself, and he had difficulty finding someone to learn with that year.

Towards the end of the school year, someone in Baltimore who had relatives in New Jersey invited Yisrael for a Shabbos. Yisrael's mother suggested that while he was on the trip, he should find out if Ner Israel had any kind of summer program since he was having so much difficulty trying to learn during the school year.

That Shabbos, Yisrael saw Rebbe at the Glen Avenue Synagogue. On the spot, Rebbe invited him to his house for lunch. While there, Yisrael

Scenes from the 1970s

In 1975 T.A. invited its boys to participate in a Shabbaton as Baltimore delegates to the National Convention of Pirchei Agudath Israel, held in Borough Park. "Entrance fee" for each boy was to memorize at least one chapter of Mishnayos. As can be seen, Rabbi Milikowsky went along.

With (l. to r.) Shalom Weiss, Neil Strauss and Azriel Siegel.

Chavrusa with the boys.
On the right is Teddy Sanders.

Learning with Mark Mazel, 1977.

asked him about Ner Israel, and Rebbe told him that he would go there with him on Sunday to make arrangements. On Sunday morning they went together to Ner Israel, where Rabbi Milikowsky began to complete the arrangements, but he wasn't feeling well, so he had his son, Shaya, represent him. Yisrael didn't know it at the time, but later on Shaya told him that his father had had a fever that day of 102 degrees. Yet fever and all, he still pushed himself to make arrangements for Yisrael to learn Torah.

The plan was that Yisrael would attend the Ner Israel Yeshiva for six weeks in the summer. During that time, two Kollel students befriended him and convinced him and his parents that he should stay there for the following year. Yisrael ended up staying at the yeshiva for approximately nine and a half years. To this day, Yisrael Beller remains grateful to Rabbi Milikowsky for the important role he played in his spiritual growth.

❧   ❧

Diamond in the Rough
An Oral Narrative by Rabbi Howard Diamond:

"Rabbi Milikowsky was an incredible human being. I am a baal teshuvah. I wouldn't have lasted in yeshiva fifteen minutes without him. He changed my life. He molded my life. I chose him to officiate at my wedding. There is not one aspect of my life that would have been what it is now if not for him."

I was a typical assimilated kid from Philadelphia. Somebody bet me that I could find something wrong with Judaism and rule it out for the rest of my life. And I said OK, fine.

In the summer of 1970, before eleventh grade, I was playing touch football on my street in Philadelphia with some friends of mine. There was a Rabbi Popack. He was a rabbi in Philadelphia. I knew him not as an important rabbi but as one of my neighbors. Me and my friends, we were standing there drinking beer, taking a break from playing touch football. It was very hot. And then this rabbi came down the street and he said, "Hey,

Howie Diamond, how are you doing? What's happening? And I said, "Nothing special. How are you?"

So he asked me, "What do you think about Judaism?" and I answered, "I think it's a lot of baloney." So he asked me, "What do you *know* about Judaism?" and I answered, "Absolutely nothing!"

I mean I went to a Conservative Hebrew School where they taught me my bar mitzvah phonetically. You know what I mean?

He said, "Look, it's like telling me that you don't like chocolate ice cream but you admit that you've never tasted it. So why don't you go to a yeshiva for two years? You can still do math and science and all that kind of stuff. And then, if you can come back and tell me that there's something wrong with Judaism, then at least I'll put stock in what you're saying."

So I then asked, "What's in it for me?" I was a real wise guy kid. And he said, "I'll make you a bet that if you can find something wrong with Judaism, I'll buy you and me a cheeseburger and you can watch me eat it."

He took me to the Philadelphia Yeshiva, which obviously laughed in my face, because I really didn't know an *alef* from a *gimel*. They had no room for someone like me. So Rabbi Popack said, "Let's go to the Talmudical Academy in Baltimore." So I said "Fine" – any opportunity to live away from home seemed nice, you know?

So at T.A. they made me a deal. They said, "You can be in the eleventh grade with the eleventh-graders for secular subjects, but for your religious studies you have to start with the second-graders."

When I first came to the yeshiva and I still didn't even know the Hebrew alphabet, Rabbi Milikowsky said to me, "Diamond, you're going to be my night *seder chavrusa*." And I came and I learned with him, but he was *adamant* that I should not practice anything that I was learning there until I understood it.

For example, the very first Shabbos that I was in the dorm, he came to me in the dorm and he said to me, "I understand that you smoke." And I answered, "Yes, I do smoke."

So he said, "Well, you don't understand yet why you shouldn't be smoking. I don't want this to be oppressive to you, *so if you want you can smoke this Shabbos.*" He said this because he understood that it would be *very* oppressive to me if I couldn't smoke. You understand?

So I said, "Rebbe, if I smoke a cigarette right here in the dorm these people will kill me." So he said, "Not while I'm standing here, they won't." So I stood there and lit up a cigarette. And needless to say, the very next day at night *seder* we learned about the things you can't do on Shabbos.

Obviously I could move up quicker than a second grader could. By the time I graduated twelfth grade, in 1972, I was in Rabbi Milikowsky's *shiur*. And then he was absolutely instrumental in my going to Ner Yisrael afterwards, although most of my friends whom I had made there were going to the *Sha'ar Yashuv* Yeshiva in Far Rockaway. He felt that I could be a Ner Yisrael person. He got me into Ner Yisrael, *because I certainly wasn't Ner Yisrael material at that time.*

I had problems at Ner Yisrael. There were times when he would come and literally be my *chavrusa* some days. Because he wanted to keep me there and he wanted to keep me learning. I could learn with him because he understood *me*. I was a typical child of the sixties, and he just understood where I was. Where my head was.

So it was an incredible experience. Yet it would not have been so if not for the fact that Rabbi Milikowsky literally became part of my life, both in terms of the dorm and in terms of where I was going and what I was doing. I mean, I became closer with him than I was with my own father. He was an incredible, incredible man. Sure, he was brilliant and a *talmid chacham* – I'm not taking that away from him – but what was really special about him was that he understood American kids *really* well. Yes, I could sit and learn *gemara* with him and yes, I could sit and learn a *tosafos* with him, and all of that kind of stuff. But more important to me was the fact that he taught me a path in life, a way of life. He was much more concerned about people treating one another properly than about anything else in the world. And that's who he was!

Another individual grateful to Rabbi Boruch Milikowsky was Rabbi Joel Feldman. Rabbi Feldman had contact with Rabbi Milikowsky during two periods of his life. First, in 1948–1949, he was privileged to be a student in Rabbi Milikowsky's eighth-grade class, during only the second year that Rabbi Milikowsky taught at T.A. Then, from 1969 to 1974, Rabbi Feldman returned to his alma mater to serve as its principal, seventeen years after he had graduated.

Rabbi Feldman had mixed emotions about taking up this position. There was the nostalgic thrill of returning to the beloved institution where he had spent twelve years of his childhood and youth, mixed with apprehension at being placed in a position of authority over spiritual figures whom he revered and who had helped to make him what he was. Indeed, seventeen years after he left T.A., some of his former rebbeim, and some of his secular teachers as well, were still employed there, and he would be their "boss."

The year 1951, the start of Rabbi Feldman's twelfth-grade year, had seen the arrival of the much-revered math teacher, Mr. Hyman Sacks. In 1969, Mr. Sacks was still employed at the school. Rabbi Feldman relates the following:

"We had a rough class and he tamed us and the other classes. When I became principal, I was still afraid of him. One day he walked into my office, holding an old black ledger, and he said in a stern voice, 'Rabbi Feldman, I have a bone to pick with you! It says here in this ledger that in 1951, on such and such a day, you did not hand in a homework assignment, and you still owe it to me!' At this point Mr. Sacks broke into a broad smile."

The ice was broken. After that, a more natural relationship developed between the two men.

His old rebbeim were no less kind in trying to understand his predicament and to help make it easier for him. Over time, a mature relationship developed between Rabbi Feldman and his old Rebbe, Rabbi Milikowsky. Rabbi Feldman relates the following:

Rabbi Milikowsky was very helpful to me. I used to seek his counsel. I had problems in dealing with the boys, with the administration, with the laymen. He was very helpful! He used to come in and sound me out. Then he would offer fine advice. He was like a wise sage from whom I sought counsel.

There were questions involving whether certain boys in the dormitory should be removed from the school for certain crimes. It's a big responsibility to expel a kid from school! I used to discuss it with him, because he knew the kids very well. He used to spend Shabbosim with them. Even though we had a dorm counselor who lived in one of the apartments in the dorm building and Rabbi Milikowsky only came for Shabbosim, he still knew the kids very well. There were times when I had one opinion about what should be done with a boy and Rabbi Milikowsky had a different opinion, and he swayed me. He was usually right. I used to seek his counsel over anyone else's.

On Saturday night, January 23, 1971, the P.T.A. of the Talmudical Academy honored thirteen of its veteran teachers with an evening of poetic tribute. Professor of History Dr. Arnold Blumberg, who composed the poetry and recited it for the occasion, had the following to say about Rabbi Boruch Milikowsky:

A guide through the forests of logic, along Gemara's road,
Whose *Tosefos* and *m'forshim* give light to the student's path,
He leads our sons so gently, helping them when they fall,
Bearing their problems in their heart, responsive to their woes.

He has followed Mir Yeshiva from Poland to Shanghai,
Bearing troubles with true courage beneath oft-darkened skies,
He made the dormitory a home away from home,
And earned his place in countless hearts where'er our students roam.

We thank Rabbi Boruch Milikowsky for twenty-four years of faithful service; for the upbuilding of our dormitory; for giving of his heart and soul, nights and Shabbosim, to the ease of lonely, angry or frightened boys living far from home.

The following story is from Rabbi Eliyahu Rabovsky, '74:

Trying to Make Men out of Boys

Once a dorm student was upset that the school would not let him do something. He was really upset. I think he walked out of class. There was a tension at a perceived injustice. Against that setting, Rebbe felt the need to say something to us, without violating any confidence, that might help us understand a bigger picture:

"Boys get angry because they feel the principal, dorm counselor, or rebbe are not being fair. But let me tell you, there is more to a story than what you just see. An example: Sometimes a boy wants to go home. His parents tell him to come home, and he is bewildered and angry when the school says no. Little does he realize that his parents are telling us not to let him come home. They have a reason why we should be the bad guys, why they feel they cannot say no to something that should be forbidden, and we go along with it, at the parents' request." As the words came out of his mouth, I saw the lights go on in our minds, and I sensed what I now know was a profound moment of adolescent growth.

They Always Come Back for More

During the 1970s, older alumni would often make surprise visits to Rabbi Milikowsky's class. If Rabbi Milikowsky was in the middle of giving his *shiur*, the alumnus would tiptoe into the room and find a vacant seat. If, however, the boys were studying or reviewing on their own at that moment, Rebbe would introduce his old *talmid* to the class and tell them something about him. Rebbe and *talmid* would then leave the room for a few minutes to catch up on old times.

At the end of such visits, when the old alumnus had left, Rabbi Milikowsky would often tell the class the following:

"You know what he said when we were outside? He said, 'If I had known back then what I know now, I would have learned more seriously when I was in your class. I'm sorry that I didn't take things as seriously as I could have.' Boys! Listen to that and take the learning seriously now so that you don't have to come back in ten years and tell me this!"

❧ ❧

Rabbi Yisrael Beller relates the following three stories, told to him personally by Rabbi Milikowsky:

I

When the Chafetz Chaim died, Rabbi Milikowsky was at the funeral. Pictures were taken, and he was in some of the photographs. In 1972, Rabbi Milikowsky told his students that Rabbi Moshe Londinsk delivered one of the eulogies. When called upon, he got up and said the following:

"*Es shteit az misas tzadikim brengt a kaporah af a gantz klal yisroel* – It says that the passing of the righteous brings an atonement for the entire Jewish People. But look, Master of the Universe! Our plight is not improving at all! Pretty soon there won't be any of us left!"

Reb Moshe gave a bang on the podium and sat down.

Rabbi Beller concludes the story by pointing out that at the time, in the summer of 1933, the fires of the Holocaust had already been lit, since Hitler had already taken over Germany.

II

In 1946, the Chafetz Chaim's second wife came to America, arriving at the port in Seattle, Washington. Two yeshiva *bochrim* met her at the port and drove her to a hotel. A Polish non-Jew offered to purchase the car from the two *bochrim* for a thousand dollars over the list price at the time, just because the Chafetz Chaim's second wife had ridden in the car one time. Even the Polish non-Jews had great awe and respect for the Chafetz Chaim, even if Polish non-Jews were not well known for their love of Israel otherwise.

As the previous two stories demonstrate, such stories were important to Rabbi Milikowsky, even if he only rarely told them to his students.

III

At various times Rabbi Milikowsky would comment on that special relationship we have with God, and all He does for us. When Rabbi Beller was attending the wedding of Rabbi Milikowsky's son, Avraham Yeshayahu, in Washington D.C., Rebbe commented to him, "Look how many good things God does for us, and what do we do for Him? We *daven* a little bit…"

Jay Neufeld came to the Talmudical Academy in eighth grade and spent five years in the dormitory. When Jay arrived in 1968, T.A. was already in its beautiful new building in the suburbs of Baltimore.

Today there are many wonderful things that Jay remembers about T.A., but his most treasured memory from that period is of his relationship with Rabbi Boruch Milikowsky. The atmosphere at T.A. on Shabbos was very beautiful and positive, and this was due in large measure to Rabbi Milikowsky's presence there week after week. He was always there, without fail. Through Rabbi Milikowsky's presence, the Baltimore suburbs became the Mir Yeshiva in Poland; they were transformed into Shanghai, China. Thanks to Rabbi Milikowsky, Shabbos at T.A. transcended time and place. When the boys went to the *beis midrash* to learn Torah after the meal, they were in Radin.

Who could forget Rebbe's *zemiros*? Who could forget his *Ka Ribon* on Friday night? Rebbe would push his glasses up over his forehead, close his eyes and cover his face with his hands, swaying gently back and forth, turning all of *Ka Ribon* into an expression of faith like the recitation of the

Shema. Rebbe would sing with the boys. He would say *divrei Torah* and tell them stories of the Chafetz Chaim. Nobody could sit in that room and remain unmoved.

Radin…

In the sefer *Torat HaParashah* a story is told about the Chafetz Chaim. One time some students came to him and asked him to reprimand them for their sins. The Chafetz Chaim sighed and responded, "How can *I* reprimand you? How can I rebuke others when I myself sin, and I neither fear God nor study Torah as much as I should?" The students were shocked. The Chafetz Chaim's simple words penetrated deep into their hearts, and each said to himself, "If the Chafetz Chaim thinks this way about himself, how much more should we think thus about our own selves?"

T.A.…

It was Erev Yom Kippur. The boys were *davening minchah* before the meal preceding the fast and naturally Rabbi Milikowsky was with them. Rabbi Chaim Samson, the Rosh Yeshiva, was serving as the chazzan. During the repetition of the *Shemoneh Esreh*, when he came to the words, "Father! Forgive us, for we have sinned!" Rabbi Samson broke down crying.

Rabbi Milikowsky took advantage of the moment to convey a message. He suddenly cried out, "Look, boys! If a *tzaddik* like Rabbi Samson is crying, how much more work remains for us to do on our own selves?"

Just Deserts

Just as boys asked Rabbi Milikowsky about the propriety of attending coeducational Young Israel youth meetings during the early 1950s, the same question came up during the 1970s regarding the religious outreach organization N.C.S.Y. (The National Council of Synagogue Youth). Sometimes Rabbi Milikowsky would discourage boys from attending that organization, while and other times he would condone it. It depended on what effect Rabbi Milikowsky thought attendance would have on the boy.

He thought that some boys still needed to attend, while other boys might be harmed.

There was one boy, Yosef*, who had become religious through N.C.S.Y. and who wished to continue his activities there. When he told Rabbi Milikowsky that he still needed the spiritual shot in the arm that came from attending N.C.S.Y., Rabbi Milikowsky would express his objections. He did not forbid attendance outright. Rather, the discussion took the form of a debate that continued over many weeks.

One time, in tenth grade, when Yosef had made his usual pitch about the shot in the arm, Rabbi Milikowsky responded, "No. That's what you *think* you need. You just have a tremendous urge to be with the girls." Caught somewhat off-guard, Yosef laughingly responded, "Rebbe, is that so bad?" Rabbi Milikowsky looked at the boy and sighed. He said, "Let me just tell you this. You know what's going to happen to you? With all your running off to see the girls, you're going to end up marrying a girl so *frum* that she covers all her hair, wears her sleeves to the wrist and her dresses down to the ankle. That will be your 'punishment.'" This was the only time that Rabbi Milikowsky expressed this "prophecy" to Yosef.

Six years passed. Yosef finished T.A. and went to yeshiva, and in his fourth year in yeshiva he married and became a full-time kollel student. Since Rabbi Milikowsky had been unable to attend his Florida wedding, soon after the wedding, when the couple were driving south past Baltimore, they decided to make a detour. Yosef wished to introduce his new bride to his Rebbe. Stopping in Baltimore, they drove straight to Rabbi Milikowsky's home without calling in advance.

When they arrived, it was late afternoon. Although Rebbetzin Leah was there, Rabbi Milikowsky was not yet home. She remembered Yosef quite well from his T.A. days and implored the couple to wait for Rabbi Milikowsky's return because she knew how important it would be to her husband to see them. Thus, for more than an hour they all sat together, engaged in animated conversation, while they waited for Rabbi Milikowsky to arrive home.

Finally, he walked in the door. For a moment he surveyed the scene in the living room. No one said a word. He looked at Yosef, and he looked at Yosef's wife, seeming to take special note of her apparel, and then he looked back at Yosef triumphantly. Wagging a finger in the air, he announced to Yosef, "Hah! What did I tell you?!"

❧ ❧

Moving Picture
During the eight years that Rabbi Milikowsky spent every Shabbos away from his family on the suburban T.A. campus, he would often give rides to dormitory students on Saturday nights, taking them to the movies or to other outings. At an agreed-upon time, sometimes quite late, he would then pick them up and bring them back to the dormitory, safe and sound.

One time he agreed that some dormitory boys could go to the movies, and he specified which movie was acceptable, driving the boys to the cinema. Later on he picked them up and brought them back.

It later turned out that the boys had broken their word and had gone to an unsanctioned movie. Sure enough, the boys were all called down to the principal's office, reprimanded and given a punishment assignment.

When Rabbi Milikowsky found out, he confronted the boys and literally wept. He said, "You told me that you were going to one movie and I dropped you off, thinking you were going to it. How could you do this to me?" They had already been reprimanded by members of the administration and had received a punishment, but neither the reprimand nor the punishment had really touched them. Yet when Rabbi Milikowsky wept before them, they felt terrible. Only then did they actually realize that they had done something very wrong. They had betrayed Rebbe's trust.

Advice Based on Experience
Alumni of the T.A. dormitory studying in New York would sometimes get together and rent or borrow a car to go down to Baltimore for the weekend. This was a chance to see the city – and the school – where they had recently

spent four years. Such visits would always include some time with Rabbi Milikowsky.

Rabbi Yaakov Neufeld thus recalls such a visit in which he went to see Rabbi Milikowsky on Sunday before returning with his friends to New York. He told Rebbe that he had just started dating. He described the sort of girl he was looking for, and he announced that he had decided to go into Jewish education.

Rabbi Milikowsky gave him some advice. He told Yaakov to save as much money as he could during the first year of his marriage. Yaakov asked why.

Rabbi Milikowsky replied, "During the second year, your wife is going to have a baby, and she won't be able to work, and even if she can work, she won't be working so much. You should save that money because during that first year you will get used to your wife's paycheck. Then, when the second year comes and you face the expenses of a new baby, you won't have as much money anymore."

Chapter 20

PORTRAIT OF AN ARTIST

Family Man

JUST AS RABBI MILIKOWSKY HAD a unique relationship with each of his students, so did he have a unique relationship with each of his own children. This was partly due to the fact that he related to all human beings as individuals. He gave his children the freedom to be themselves and, in fact, nurtured the strong points and individual characteristics of each. Yet the children were different from one another as well, so that with each child Rabbi Milikowsky faced a different challenge.

For example, the two boys, Chaim and Shaya, were both highly intelligent, scholarly and devoted to Torah learning. Yet Chaim was interested in academics as well, and after he learned in the Mir Yeshiva and Ner Israel in Baltimore, he studied for his Ph.D. at Yale University.

Shaya, by contrast, was always the most "yeshivish" of the four children. While he always excelled in his secular studies, he never expressed any interest to pursue higher degrees in them. Quite the contrary. So the challenge facing Rabbi Milikowsky with Shaya was to try to foster the moderation recommended by Rambam.

ॐ   ॐ

Enlightened Flexibility

However reticent Rabbi Milikowsky was about his background, until the end of his days he always remained what he had been when he arrived in the United States, a *Litvische* Yeshiva *bachur*. If he had specific *minhagim* that made him unique, they were more the *minhagim* of his yeshivos than of his family. Thus, for example, Rabbi Milikowsky told his daughter Malke that he did not personally view *Tashlich* as his *minhag*, since the Vilna Gaon didn't go to

Tashlich. Even so, he would take his boys. He thought it was important for his boy to have that experience. Actually, this enlightened flexibility was itself part of being a *Litvische* yeshiva *bachur*.

While Rabbi Milikowsky was a *Litvische* Yeshiva *bachur*, his wife, Rebbetzin Leah, came from a Chassidic family, and her mother, Mrs. Goldman, lived in or near the Milikowsky home for many years. Leah and her mother had come from a home with *minhagim* that differed from those of Rabbi Milikowsky. Halachically, the customs in the Milikowsky home should have followed those of Rabbi Milikowsky's parents. Yet if Leah Milikowsky had arrived in the U.S. at age twenty-two and was open to change, her strong-willed mother had arrived in middle age and was less flexible. Yet in every case, Rabbi Milikowsky was understanding and receptive to the needs and wishes of his mother-in-law. He wanted not just to show her honor but also to make her feel at home.

Thus, as a *Litvische* yeshiva *bachur*, Rabbi Milikowsky did not believe in *shlogging kapporas* with live chickens on Erev Yom Kippur. Chafetz Chaim's *Mishnah Berurah* actually frowns on the custom. Yet at his mother-in-law's urging, he would take his family to a kosher slaughterhouse in Baltimore each year and carry out this *minhag*.

Likewise, it was his mother-in-law's wish that on Pesach there be no *gebrochts* in the house, so for many years there were no *gebrochts* in Rabbi Milikowsky's home on Pesach, even if this was not his own *minhag*. For Rabbi Milikowsky, giving up kneidlach for seven days was a way to show honor to his mother-in-law.

Moreover, in Europe, the Goldman family had never used ovens on Pesach due to Kashrus problems. In Europe, the ovens were made of brick and mortar, and chametz would get into the bricks. It was impossible to get the chametz out without dismantling the whole oven. So in America, Mrs. Goldman refused to let her daughter's family use the oven as well. Her family hadn't used ovens during Pesach in Europe, and she wasn't about to let her daughter start using them here in America — such was her pure, simple faith. The fact that in America there were different kinds of ovens made of metals that could be *kashered* made no difference. Thus, on Pesach, out of respect for the wishes of Mrs. Goldman, the Milikowsky family did not use an oven.

When Rabbi Milikowsky's older daughter Malke came to Israel to study at Michlalah, a Jerusalem women's seminary, she was invited to the home of Rabbi Chaim Shmuelevitz, the Mir Rosh Yeshiva, for Pesach. The Shmuelevitzes were *Litvaks* and on Pesach they had *gebrochts*. They ate kneidlach. Malke had never eaten *gebrochts* before on Pesach, so she called her father and asked what she should do. Her father explained that since his own *minhag* was that kneidlach were permitted and that since the family had only been trying to show honor to Mrs. Goldman, Malke could have *gebrochts* herself.

Rebbe's True Greatness

Rabbi Boruch Milikowsky was a humble, unassuming man. He learned in Europe and Shanghai for twenty years and had contact with the greatest rabbis of his time. Then he taught in T.A. for most of forty years. In terms of training, he certainly had the credentials to be an important Rosh Yeshiva in a post-high school yeshiva, and indeed, he had briefly considered this upon arrival in the U.S. Yet for most of his teaching years, he never taught higher than the tenth grade. Thus he prepared boys for the top *shiur* without ever teaching it himself. Only during the 1980s, when Rabbi Mandelcorn was the principal of T.A., was he provided with the opportunity to give a high-level *shiur*. Rabbi Milikowsky never boasted or bragged about his past. Indeed, he hardly ever talked about it, and he never made his Torah a spade with which to dig. Yet as each of his children went to Israel to study, they discovered who their father was.

When Shaya Milikowsky went to learn in the Mir Yeshiva, the Rosh Yeshiva was Reb Nochum Pertzovitz, husband of Rav Chaim Shmuelevitz's daughter Etyl, and an old friend of Rabbi Milikowsky from the Mir. Rabbi Pertzovitz told Shaya that he would not need to take a test to get in. Surprised, Shaya asked why he was so privileged, and Rabbi Pertzovitz told him that Shaya's father was known in Mir circles to be a genius, obviating the need for his sons to be tested. Moreover, the family's aptitude for yeshiva learning had been confirmed three years previous, when Shaya's older brother, Chaim, had been in the Mir. Rabbi Pertzovitz pointed out that in Shanghai Shaya's father had been perceived as a *tzutzik,* a brilliant *enfant terrible* who keeps older people excited and entertained. Reb Nochum told Shaya that in Shanghai he, himself, had been the *tzutzik* of the middle aged *bochrim* in the Mir, and Reb Boruch, Shaya's father, ten years older than Reb Nochum, had been the *tzutzik* of Reb Leib Malin's group, ten years older than Rabbi Milikowsky.

Likewise, when Rabbi Milikowsky's older daughter Malke came to Israel during the late 1960s to study in seminary, her father let on that for home hospitality she could call none other than the Rosh Yeshiva of the Mir, Rav Chaim Shmuelevitz, and he gave her a phone number. When she arrived in Israel, Malke somewhat dubiously dialed the number, but when the Rebbetzin Miriam answered the phone and heard who was calling, she got all excited and cried out, "Oh! Reb Boruch! Reb Boruch! How is your father? How is Reb Boruch?" Thus Malke discovered for the first time how close Rabbi Milikowsky had been to the Rosh Yeshiva Rabbi Chaim Shmuelevitz and his family.

Rav Shmuelevitz had temporarily assumed the post of Rosh Yeshiva when his father-in-law, Rav Eliezer Yehudah Finkel, went to Eretz Yisrael in 1941. Shepherding his flocks through six years in Shanghai, he had gotten to know each of the two hundred fifty students of the Mir personally – a mark of his greatness. Yet with Rabbi Milikowsky he had a special relationship that went beyond that. It was hinted to Malke that during the Shanghai years Rabbi Milikowsky had undertaken to help Rav Shmuelevitz with part of the logistical burden of feeding 250 students each day, whether this involved planning, purchasing or actually preparing the food for the meals.

The institution that Malke had chosen for her studies in Israel was the Michlalah College for Women in Jerusalem, a new Torah institution at that time. In terms of outlook, it was not exactly Bais Yaakov. Malke had been raised in Baltimore and had studied in Baltimore Bais Yaakov. Michlalah was a bit more modern. Rabbi Milikowsky, concerned about the school's newness and by the rumors about its modernity, wanted to clarify whether it was a good institution. The alternative was for Malke to go to one of the institutions in Jerusalem that was closer to the spirit of Bais Yaakov, but Malke very much wanted Michlalah. In fact, she had her heart set on it.

So during the year previous, Rabbi Milikowsky wrote to Rav Nochum Pertzovitz (in the days before e-mail), asking him to find out whether Michlalah was a suitable institution. Rav Pertzovitz wrote back, "It's not bad. It's not heresy, but why should girls have to learn so much?"

This half-hearted approval was enough to enable Malke to go to the school that she wanted, and she indeed went there.

While Michlalah did not have precisely the same worldview as that of Rav Shmuelevitz and his family, Malke was still welcomed into the Shmuelevitz home with open arms, as well as into the home of Rav Nochum and Etyl Pertzovitz. In fact, another American girl, Sima Bornstein, also the daughter of a Mir alumnus, was also at Michlalah and had been there the year before. The Shmuelevitzes had been hosting Sima for a year already, and Sima had made clear to them what type of *shiurim* there were in Michlalah. As a result, the Rosh Yeshiva and his family had come to realize what a fine place Michlalah really was.

In short, whenever Malke or Sima wished to come for Shabbos or for Pesach Seder, they were welcomed very warmly, like family. Rebbetzin Miriam Shmuelevitz, Rav Chaim Shmuelevitz's wife, was like a mother to Malke, who enjoyed the same warmth in the Pertzovitz home as well as in the home of the Rosh Yeshiva, Reb Beinish Finkel.

❧   ❧

In the yeshiva world, two talents that earn a student a reputation for genius are a powerful memory and analytical skills. In the elite yeshivos of Eastern Europe, such as the Mir, both talents were prerequisites for success. Anyone who lacked them could not remain there and would leave. Analytical abilities were particularly prized. As Rabbi Avraham Leventhal explains:

Rabbi Milikowsky told me a story about the Mir in Europe. He told me what it meant to be a *ben Torah* in the Mir. A person in the Mir could sit on a *sevarah* (hypothesis) in learning for hours at a time. We have enough trouble sitting through a single two-hour learning session of any sort! But a person in the Mir could sit for hours at a time on one *sevarah*, working on one piece, one *shtickel*, one *inyan*.

Rabbi Yaakov Spivak recalls that when Rabbi Milikowsky had time for it, he loved to engross himself in the *Pnei Yehoshua*, a difficult commentary on Tosafos. Rabbi Spivak points out:
"Rabbi Milikowsky could have been a very big Rosh Yeshiva. He gave it up for his dedication to his boys."

Rabbi Milikowsky was also known for his phenomenal memory. He knew parts of *Shas* by heart, especially from the more *yeshivish* tractates. Of course, in the great Lithuanian yeshivos, learning a piece of gemara ten times before moving on was an elementary requirement, something that didn't even have to be mentioned. Like his yeshiva contemporaries, he viewed really *knowing* the *gemara* as essential, both in terms of knowing the content, and in terms of having a profound understanding.

During the 1950s, in Baltimore at the Talmudical Academy, there was a limit to what extent Rabbi Milikowsky could expect such a level of study and review from American boys, but he did want them to have a taste of it. Therefore, over the forty years that Rabbi Milikowsky was involved with T.A., he would occasionally select a *gemara* that he wanted the boys to learn by heart. Many students of Rabbi Milikowsky do not remember this experience, but I do, and so does Dr. Murray Kuhr '57:

He also did some things regarding which I am not exactly certain of the rationale. There were a lot of things that I can only appreciate now – I've heard it said that it takes forty years before you appreciate your teachers. Sometimes he would select a *gemara* that he wanted everyone to learn by heart. He didn't do it a lot, but he would do it every once in a while. He would say, "I want you to be able to say exactly what the *gemara* says, to say it by heart."

236

Of course, with a man of Rabbi Milikowsky's active intelligence, his memory and analytical skills found expression outside the realm of Torah learning as well. For example, Rabbi Milikowsky was known to enjoy chess, a game that was actually popular amongst the students of the great Lithuanian yeshivos as a form of relaxation and a means of sharpening the mind. In fact, Rabbi Milikowsky's friends testified that in Europe he would sometimes play blindfolded.

On the other hand, his children told me that Rabbi Milikowsky did not play chess with them. As Shaya said, "He never played it with me. He used to play it with the T.A. boys. With me he didn't need to play chess. With the boys he thought it was necessary."

As Shaya implies, Rabbi Milikowsky played chess with the boys at T.A. mostly as a means of reaching out and becoming closer to them. Various T.A. alumni enthusiastically described the games that Rabbi Milikowsky would play. One student from the 1960s related how there would be *melave malkas* in which Rabbi Milikowsky would play five or six boys *at once*, thereby flaunting both his memory and his analytical skills to the delight of the students.

While Rabbi Milikowsky did not play chess with his children, he did give them a glimpse of his skills in other ways. Rabbi Milikowsky's daughter Malke points out:

My father had a very good memory. I remember when I was young he would say to us, 'Make up ten numbers, and then write them down.' He himself couldn't write them down. He would play with us for a few minutes, and then he would have to repeat the numbers in their correct order. He always succeeded in reciting back the ten numbers.

As the following story will demonstrate, Rabbi Milikowsky found still other ways to make use of his good memory.

Closed Books

Conscientious yeshiva rebbeim do a lot of behind-the-scenes work before the beginning of each new year. They consult with the previous year's rebbeim for general information about the academic level of the class, the class's social cohesion, and perhaps are also interested in finding out something about each student in particular. If a student is a newcomer to the school, they may consult with the office to see the boy's entrance examinations and record.

Rabbi Milikowsky raised this level of conscientiousness and preparedness to new heights, as the following story will illustrate.

One class in T.A. included a group of boys who were far from Torah Judaism. Their Jewish knowledge was very lacking, to put it mildly, and perhaps because they despaired of succeeding in their Torah learning, these boys would try to find other ways of passing the time of day or at least the part of the day that they had to spend in T.A. Some would try to devour rebbeim, especially older rebbeim with greyish beards, who often seemed more then ready to play Jacob to their Esau (with no Rebecca to protect them). Thus, when the boys came into Rabbi Milikowsky's class on the first day of the year, they sized him up as an easy mark based on his appearance. One boy was even heard saying to the others, "Oh, boy! This is going to be fun!" not meaning the words in the innocent way that they are usually meant.

But Rabbi Milikowsky was well prepared. At the end of the first morning, with about a half-hour left, he told the boys to close their books. He looked at them in silence for a moment. They were waiting. Then he said, "Boys! I want you to know that I know everything that is going on with every one of you!" Some of the boys started laughing, and one boy called out, "Rebbe! You don't even know my name!" Rebbe stared back at him and said, "Oh, yes, I do!"

He knew every boy's name, and he went around the room and proved it.

One of the wild group, his fingers now somewhat burnt, still managed to blurt out, "Oh, yeah? Well, you don't know 'everything about us.' That's impossible!"

Rabbi Milikowsky now proceeded to go around the room a second time, this time providing a personal detail about each boy, and in the case of some of the boys, he provided the names of girls that the boys were dating.

Nobody ever figured out how Rebbe was able to do all of this, and however much we know about Rabbi Milikowsky's phenomenal memory, a tremendous amount of toil and research must still have been involved. Anyway, for the rest of the year, the whole class all assumed that Rabbi Milikowsky had *ruach hakodesh* (prophetic intuition). As the boys went to lunch, one thing was absolutely clear. This year, it was not going to be so easy to put anything over on their rebbe.

∾ ∾

Together with the Boys

In 1969, when Rabbi Milikowsky's daughter Malke was an upper-level student at Michlalah, a friend of hers introduced her to Rabbi Aharon Bina. Rabbi Bina, son of the illustrious Rabbi Aryeh Bina, founder and longtime Rosh Yeshiva of the elite Netiv Meir Yeshiva High School, was himself an outstanding Torah scholar who had been learning in the Ponovezh yeshiva for ten years.

The couple decided to wed, and their wedding took place in Baltimore. Rabbi Yaakov Ruderman, founder and Rosh Yeshiva of the Ner Israel Yeshiva in Baltimore, was unable to attend the wedding. It is indicative of Rabbi Milikowsky's wonderful relationship with Rabbi Ruderman and his tremendous regard for him that he made sure soon after the wedding that he and his new son-in-law would go to visit Rabbi Ruderman. After they spoke in learning, Rav Ruderman gave Rabbi Bina a *berachah*.

Soon after the wedding, Rabbi Bina began a long career as a *maggid shiur* [a Talmudic lecturer] at a *yeshiva gedolah* in Jerusalem. Soon he was placed in charge of the large program for students from abroad, and ultimately he became *Rosh Yeshiva.*

On Rabbi Milikowsky's visits to Israel, he now had a second yeshiva in Israel, besides the Mir Yeshiva, where he could feel "at home." When Rabbi Milikowsky, then in his seventies, walked into the *beis midrash* to learn, he would often strike up conversations with his son-in-law's students. Although he had been retired from T.A. for ten years, he was still the *mashgiach* with whom everyone shared their problems. Rabbi Bina did not advertise that his father-in-law was going to be visiting. The boys sensed that he was a person to whom they could bare their hearts.

One time Rabbi Milikowsky was going to be with the Binas for Yom Kippur. Erev Yom Kippur found Rabbi Milikowsky making his spiritual preparations in the *beis midrash*. His daughter Malke informed him that she would be serving the *se'udah mafsekes*, the meal consumed before the fast, in their home at a certain time. Rabbi Milikowsky, however, had other plans. The boys would be eating their *se'udah mafsekes* in the yeshiva. Rabbi Milikowsky preferred to be with the boys.

As Rabbi Bina explains, more than a Rosh Yeshiva or *mashgiach*, Rabbi Boruch Milikowsky always remained the European yeshiva *bachur* he had been fifty years before. Like his old *chavrusa*, Rabbi Avraham Bayarsky, *yibadel lechaim*, he too was "still there."

The Rebbe-Talmid Relationship
Rabbi Edward Davis, '64:

Rebbe came with Rav Bina to visit me in Richmond, where I was serving as a pulpit rabbi. I forget the reason. Possibly Rav Bina was touring around recruiting students for his yeshiva. Rebbe went with him because Rebbe knew me, although we hadn't had contact in years.

When they called to say they were coming, there was a certain apprehension, with me thinking, "What am I getting myself into here?" But he came and it was all just tremendous warmth and reminiscences. He was *shepping nachas* that I had gone into the rabbinate. He was so pleasant. He made me feel like I was a favorite son who had excelled, placing a crown on his head. That's the feeling I got when he came to visit me in Richmond.

It made such an impact on me personally that when he passed away, I made a big thing about it in my own shul, about the ideal Rebbe-talmid relationship and how it goes far beyond just learning a page of *gemara*.

❧ ☙

"Who Has Time…"

In the great yeshivos of Europe, where all day long brilliant students would thrash around ideas in their attempts to understand difficult Talmudic texts, they developed a tolerance for new thoughts, and a willingness to at least hear out controversial or revolutionary theories. Within his family, Rabbi Milikowsky would occasionally hint at this sense of tolerance, but he also demonstrated it through his own behavior.

Rabbi Milikowsky's daughter Malke earned a master's degree in biblical studies at the Bernard Revel Graduate Program of Yeshiva University. Among the various courses in the program was one called Introduction to Amoraic Literature, an academic course about the layers theory. It dryly analyzed the Talmud as a corpus of literature, talking about how it was put together and theorizing about it in a way analogous to Biblical Criticism. At the end of the academic year, Rabbi and Mrs. Milikowsky drove up to New York to help Malke pack for aliyah to Israel. Lying on Malke's bed was a Hebrew book by one of the *maskilim* about the layers theory that Malke had read to fulfill a course requirement. As Malke ran around her room, packing up and organizing, she suddenly noticed her father sitting on the bed, engrossed in the book. "Uh-oh!" she thought. "Now I'm going to get it! My father is going to ask me, 'What are you doing? What kind of courses are you taking?'" Rabbi Milikowsky read the book for a while, and when he closed it he did not say anything.

A few days later, Malke asked her father, "Nu, Daddy, what do you say about that book you were reading in my room? What is your opinion?" She was eagerly waiting to hear her father's opinion of the book and its theories. For her own part, while she had taken the course to fulfill an academic requirement, of course she did not view the course's theories as Torah from Sinai.

Rabbi Milikowsky looked at his daughter and said, "Look, Malki. Most of what's written here is correct. You know, there *were* layers. It *was* put together. But we're so busy learning the *Tosafos*, learning the *Rishonim*. We don't have time for this!"

❧   ❧

Rabbi Milikowsky's tolerance extended in other directions as well. I have described his closeness with his Mir Yeshiva colleagues and rebbeim, a closeness which continued in the next generation as well. Yet Rabbi Milikowsky's family also developed close relationships with their less observant relatives in Israel, of whom there were many. Rabbi Milikowsky loved those relatives and got along well with them – not only his own relatives but those of his wife, Leah. As Rabbi Aharon Bina explained, when it came to his love of Israel, Rabbi Milikowsky had a sort of "shine in his eyes."

In Haifa was Rabbi Milikowsky's Uncle Velfka, or Zeev. On his mother's side were all the Dickenstein cousins. Rebbetzin Leah had an aunt and uncle who lived on a *Ha-Shomer ha-Tza'ir* kibbutz. For a time, this uncle had been an editor of *Al ha-Mishmar,* the Mapam (United Workers' Party) newspaper.

Yet all of them very much loved Rabbi Milikowsky and his wife. One of the aunt's sons became an emissary of the Jewish Agency to Columbus Ohio. Although he had been raised "in the path of his fathers," he would visit Baltimore every chance he could get just to see Rabbi and Mrs. Milikowsky. They knew how to make him feel comfortable. Visits to the Milikowskys were pure pleasure.

Quality Time with the Family

Elsewhere in this book I talk about Rabbi Milikowsky's skills of memory and analysis. He had developed these skills over the years for his own benefit, to help him with his learning, but he did not stop there. As an intellectual and the father of four intellectual children, he worked hard and successfully to foster his children's intellectual skills as well. Here is Malke Milikowsky Bina's testimony about her father's efforts in this realm:

My father began to teach me about multiplication before I was yet in school. He would work with numbers with me. I remember at age five him teaching me two times three. Then he wanted to keep me busy for a while, so he introduced me to nine times nine without telling me what the answer was. I remember that he had me count it out and write it down. He showed me the mechanism of nine times nine and what I would have to do to get the right answer. I figured out that it was the same technique as two times three, but I would just have to write more. And then I came back with the right answer, and he was so proud of me! He always used to encourage us in this way. I remember his pride that I was able to figure this out.

It's so funny how you have these memories! I picture us outside in the back yard. I was playing, and he was with someone and he wanted to talk to that person. I asked him to give me some math questions. I wanted his attention too! He gave me a few questions, but those were easy ones, and I came back after a minute. And then he said, "OK, now I'm going to give you a harder question because I have to speak to this person." And I think I still came back quickly. I came back before he thought I would come back, and I even had the right answer!

Despite the preceding, it would be a mistake to think that Rabbi Milikowsky's relationship with his family was entirely intellectual. He knew how to have fun with his family as well. During the summer, especially during the early years, Rabbi Milikowsky would always do something nice with his family on Sundays. Every week he would take them somewhere special whether it was to a park, out on a picnic, or to a secluded part of the beach. He felt that this was healthy. It was good for a person to be out with nature.

It is true that Rabbi Milikowsky loved learning, perhaps more than anything else in life, but he also loved life's pleasures. He was a person who liked to go out in the sun. He would take a *sefer* – or a newspaper – and read outside on a warm day. Rabbi Milikowsky did not ignore the physical elements and aspects of this world.

Of course, one special weakness of Rabbi Milikowsky was that he loved going to the Y (the Baltimore Jewish Community Center) to go to the *schvitzbud*, the steam room. This was his *me'eyn ha'olam haba*, his taste of the World to Come. Rabbi Milikowsky, who appreciated God's gifts, used to say: "My car – when I have to go to the Y, it goes itself. I don't have to drive the car. The car knows the way to the Y by itself and it drives itself there!" Every opportunity he had, he would drive his old car to the J.C.C. That was his special pleasure in life, and his car, which he used to perform so many acts of kindness, had the further mitzvah of bringing a *talmid chacham* to his desired destination.

Outside of his learning and teaching, Rabbi Milikowsky had other skills and hobbies that he loved to indulge as well. He was a skilled carpenter who built his family's bookcases. He loved to tend the garden. He made liquor from cherries and plums. He was very handy with a hammer, a hoe, or in the kitchen in a chef's hat. The fact that his father had been a farmer may have contributed to development of these interests and abilities. After all, he had lived at home before going off to learn at twelve years old. Yet we cannot be sure. There is no one alive to tell us one way or the other. His sole surviving sister, Minna, was only three years old when he left for Radin.

Striving towards Perfection

When Rabbi Milikowsky's younger daughter Frady was twenty years old, she was already enrolled in graduate school for social work. Young and very sure of herself, she once told her supervisor regarding the skills she was being taught, "I really know all of this! My father was just a very special person and I learned it all from him." Her supervisor, a religious man who knew of her father's reputation, explained to her that while she really had gained a lot from her father, social work school would polish her skills further.

Rabbi Milikowsky never studied social work, psychology, or psychiatry, even if his students at various points attributed to him the skills associated with those various fields. Rather, he simply recognized what kind of help people needed in order to progress. It was a natural talent of his. As Frady explains:

> He did what had to be done. He knew. I don't think he could tell you why he was doing a particular act, why such-and-such would work for this student but something else would be necessary for another. It was just a part of him. Like eating is for the rest of us, he just inherently knew about people. It was an unbelievable, uncanny thing to watch.

The fact that Rabbi Milikowsky never went on to earn formal degrees in the areas in which he excelled is no indication that he had anything against secular education. Indeed, his wife Leah completed high school with his encouragement. Since World War II broke out when she was thirteen years old, she had missed years of education. For years she went to night school in America until she finished high school. She went on to earn a teacher's degree from Baltimore Hebrew College, after which she began a teaching career that lasted many years.

But Rabbi Milikowsky was already a teacher. He had his job, which filled up his day, to put it mildly. Whatever interest he may have had in attaining secular degrees for himself, he really had no time. He did not really need a teacher's degree. T.A. recognized his years of yeshiva learning.

Even as Rabbi Milikowsky grew older and T.A. began to bring in younger, more modern American rebbeim, it was recognized that he was far ahead in his psychological understanding of students and in his ability to relate to them. The younger rebbeim and administrators, some of whom were former students of his, often came to him for advice about how to deal with particular problems. Using the gifts God had given him and that were further honed by his yeshiva and life experiences, he was able to deal with matters that came up with his students and in the classroom. On various matters, he would peruse Hebrew books and journal articles, Yiddish textbooks, material in easier English, or he would consult with professionals.

He did not feel the lack of anything, with one exception. As his daughter, Malke Bina, explains:

> English! He felt a lack with English. He always wanted to improve his English so he could speak better. *That* was a bit of an impediment. There were *Roshei Yeshiva* like Rabbi Yaakov Weinberg who were American-educated, who had more beautiful language. That he always felt, that he wasn't as articulate with his students as he could have been if he had better English.

Throughout his years in America, Rabbi Milikowsky did what he could to remedy this situation. Whenever he was reading a newspaper or a book and he was stuck on an English word, he would be sure to determine what it meant. The same was true with the spoken word.

One time when he was listening to a song on the radio, he heard the words, "I never promised you a rose garden." So he asked one of his daughters, "What is this 'rose garden'?" and she explained to him, "I didn't promise you *olam haba*. I didn't promise you Paradise." Later on, one of the T.A. boys was visiting the Milikowsky home and he said, "You know, I don't believe it! Your father sang to me, 'I never promised you a rose garden.'" He was fascinated by the idea that something bad could be called a "lemon." He would try to get idiomatic expressions right, so he could talk to the boys in their own language and they could understand what he was saying.

Sometimes his self-education backfired. One time he learned that when you say, "No strings attached," it means no monkey business, no tricks. Months later he was in the supermarket, and there was a big sign advertising a hundred tea bags for a mere fifty cents, and at the bottom the sign said, "No strings attached." From this he understood, "No monkey business. They're selling them inexpensively, no strings attached." Thus he purchased the teabags.

When he got home and opened them up, he cried out, "Where are the strings?" His daughter Malke responded, "Daddy, the sign said, 'No strings attached,'" but Rabbi Milikowsky insisted, "No! That means no monkey business!"

Although he was always trying to learn the idiomatic expressions in order to improve his communication with the students, sometimes he felt frustrated in his efforts. Yet the final judge of his success in communications was the students themselves, and looking back over the years, Rabbi Milikowsky passed the communications test with flying colors thanks to the bond that he created through his efforts. It was a bond that transcended the spoken word. In the words of Joseph Friedman:

> I'll tell you something. It was more important how he said it than what he said. It was more important that you felt connected to him than the actual words that were coming across. It was more important the bond that he had with us than the actual sayings. You could approach him at any time. You could talk to him at any time.

Or in the words of Rabbi Yaakov Spivak: "Rebbe was like an emotion. It was not always words. It was a feeling."

It didn't matter that Rabbi Milikowsky's English was imperfect. His relationship with the boys at T.A. went far beyond language.

End of an Era

In 1975, the Talmudical Academy closed down its dormitory, if only temporarily. It was at this point that Rabbi Boruch Milikowsky decided to retire officially, even if he actively continued his work at T.A.

For the first time in twenty years, Rabbi Milikowsky would now be free to enjoy all of Shabbos with his family. Moreover, if the boys of the Talmudical Academy had previously been the main benefactors of Rebbe's knowledge and experience, the Baltimore Jewish community at large would now be able to benefit in that way.

Starting in 1975, one of the shuls where Rabbi Milikowsky now became a prominent regular on Shabbos was the "Adas" on Rodgers Avenue. Besides doing some of his learning there with Rabbi Bayarsky, every

Shabbos morning he would give a *shiur* there in *Ein Yaakov* before morning prayers. Also, since the Adas didn't have a rabbi for many years, the speakers at *shalashudes* rotated among four rabbis, one of whom was Rabbi Milikowsky. The late Mrs. Annette Klein recalled how her husband, Yoel Moshe, came home from a *shaleshudis* at which Rabbi Milikowsky had described his encounters with the Chafetz Chaim in Radin. Her husband told her, "Everyone was so inspired by Rabbi Milikowsky that they felt as though they had been there too."

Chapters 22 through 24 will describe many of the ways in which Rabbi Milikowsky remained intimately connected to the Talmudical Academy until his passing.

Chapter 21

LOVER OF ZION

DURING THE 1880S, when disciples of the Chafetz Chaim reported to him about the first pioneers coming to Israel and working the land, his response was, "It's starting! It's starting!"

"Moshe Is Truth"

Simchas Torah morning, 1973, found Rabbi Boruch Milikowsky dancing with a *Sefer Torah* at the "Adas." The Yom Kippur War had been raging for eleven days and the situation in Israel was still touch or go. With the war in the background, the Jews of Baltimore were doing their best to celebrate their completion of the Torah with joy.

In the Adas, the congregants, led by a very lively Rabbi Milikowsky, were singing a rousing chorus of *"Moshe emes vesoraso emes,"* "Moshe is truth and his Torah is truth," when suddenly he signaled to everyone that he wished to say a few words:

"Moshe is truth and his Torah is truth!" he began. "That refers to Moshe Rabbenu, but right now we also have to strengthen Moshe Dayan. Because he's leading the battle of *Am Yisrael* (the Jewish people), and we should all pray for him to be successful in the wars of *Am Yisrael*, the wars over *Eretz Yisrael!"*

Whatever one might think about such an address today, in the early 1970s the State of Israel was viewed differently by much of the American yeshiva world from the way it is now, thirty years later. At that time, Israel was not yet the undisputed world Torah center that it has become. Menachem Begin had not yet brought Agudas Yisrael into the government.

There was not yet a religious revival like the one that had begun in the United States during the 1960s. There was not, as yet, any large scale yeshivish aliyah from America. In some American yeshivos, the State of Israel was still associated with the cutting off of *payos* during the 1950s, with Ben Hecht's *Perfidy*, and with arrogant atheism or at least complacent agnosticism. In short, many still viewed it exclusively as a place of spiritual danger, in spiritual decline, and a place that Torah Jewry must relate to with caution. In some Torah circles, even to refer publicly and approvingly to certain aspects of the modern State of Israel was considered taboo or at least socially gauche.

What was there in Rabbi Boruch Milikowsky's background that made him different? How was he so preoccupied with the State of Israel's survival as to be ready – perish the thought – to mention Moshe Dayan publicly in the same breath with "Moshe is truth and his Torah is truth"?

Blessings and Curses

As noted at the beginning of this book, Rabbi Milikowsky's mother's family were Zionists and *maskilim*. Some of them were connected to the local He-Chalutz pioneer movement in Vishnevo. As a boy, Boruch Milikowsky would discuss Zionism with his aunts and uncles on his mother's side, with Eliezer and Matle and Avraham and Benzion, some of whom were not that much older than he, his mother being the oldest and most settled of the siblings. Later on, when he went off to yeshiva, he continued these talks in return visits, and the talks were now more profound, as he was increasingly able to hold his own with a Torah perspective. As he sat with his mother's family, whom he loved, they would tell him about the most beautiful aspects of secular Zionism. Sometimes he would get into heated debates with them, and with other young people in Vishnevo, on the meaning of life. Both he and the secular Zionists were preoccupied with finding what they called "the *emes*," the true purpose of life.

Young Boruch Milikowsky learned secular Zionism from the inside. He realized that while the points his aunts and uncles raised contained some truth and beauty, they were not the whole truth by any means.

At first the conversations seemed entirely hypothetical, pipe dreams with no basis in reality for parlor intellectuals. Then, in 1926, there was a surprise. The uncles and aunts suddenly began to make good on all of their talk. The Dickensteins began to move to Israel.

At that time, as far as Boruch's parents were concerned, Hitler – if they had heard of him at all – was a rising force in a small, eccentric political organization based mostly in Austria. Mostly he was viewed as a clown, not to be taken seriously. Shmuel and Malke saw no reason to uproot themselves, nor would it have been easy to do so, given their businesses and their wealth.

As the 1920s came to an end, the situation in Germany began to change. The Depression struck there, creating instability. Uncle Avraham began to talk to his sister Malke in increasingly strident terms about the importance of getting out while it was still possible. Letters arrived from those who had already made the move. "Come to Israel!" they warned. "It's no good where you are!"

But Shmuel and Malke resisted. Business was going exceedingly well, and there was no proof that the insanity slowly consuming a minority of German society was going to consume the majority or that it would somehow spill over into Eastern Europe. Why should such a thing happen? Just fifteen years before, the Jews of Vishnevo had come into contact with German soldiers who were fighting the local anti-Semitic Slavs. The Germans had seemed so much more genteel. They would enter a Polish village and seek out the Jews who, as Yiddish speakers could serve as adequate translators for the Germans, and then they would give those people privileges. It seemed impossible that these Germans could ever become anti-Semites. And anyway, hadn't the German Weimar Republic been an enlightened democracy since 1918? Unlike distant America, a Jew in Germany could live *anywhere*. How bad could things get?

The Chazon Ish, in his sefer *Emunah u-Bitachon*, writes that in light of the events of our generation, the term *bitachon*, trust in God, cannot be defined to connote the belief that if I pray hard enough for something, I will get it. Rather, in our times, *bitachon* must mean the belief that whatever happens, whether it seems good or bad to us, comes from God and is for our own good.

We cannot know what constitutes a blessing and what constitutes a curse. During World War II, some Jews remained in Eastern Europe and perished while others fled in time to save their lives.

Boruch Milikowsky observed these events. He recalled the philosophical conversations of his childhood. The secular Zionists in his family had survived, while his parents and most of his siblings perished.

Rabbi Milikowsky's background clearly influenced the person he became, the beliefs he held, and the way he chose to express himself. For a man who had learned for over twenty years in the yeshivos of Europe, he was unique. Here follow some further examples:

Rabbi Milikowsky developed a beautiful mastery of modern Hebrew and would read it a great deal. For many years he kept up a subscription to *Ha-Doar*, the American Hebrew literature magazine. He enjoyed reading Hebrew poetry. In his daughter Malke's words, when it came to modern Hebrew literature, "He read Bialik, he read everything!"

One time one of his high school students, himself a lover of Hebrew literature, was sitting during *Gemara* class reading *Ha-Doar* under his desk. As was his practice, Rabbi Milikowsky quietly approached the boy in the middle of explaining a point of *gemara* to the class and, without embarrassing the boy in any way, gently removed the journal from the boy's hands. A week later he approached the boy and returned the journal to him, but first discussed some of its articles and poetry with him. He made it clear that he had read through the entire journal.

Nevertheless, Rabbi Milikowsky's enjoyment of modern Hebrew was not simply a recreational pastime like watching television. He believed that the literature he read had intrinsic value as a form of enrichment.

He once asked Malke to describe her Bais Yaakov high school curriculum for that year. When she had finished describing both her Jewish and secular studies, he then asked, "What do you mean? In Bais Yaakov you don't learn Bialik?" He was surprised and sorry to hear that it was lacking.

Rabbi Milikowsky's connection to modern Hebrew did not limit itself to the written word. He also spoke a fine modern Hebrew.

Rabbi Eliyahu Rabovsky '74 relates the following:

One day during *shiur* an alumnus came by for a visit. The *talmid* had come from a kibbutz program in Israel. They greeted each other warmly, and Rebbe began a conversation with him in modern Hebrew. The fellow left and most everyone had the same question – "Where did Rebbe learn how to speak modern Hebrew?" With utter sincerity he said, "Boys, if you learn and know one hundred Rashis on *Chumash*, you can speak Hebrew!"

(It should be noted that you cannot really speak modern Hebrew based on the knowledge of one hundred Rashis, but Rabbi Milikowsky never missed an opportunity to encourage his students to learn!)

There was a period of time during the mid-1970s when Rabbi Milikowsky actually thought seriously about moving to Israel. All his relatives were in Israel, and he had many Mir Yeshiva connections in Israel as well. Moreover, he already had one daughter living in Israel, and his older son was preparing to move there. Since he had just retired from T.A., the move was more possible than it had ever been.

Rabbi Milikowsky grew more and more excited about the idea. On one of his trips to Israel, he went with his son-in-law Rabbi Aharon Bina and visited Yesodot, an Israeli moshav where one of his former T.A. students lived. When that *talmid* showed him the fields where he did agricultural work with his own hands, Rabbi Milikowsky, now in his sixties, asked for permission to share in that work and spent an hour digging in the field, working the holy soil of Eretz Yisrael.

During that time, many conversations took place over the move. Rabbi Milikowsky made it clear to all that for the sake of moving to Israel, he would be willing to do anything. He said, "There are so many rabbanim already in Israel, so much Torah! What, am I going to be a yeshiva rebbe in Eretz Yisrael? Better I should be a taxi driver!" He was serious.

The truth is that in his visits to Israel he had come into contact with many Israel taxi drivers and he enjoyed them. He found their gutsiness, their brash openness, very appealing. Perhaps he was reminded of himself in some way.

Unfortunately, in the end the move never happened. Rabbi Milikowsky's mother-in-law fell ill and the entire project became impossible. Still, we know that when a Jew even thinks about doing a mitzvah, God treats his intent as though he had actually carried out the deed.

Chapter 22

THE LAST DECADE

ALTHOUGH RABBI MILIKOWSKY officially retired in 1975 when the dormitory closed down, he remained actively involved with T.A. through the 1980s until the end of his life. In fact, when the dormitory reopened in 1979, once more Rabbi Milikowsky developed close relationships with the dormitory boys just as he had had during his first thirty years. Although he no longer spent Shabbos with the boys, every year he would still spend Rosh HaShanah and Yom Kippur, as well as the *Yomim Tovim*, in the dormitory, to the great benefit of the boys who stayed there. When Rebbe arrived on such an occasion, he did not stay with families in the neighborhood. Rather, he stayed with his family in the dormitory, and he and his family would eat all their holiday meals together with the yeshiva boys.

Students of Rabbi Boruch Milikowsky who were in the dormitory during the years that T.A. was on Cottage and Springhill Avenue and Rabbi Milikowsky lived a block away tend to assume two things. First, they assume that no city boy could ever be as close to Rabbi Milikowsky as the dormitory boys were. Second, they assume that no student who graduated after 1967, when T.A. moved to its new, suburban campus, could ever be as close to Rabbi Milikowsky as were those boys who graduated beforehand.

The facts are different, however. Some of Rabbi Milikowsky's closest relationships developed during the 1970s and 1980s with city boys. Consider the following testimony of Rabbi Benyamin Fleishman, 1981:

> Rabbi Milikowsky gave a *chumash shiur*, a *parasha shiur*. It was during the two years between 1979 and 1981, my junior and senior years. Rebbe had a way of making the *shiur* come alive, so the material was

never dry. Moreover, he had a way of relating to each of us on our own level, even though we were in a group. Rebbe just knew every *bochur*. As my father said, "Rebbe knew your thoughts before you knew them." He had warmth. He had understanding. He had compassion. There was unfortunately no one like him.

Later on, during the two and a half years that I was a synagogue rabbi, I definitely tried to emulate Rebbe and to do the same thing in the *shiur* that I taught.

…Rabbi Milikowsky came in to give a *chumash shiur*, and he would give some other classes as well. Even the worst kid would sit there with rapt attention. There was one boy who was a troublemaker in all his classes, but Rebbe had his thumb on him. It was amazing! If you compared the boy's behavior in Rebbe's class with his behavior in other classes you could almost think that the boy was schizophrenic. In fact, a few years ago I met this kid, who is now an adult. What a mensch he has become! He's not Sabbath observant. He's not *frum*, but he's a mensch. And I wouldn't be surprised to find out that his *menschlichkeit* could be directly attributed to Rabbi Milikowsky's influence.

I remember when my grandfather passed away. Rabbi Milikowsky knew before I did. My parents had come in from Harrisburg, their hometown, and they had told him. When I came out of my house, my parents told me. Rabbi Milikowsky was there, and he put his hand on my shoulder. I don't remember what he said, but it really made me feel better.

To say that I have fond memories of Rebbe would be a mild understatement. He was always warm, always had a smile, a kind word. He always understood everyone! Rabbi Milikowsky officially retired in the mid-seventies? He never retired! Not until the day he passed away. Rabbi Milikowsky could not retire. He was there! He was the yeshiva.

જ ๙

FORTY YEARS OF TORAH EDUCATION

Rebbe.

Sunlight

Rabbi Peretz Dinowitz, who went all the way through T.A. during the 1960s and 1970s, later returned and became an elementary school Rebbe in his own alma mater. For three years, in fact, during the early 1980s, he served as dormitory *mashgiach*.

When Rabbi Dinowitz was a *mashgiach*, he dealt with the problems of different boys devotedly and conscientiously. Sometimes, when a case was particularly difficult, he would go back to his old tenth grade Rebbe, Rabbi Milikowsky, for advice and assistance.

There was one boy in the dormitory who had come from a non-observant family and was now seeking to become observant. Unfortunately, the yeshiva staff found him hard to bear because he talked endlessly and monotonously about his own problems to the exclusion of all else, and once he began speaking it was impossible to end the conversation. Matters developed to the point that the boy was considered both by the staff and students to be "a tremendous *nudge*." Whoever saw him coming would turn around and head in the opposite direction. Day and night he would come and complain about the same issues over and over again.

Rabbi Dinowitz was beside himself about what to do. He felt guilty for avoiding the boy and even worse over his failure to deal with his problems, which frankly overwhelmed him. He went to Rabbi Milikowsky and spoke to him at great length. Rabbi Milikowsky said, "Send him to me," and Rabbi Dinowitz did.

Soon afterwards, Rabbi Dinowitz began to see Rabbi Milikowsky learning with this boy every evening at night *seder*. Moreover, when *seder* was over, he would sit and talk with him. These activities stretched from days into weeks, and it was clear to all that Rabbi Milikowsky was giving the boy quality time, on the boy's terms, on a daily basis.

The results were not long in coming. Like a long dormant house plant brought into the sunlight, the boy began to flower. Previously he had had a difficult time getting up for morning prayers. Slowly he became one of the first to arrive each day. In fact, he would walk in early and study

FORTY YEARS OF TORAH EDUCATION

Classroom scene from early years

…and during the late 1960s, still using a
gemara he brought from Shanghai

…and after "retirement."

something on his own. Rabbi Milikowsky had done such a good job of nursing the boy's wounded ego that he began to feel better about himself. As he slowly stopped being obsessed with his own problems, he became a more pleasant person. The day came when Rabbi Dinowitz was able to approach the boy and ask him to assist him as *"veiker,"* the student honored with the task of waking up the dormitory boys for morning prayers. He was getting up early anyway and he was dependable, so he was a perfect candidate for this post.

When Rabbi Dinowitz went to Rabbi Milikowsky for advice, he expected precisely that – advice. What he got instead was an object lesson in how to save a Jewish boy's soul. Such was the influence that Rabbi Milikowsky had on everybody even during the 1980s, ten years after he retired.

Even during the 1980s, just as during his own time as dorm *mashgiach*, when the dormitory boys would come back from the long Pesach and Succos holiday breaks, Rabbi Milikowsky would call all of them over to him, individually, to ask them how their holiday had been and how their family was doing. He went out of his way to do that because he wanted to maintain close contact not only with each boy but with the boy's family. Even during the 1980s, Rabbi Milikowsky knew everything about each family.

The parents of the dormitory students, many of whom were less observant, were aware that this was happening and were happy to see it. Whenever they came to the school to take their sons home, Rabbi Milikowsky would approach them and address them by their first names, like old friends. He would approach a boy's father and say, "Michael, how are you doing?" as though each dormitory boy were a regular student of his. Maintaining that human contact with each boy and his family remained important to him long after he reached retirement.

Not only did Rabbi Milikowsky spend his holidays at the yeshiva, but he also attended night *seder* all the way through the 1980s, even near the end of his life. Just as he had always done, he would devote his time at night *seder* to fielding questions on any and every realm of Torah knowledge. He also learned individually with those selected students whom he felt needed encouragement.

Rabbi Avraham Leventhal, '84, was one such student. Avraham's family had been in a process of becoming more religious when they moved to Salisbury, Maryland on the Eastern Shore. When they arrived there in 1979, they immediately placed Avraham in the T.A. dormitory. Avraham was thirteen years old, in the eighth grade. One evening at night *seder*, soon after Avraham's arrival in the school, Rabbi Milikowsky approached him and invited him to learn with him. He saw a serious boy, one of the two youngest in the dormitory, newly arrived in Baltimore from a town where there were no Jews. He jumped at the opportunity to have positive input there.

Avraham recalls the wonderful experience of learning one on one, every night, with Rabbi Milikowsky during his first two years at T.A. They had a *seder* in *Mishnah Berurah*. Initially Rabbi Milikowsky had suggested this. The High Holidays were approaching, and Rabbi Milikowsky wished to study the appropriate laws. The *chavrusa* between Rebbe and Avraham went very well. Rebbe was an excellent teacher, and Avraham an excellent student. Eventually they learned all of Book Six together and continued to Book One.

Rabbi Milikowsky's shared learning experience with Avraham was an unparalleled act of kindness performed for its own sake. Yet, as so often happen with our kind deeds, Rabbi Milikowsky's act brought dividends in this world. Avraham went on to study in yeshiva after finishing high school. Later he decided to study for the rabbinate and to go into Jewish education, and he has devoted the last eleven years to teaching Torah in his own alma mater, T.A. Like so many other T.A. boys who later became teachers of Torah, one of the main influences upon him to do this was Rabbi Boruch Milikowsky.

Not so Simple

When can one cite the behavior of the Chafetz Chaim as a precedent for ourselves? The following two stories involving one student from the 1980s indicate that it isn't always so simple…

One time a student saw Rabbi Milikowsky picking up some garbage from the hallway floor. The garbage consisted of objectionable items such as squashed fruit and peels. He asked Rabbi Milikowsky why he was doing something so far beneath his dignity. Rabbi Milikowsky replied briefly that as a young student in Radin he once saw the Chafetz Chaim do the very same thing.

Who can argue with such a response?

A few years later, that same student graduated T.A. and went to learn in yeshiva in Israel for a year. He returned the following summer. At that point, he was still a relative neophyte in Talmudic study, although a year away from certain friends had pushed him spiritually in the right direction.

One tangible change in this student was that while he was away he had grown a beard. When he came back to Baltimore and went to visit Rabbi Milikowsky, he thought Rebbe would be proud of him for growing a beard. What a shock he had! As soon as Rabbi Milikowsky saw him he said, "You look terrible! Shave that beard off right away!" The student asked why, pointing out that the Chafetz Chaim had had a beard. Rabbi Milikowsky answered, "When you are the Chafetz Chaim, you can have a beard."

The alumnus who told me these two stories is today a rabbi and a teacher involved in religious outreach. He had the following to add:

"I think Rabbi Milikowsky's main motivation for objecting to my beard was that he knew my parents, especially my mother, wouldn't like the beard at all, and indeed he was right. Rebbe didn't want me trying to be more pious in a way that would cause my parents pain."

In my research for this book, at various times I asked family members of Rabbi Milikowsky to whom he turned when he had halachic questions. From the section of the book on the 1970s there is a single story on a letter he sent to Rabbi Nachum Percowitz, seeking advice. Otherwise, the family's answer may be summed up in the response of his son-in-law, Rabbi Yitzchak Koff:

"I don't know who he asked halachic questions of, because whenever we asked him a halachic question, he always immediately gave an answer. He didn't have to look anything up. I never saw him turn to anybody else."

All the same, it is a mark of Rabbi Milikowsky's great humility that as the years passed, he deferred more and more to the younger rebbeim at T.A. Presumably this was a means of encouraging his own students to give those rebbeim respect. Thus, during the 1980s, when his own students asked him halachic questions, he would sometimes send them to ask those questions of the younger rebbeim, even when he certainly could have given the answers himself.

This does not mean that he degraded himself. He continued to sit in his red upholstered chair on the left side of the eastern wall of the *beis midrash*. There was no denying who he was or where he had come from. Nevertheless, he stood back and let the younger *rebbeim* have their moment in the sun. Consider the following.

Rabbi Joseph Rottenberg was the twelfth grade Rebbe in T.A. for many years and was later T.A.'s Rosh Yeshiva. During the 1980s, his *shiur* was moved from its regular location in a classroom in the high-school building to the *beis midrash*, presumably to create a more reverential environment for the older boys who attended it. All week long, Rabbi Rottenberg would give his *shiur* in the *beis midrash*. On Fridays, however, the *shiur* would have an additional student. Rabbi Boruch Milikowsky would sit quietly behind the partition, in the women's section of the *beis midrash*, marveling at and reveling in Rabbi Rottenberg's *shiur*.

He never came into the main section of the *beis midrash* where the boys sat. Perhaps he did not want Rabbi Rottenberg to feel uncomfortable. Yet although he stayed in a corner of the women's section, it was obvious that Rabbi Rottenberg knew he was there. Rabbi Milikowsky's expressions of pleasure were audible.

Rabbi Avraham Leventhal, mentioned above, eventually became a fourth-grade rebbe at T.A. in 1990. Before that, towards the end of his studies, he began to work as a substitute rebbe at T.A. One Friday morning he wanted to ask his old dorm *mashgiach* for some advice on teaching and approached the *beis midrash*, knowing that he would find Rabbi Milikowsky there, listening to Rabbi Rottenberg's *shiur.* Quietly he entered the *beis midrash* and approached Rabbi Milikowsky, asking him if he could receive some advice at that time. Rabbi Milikowsky gently replied that Avraham would have to wait until the end of Rabbi Rottenberg's *shiur.*

                                                        ৵ ৶

During the 1980s, Rabbi Milikowsky also spent much time as a substitute Rebbe. His presence was exceedingly valuable for T.A. because he could be counted on to step into any class, seventh through twelfth grade, and keep control so that days did not go by, wasted. As one alumnus put it, "I guess it was a smart move by the administration. Although we were a wild class, we were still very respectful of Rabbi Milikowsky."

Quite apart from that aspect of it, when Rabbi Joseph Rottenberg, the twelfth-grade rebbe, became ill for an extended period of time, Rabbi Milikowsky filled in and gave the high *shiur* in Rabbi Rottenberg's place.

Likewise, during the 1980s, when a particular ninth-grade rebbe became engaged to be married and had to miss classes for long periods of time, Rabbi Milikowsky stepped in and became the rebbe. Throughout those years, he continued to be a constant presence in the school.

During the mid- and late 1980s, besides substituting, Rabbi Milikowsky also gave what was called his "enrichment *shiur.*" It wasn't an official *shiur*, but all T.A. boys between ninth and twelfth grade benefited from it. Rabbi Milikowsky came to T.A. every day in order to sit and learn in the place that had been his life for forty years, and he began to pull boys out of the high school to learn with him. Mostly he would do this during *gemara shiur.* Sometimes he would pull out boys who were weaker in Torah learning and who needed more help and sometimes boys who were stronger, relating to each boy in the way that he needed.

At some point during the 1980s, Rabbi Milikowsky began to talk a bit more about his memories from Europe, although his students still had to press him before he would agree to do so. Perhaps some of his wounds had healed with the passage of time, or perhaps he was no longer afraid that he would be overburdening his students if he shared his memories with them. Quite the contrary, they were now starved for this knowledge and felt frustrated that the European experience remained a big blank for them.

This change evidenced itself in various ways. As Rabbi Akiva Houghtling relates:

"One time, (after we pressed him), he brought in an old type of visa card, written in Japanese or Chinese. This card gave him the authorization to go certain places and get food for the yeshiva. It turned out that he was one of the people responsible to get food for the Mirrer Yeshiva when they were in Shanghai. I guess this was a pretty big responsibility, as at the time, from what I understand, food was scarce and people were dying from malnutrition."

Another example is that during the 1980s he began to call his out-of-town students by the name of the city they were from, after the custom in the European yeshivos. Thus, for example, Avraham Leventhal of Salisbury, Maryland, became "Avraham Salisbury." Of course, Rabbi Milikowsky had more than one motive for doing this. Humor and the desire to liven things up were surely part of it. No one can deny that "Avraham Salisbury" sounds ludicrous, compared, for example, with Chaim Lomzer, the name by which the school's founder, Rabbi Chaim Samson, was known in Europe.

Second, it was always important to Rabbi Milikowsky to show his boys that he knew them and he knew about their lives, and this was one way of doing that.

Third and perhaps most important, by adopting a custom of the European yeshivos, Rabbi Milikowsky was transmitting a subtle message that Jews learning Torah, even during the confused 1980s in America, could legitimately hope to carry on the great tradition of Torah learning from Europe.

"Make Us Not Dependent on the Gifts of Human Beings"
Rabbi Peretz Dinowitz recalls that during the 1980s when he was the dorm counselor, for at least a few years a special custom was maintained at T.A., initiated by Rabbi Milikowsky. The entire junior and senior high school would assemble after morning prayers on the day before Rosh HaShanah or Yom Kippur and all the boys would line up, the way boys do when they are wishing "Good Shabbos" to a Rosh Yeshiva on Friday night after davening. Each boy would ask Rabbi Milikowsky for a piece of cake. Rebbe would give him a piece, and then it would be the turn of the next boy.

What was the purpose of this custom? As Rabbi Milikowsky patiently explained before initiating this custom, on Rosh Hashanah we pray for our spiritual and material welfare for the coming year. If, God forbid, it was decreed for a Jew to become so poor during the year that he has to ask his fellow Jews for help, it was hoped that this ritual, in which students "asked Rabbi Milikowsky for food," would suffice to fulfill the decree.

The NCSY organization of Baltimore always sponsors a *Chol HaMoed* excursion to a large amusement park, and this custom goes back at least to the 1980s, when they would take young people to the Great Adventure amusement park in New Jersey. Rabbi Milikowsky, who was already in his seventies by this time, would come along on these trips and, to the great surprise of the youngsters, would accompany them on the roller coaster rides for which the park was famous.

It is not clear whether or not he actually enjoyed these rides. After all, many older people, even those who in earlier years enjoyed driving quickly or even recklessly find fast car travel unpleasant, even disorienting, as they grow older. Even many people in their forties cease to enjoy the physical sensation created by small carousels in children's playgrounds. One can assume that the same is all the more true regarding modern roller coasters.

Much more likely, Rabbi Milikowsky found this a way to break the ice with the T.A. boys, and whatever physical discomfort may have been involved for him personally was immaterial.

During Rabbi Milikowsky's retirement years, he also went far out of his way to break the deadly pattern of "Torah-teacher as enemy." He often looked beyond the short-term effect of keeping boys in class to learn an extra page of material towards the long-term goal of gaining loyal, Torah-true members of the Jewish community, people with positive memories and good feelings about the education they received. The following testimony, from a "city boy" in around 1979, demonstrates this.

"I don't remember which grade we were in, it must have been 10th or 11th, but we decided that we wanted to take a day off and go to an amusement park. The administration told us we had to get a teacher's permission. We asked one of the English teachers and were given an OK. The administration then told us that we had to get one of the rebbeim to give us permission to miss our religious studies. Rabbi Milikowsky said OK.

"Running out of options, the administration said we had to get one of the teachers to go with us. The only one that would agree to go was Rabbi Milikowsky. We headed off to King's Dominion (Amusement Park in Virginia) in two cars. I was in the car with Rabbi Milikowsky. One of the boys in the car asked Rabbi Milikowsky if it was OK to smoke. His reply was 'I don't see it.'

"What I remember most about that day was being on a flying, spinning ride that terrified me. I got up the courage to turn around, and flying in the car behind me, looking calm, almost bored, with his hat in his lap, was Rabbi Milikowsky. I remember being surprised that a rebbe would go on a ride at all, and being really amazed at how calm he was."

The person who told me this story concludes:

"He was the man I chose to officiate at my wedding. When I went to ask him, he told me that he didn't sing or do fancy weddings. I didn't care; he was the person that I wanted."

Students recall that during the 1980s, whenever T.A. would take students roller-skating, Rabbi Milikowsky would always accompany the school on the trip even if no one recalls him actually roller-skating. Here again, the purpose was to build up his connection to T.A.'s students.

Rabbi Milikowsky made a special effort to participate in activities earmarked for the dormitory boys. Although he was retired and no longer the official *mashgiach,* he had been officially responsible for the welfare of the dorm boys for twenty-six years, and that feeling of responsibility continued long afterwards. Thus, besides his daily participation in the night *seder,* Rabbi Milikowsky also made it a point to *daven* with the dormitory boys in the morning and to eat both breakfast with the dorm boys and lunch with the entire student population every day. It is thus no surprise that so many students from the 1980s, both city boys and dorm boys, developed personal relationships with Rabbi Milikowsky.

Sharing in Their Joy

Through most of the 1980s, any event that T.A. arranged for the boys, especially those involving the dormitory boys, saw Rabbi Milikowsky as an active participant, and his joy and liveliness would add to any occasion. When T.A. held its annual *Simchas Beis Hashoeva* during Succos he was always there, and the same goes for Purim and Chanukah celebrations.

The same was true regarding all joyous life-cycle events, weddings, *sheva berachos* (festive dinners held nightly during the week after a wedding), bar mitzvahs, etc. In 1985, a young dorm counselor became engaged and got married. Avraham Leventhal, '84, who had been close to this dorm counselor, was learning in the Scranton Yeshiva, but came down to Baltimore for the *sheva berachos,* where he saw his old Rebbe, Rabbi Milikowsky.

Rabbi Milikowsky, ten years retired as dormitory *mashgiach* and no longer living in the T.A. area, was still spending *Yom Tov* in the T.A. dormitory. A joyous occasion in the T.A. dormitory was a joyous occasion for him as well, however much actual contact he may or may not have had with the young bridegroom. So he came to the *sheva berachos* to bring joy to the bride and groom. Avraham Leventhal vividly recalls the great joy with which Rabbi Milikowsky danced and sang at that *sheva berachos.*

ALWAYS THE EDUCATOR

Participating in a siddur party for young T.A. boys.

Lighting Chanuka Candles with a grandchild.

Introducing a grandson to *tzitzis*.

Chapter 23

BIRDS OF A FEATHER

DURING THE 1930S, not too long after Rabbi Milikowsky's arrival in the Mir yeshiva, a young student by the name of Yaakov Kafkevich was accepted as well. Yaakov was part of a learning group ten years younger than Rabbi Milikowsky. The Mir Yeshiva was divided into learning circles based on age, and the older boys did not mix very much with the younger boys. Even so, Rabbi Milikowsky got to know this boy, and they became friends. There are two explanations for why this occurred. First, Yaakov Kafkevich was always known as an enormously diligent student, and as a result, Rabbi Milikowsky heard about him and held him in great esteem. Second, Rabbi Kafkevich, like Rabbi Milikowsky himself, learned in the Mir for a long time, and accompanied the Mir to Shanghai. Today, there is still a photograph of the two men standing together on the boat going from Japan to Shanghai.

True Greatness

Approximately forty years after that picture was taken, Rabbi Milikowsky's daughter Frady and Rabbi Kavkevich's son Yitzchak met and became engaged. After the engagement, Rabbi Milikowsky invited Yitzchak for Shabbos, and he came. On erev Shabbos, they walked to Rabbi Milikowsky's regular Friday night minyan, the Shearith Israel synagogue. Although Yitzchak had been learning in Baltimore for eight years, he didn't really know anything about his future father-in-law. Because Rabbi Milikowsky was an important *talmid chacham* and educator, Yitzchak expected his father-in-law to have a seat by the eastern wall, but they *davened* quietly in the middle of the shul. As Yitzchak put it, "no one made a big deal out of him."

Yet as they were walking out of the shul, numerous Talmudical Academy alumni from a thirty-five year period started coming up to Rabbi Milikowsky to wish their old Rebbe a good Shabbos. For each "boy," Rabbi Milikowsky had an appropriate comment. He asked one boy who was wearing a black hat: "What are you learning and who are your *chavrusos*?" Then, when he was approached by a boy with longish hair and no hat, he started complimenting the boy on his clothes. "That looks like a new pair of pants!" and so forth. As he left the shul, Rabbi Milikowsky was approached by all kinds of former students, some married and some not, some yeshiva students and some deeply involved in the secular world, and he talked to each student about what interested them. This was Yitzchak's first contact with Rabbi Milikowsky's greatness as an educator. Yitzchak saw firsthand that just as Rabbi Milikowsky's own *rebbeim* in Europe had related to everyone they encountered on a personal level, Rabbi Milikowsky talked to everybody on their own level. Most important, Yitzchak saw that Rabbi Milikowsky's aim was to show personal interest in each student, so that each one should feel special and good about himself.

Talmidim for Life

Henry Lazarus '59 was a *talmid* of Rabbi Boruch Milikowsky. As long as he lived in the United States he always stayed in touch with his Rebbe, and after he came on aliyah in 1980, he did so as well.

Henry has two sons, and he named his older son Boruch. As it turned out, Boruch went through the Chorev Elementary School and the Netiv Meir Yeshiva High School with Rabbi Milikowsky's oldest grandson, Moshe Bina.

In 1985, when it came time for his own son Boruch's bar mitzvah, Henry called Rabbi Milikowsky to tell him the good news. Rabbi Milikowsky asked when the bar mitzvah would be taking place, and Henry answered that it would be a week and a half before Pesach. Henry knew from his own son that Moshe Bina's bar mitzvah would be six weeks later, a month after Pesach, and that Rabbi Milikowsky was planning on coming to Israel especially for that. Thus, he had very little hope of Rebbe being able to attend his son Boruch's bar mitzvah a month earlier.

Yet when Rabbi Milikowsky heard the date of Boruch's bar mitzvah, he said simply, "I'll be there."

Henry gasped in surprise. "Rebbe!" he said. You're coming special to Israel a month later for your own grandson's bar mitzvah. How will you be able to be at my son's bar mitzvah too?"

Rabbi Milikowsky responded firmly, "There's nothing that's going to stop me from coming to your bar mitzvah. Your bar mitzvah is a bar mitzvah of my own family." On the spot, Rabbi Milikowsky had moved up his plans by six weeks. When the time came for Boruch Lazarus's bar mitzvah, Rabbi Milikowsky was a bit under the weather, but he flew to Israel and was there with his *talmid* to celebrate.

Magic Formula

The following vignette is from Rabbi Eliyahu Rabovsky:

"When Rebbe and his Rebbetzin were on a visit to Miami Beach in about 1988 or 1989 we were privileged to host them for lunch. I was learning in the Yeshiva Toras Chaim Kollel at the time and had much involvement with the high-school students. I asked Rebbe for his magic formula in dealing with American teenagers. His answer was simple and direct:

"Treat them like adults – expect them to act like babies."

The Banquet

In 1985, the Talmudical Academy decided to honor Rabbi Boruch Milikowsky at its yearly banquet. The idea was initially suggested by two alumni, Emanuel Friedman, a dormitory student, and Dr. Arthur Lebson, a Baltimore boy. They each gave a large donation to T.A. in honor of Rabbi Milikowsky.

The banquet, which was held at the luxurious Beth Tefilah Synagogue auditorium, was ultimately attended by over 980 people, including over 400 students of Rabbi Milikowsky.

Before the dinner, a special reception was held in a side auditorium. The only people allowed into that room were former *talmidim*, and Rabbi Milikowsky had a hug and a kiss for every single one of them.

The main speaker of the evening was a close *talmid* of Rabbi Milikowsky, Rabbi Yaakov Spivak, not only a *talmid chacham* but a noted Jewish radio personality in the New York area.

Of course, it was a great honor for Rabbi Yaakov Spivak to be asked to be the guest speaker at the dinner honoring Rabbi Milikowsky. Rabbi Spivak had to get from New York to Baltimore for the dinner, and then to get back to New York, and he decided that the best way to do this was by what is called a "Chassidishe Car Service." He figured that the alternative, taking a few buses and a train and a cab or two, would waste a great deal of time, lose him a great deal of sleep, and end up not saving him any money.

The dinner was held before Rabbi Spivak had become a Rosh Kollel. He came in a regular, short suit, while his Chassidishe driver came in a *lange rekel,* a long black coat, with a chassidishe hat. The driver parked the car outside the auditorium where the dinner was to be held, and the two men entered the building together and walked up together in front of Rebbe. Rabbi Spivak figured that now, as the guest speaker, and as one of Rebbe's *talmidim* returning triumphantly to honor him, he was going to enjoy a moment of glory.

Rabbi Boruch Milikowsky, among the humblest and most down-to-earth of men, had little tolerance for anything smacking the least bit of pomposity. Rebbe looked at his *talmid* Yaakov, who had obviously just come hundreds of miles with a personal chauffeur, and then he looked at the driver in the long coat, and then his eyes narrowed. He turned to Rabbi Spivak and he said slowly, with a gleam in his eye, "I don't know who is the Rebbe and who is the *talmid!*"

Rabbi Spivak laughed until his sides ached. But Rebbe wasn't done yet.

He said, "Tell me. You're making a lot of money there as a *rov?*" And Rabbi Spivak answered that he was not. So Rebbe said, "So what are they making such a big deal over you?"

Rabbi Spivak was hysterical now, and between laughter and tears he answered, "I don't know, Rebbe! Maybe I should go home!"

Both Rabbi Spivak and Rabbi Milikowsky delivered memorable speeches. Two aspects of Rabbi Milikowsky's speech were particularly noteworthy. First, he began his speech with the words, "I would like to thank the Talmudical Academy for not firing me for smoking all those years!" Second, he concluded his speech with the words, "The Chafetz Chaim gave me a *birkas kohanim* [a priestly blessing], and I am going to pass on to you a *birkas hedyot* [layman's blessing]."

As soon as his speech was over, dozens of boys rushed forward to shake his hand once more and to express their gratitude for all his love and help.

It was a glorious evening, and it was well timed too. Rabbi Milikowsky was able to enjoy the evening in good health, while he still enjoyed the abundant strength and vitality that God had given him.

Rebbe honored at T.A. Banquet.

Chapter 24

SUNSET

During the late eighties, Rabbi Milikowsky would come every morning to davening. He would walk around, shake the boys' hands, give boys a little pinch on the cheek. Very affectionate! Very warm to the boys! He would tutor. He would be around, whether he was giving a shiur or not. It was his yeshiva! He would be there to help, to work, to tutor, to learn, to smile, to speak to bochrim about personal issues.

And he was beloved! He was the rebbe, the zeide image to the boys. It was just a beautiful sight to see. His presence was very evident day in and day out.

–Rabbi Yudie Levkowitz, Executive Vice President since 1987

During the late 1980s, the Talmudical Academy fell into serious financial trouble. Rabbi Milikowsky's sense of loyalty to the Talmudical Academy was such that in the last few years of his life, when he was no longer in his prime, he would sometimes accompany Rabbi Yudie Levkovitz, T.A.'s new Executive Vice President, on fundraising trips. They would go around together and visit alumni who were close to Rabbi Milikowsky, seeking help for the yeshiva. Here is Rabbi Levkovitz's recollection of a visit to Mr. Emanuel Friedman in Washington D.C.:

> Mr. Emanuel Friedman was CEO of a brokerage firm with approximately seven hundred people working for the firm. We walked into this facility, a large open room, with all the brokers working on computers in public view. They weren't private rooms.

Mr. Friedman is a soft-spoken, quiet and reserved individual. Yet when Rabbi Milikowsky walked in, Mr. Friedman walked towards him and embraced him in front of all those people as if it was his father. I was quite surprised at that moment to see this.

Yet as times goes on, I have occasion to visit with this Mr. Friedman and to know him better and better. With each visit, it becomes even more shocking, knowing his personality and how reserved he is, and how private a person he is, to have seen him embrace the rabbi so lovingly, so publicly. Here a rabbi with a hat and a beard comes in, and this is not exactly Williamsburg, or the Holy City of Jerusalem, *lehavdil*.

But to have watched Rabbi Milikowsky embrace this individual, to have seen that *talmid* embrace *him* – it was magnificent. It was an extremely emotional high for me. Here is a *talmid* who had been out of the yeshiva for many, many years and who was not in an environment conducive to such an embrace. Yet he had no hesitation about this public display of emotion and he made no effort to hold back his affection towards his rebbe.

Rabbi Milikowsky was always known as a man of almost infinite energy and robust health. Certainly during the almost twenty years that he was living a block away from the school, intimately involved with the dormitory, he subsisted on very little sleep. He was also very strong physically. Thus, it came as some surprise when early in 1989 Rabbi Milikowsky began to complain chronically about his health. He was eventually diagnosed as suffering from kidney cancer.

Although Rabbi Milikowsky underwent treatment for this cancer and was officially "cured," the last two years of his life were difficult and sometimes painful.

Rav Yeruchem Levovitz once said: "A person who does not recognize his abilities cannot understand Torah."

As the following story will demonstrate, Rabbi Boruch Milikowsky had a clear sense of his own potential:

One day, the Talmudical Academy phoned and asked him to come and give a *mussar* talk. At this point in his life, Rabbi Milikowsky was using a walker. On the morning of the talk, he was at the home of his son, Rabbi Shaya Milikowsky. When it came time to go to T.A., Shaya helped him with the walker to the back door of his house. Then Shaya helped Rebbe go down the steps. Sitting there at the bottom of the steps was a wheelchair. Shaya wheeled his father down the alley to where his car was sitting, helped him into the car, packed the wheelchair into the trunk, and drove him to T.A. Then Shaya removed the wheelchair, placed it near the front right seat of the car, opened the door, helped his father into the wheelchair and wheeled him into the building, right up to the *beis midrash*.

The *beis midrash* was packed with boys, most of whom remembered Rebbe from his very recent, active days. At the door of the *beis midrash*, Rabbi Milikowsky told his son that it would be inappropriate for him to enter the room in a wheelchair or even with a walker. In fact, he asserted that he would give his entire talk standing up, and that is just what he did. He walked from the door of the *beis midrash* to the *bima*, holding on to somebody. As he entered the room, all of the boys immediately rose in reverent silence and remained that way until he reached the *bima*, where he delivered his talk. In the meantime, Shaya quietly entered the women's section to listen to his father's talk. Shaya assumed that the talk would take only three to five minutes. After all, how much strength did his father have? He would say a bit of *mussar* and then they would leave.

To Shaya's utter surprise, Rabbi Milikowsky spoke for thirty-five minutes, standing at the *bima*. Moreover, he managed to speak in a loud voice.

Rabbi Shaya Milikowsky concludes this story as follows: "They say that this phenomenon holds true for a lot of people: When you give your life for something, you have unbelievable resources that you can tap into."

Rabbi Milikowsky, as someone who had given his all in Torah learning, and then had once more given his all in teaching and helping Jewish boys, knew what he was capable of. Yet as the following story shows, he also had a clear understanding of the human potential of those around him.

During much of the time that Rabbi Boruch Milikowsky served as *mashgiach* and tenth-grade rebbe, the ninth-grade slot was filled by Rabbi David Krasner, an exceptional talmid chacham in his own right. In the late 1980s when Rabbi Milikowsky was very sick, Rabbi Krasner's wife suffered a very serious, debilitating stroke. Rabbi Krasner sat by her side for long hours and took meticulous care of her. On witnessing this, Rabbi Milikowsky told his son, "You'll see, Shaya. He's going to bring her back to life."

When Shaya told Rabbi Krasner what his father had said, tears started rolling down his face. He said to Shaya, "Your father always knew what was right." In the end, Rabbi Krasner did bring her back, and as of this writing, twelve years later (2004), while Rebbetzin Krasner, *ad meah ve'esrim*, is indeed confined to a wheelchair, she can speak and do many things for herself.

❧ ❧

The following story is from Rabbi Yisrael Beller, who learned in Ner Israel into the 1980s.

"As Rebbe got older, his health began to deteriorate and he didn't always feel up to par. One time Rebbe was sitting at a table near the back of the Ner Israel *beis midrash* and Rabbi Mordechai Gifter, the Telshe Rosh Yeshiva entered. As Rav Gifter passed by, he gave Rebbe a big *shalom aleichem* and asked Rebbe how he was feeling. Rebbe replied, '*Men shlept zoch*,' 'I'm shlepping along.' Rabbi Gifter shot back and said in his loud voice, '*Boruch Hashem, men shlept zoch*,' Thank God one has what to shlep.

❧ ❧

In the fall of 1988, Rabbi Avraham Leventhal was a new rebbe in T.A. At that time, his wife worked as a teacher in the same afternoon Hebrew school

Rebbe and his wife with two of
Malke's children.

Three of Frady's children.

With one of Malke's
children. Behind Rebbe is
Malke's husband,
Rabbi Aharon Bina.

At son Chaim's wedding. Second from left is
Chaim's new father-in-law, Rabbi Shmuel
Rozovsky, Rosh Yeshiva of Ponevezh.

where Rebbetzin Leah Milikowsky taught. Soon, he noticed that every day, when he was picking up his wife from her job, Rabbi Milikowsky would be picking up his own wife as well. Seeing this, and not wishing his old tenth-grade Rebbe and *mashgiach* to have to make this effort, Rabbi Leventhal offered to pick up Rebbetzin Milikowsky and save Rabbi Milikowsky the trip. "Please! It would be my pleasure," he said, but Rabbi Milikowsky answered, "No! Absolutely not!" He wanted to perform the kindness of picking up his wife up by himself. In the end, however, he agreed to form a carpool with Rabbi Leventhal.

The carpool got off the ground and by Erev Rosh Hashanah of 1990, it had been going on for two years. That day, Rabbi Leventhal received a phone call from Rabbi Milikowsky. Rabbi Milikowsky apologized to him for those times that he might have been late or for when Rabbi Leventhal might have had to cover for him on short notice. He thanked Rabbi Leventhal for taking the burden off him and enabling him to drive less.

Rabbi Leventhal was at a loss for words. As he told me, "It was not a big deal for a *talmid* to do such a thing for a rebbe. It's not like his wife was very far away. He was only five blocks away."

No matter. Rabbi Milikowsky always said "Thank you" for any kindness he received, and this thanks to his *talmid*, Avraham Leventhal, came at a good time. After this Rosh Hashanah, there would be no other.

During the late summer before that Rosh Hashanah, Rabbi Milikowsky made a final visit to Israel. He went to visit his family there, spending his time resting in his daughter's home in the Old City. It was unclear whether he would ever see Israel again. As in previous visits, he made surprise phone calls to former *talmidim*. This time, however, it was the students who came to visit him, one by one, in the Old City. Many an emotional reunion was held during that time. Before Rosh Hashanah he returned to Baltimore.

At first, Rabbi Milikowsky remained at home, going into the hospital occasionally to be treated. Indeed, he was still managing to go to T.A. at least once or twice a week. Yet in late October he went into Sinai Hospital and remained there.

Isaac Kinick, '53, a devoted student of Rabbi Boruch Milikowsky, visited his Rebbe when he was critically ill at Sinai Hospital. During the visit, Rabbi Milikowsky asked for a Coke, and Mr. Kinick went to get it for him. Yet when the nurse saw him at the Coke machine, she told him that he must not buy a Coke for Rabbi Milikowsky because in his condition it would be very bad for him. Mr. Kinick felt terrible. The man who had brought so many hundreds of bottles of Coca-Cola to ailing students over forty years' time could not have one himself. He was now very, very ill.

During the last several weeks of Rebbe's life, one frequent visitor to the hospital was Dr. Chaim Botwinick '67:

> I remember when he was in the hospital. Those last couple of weeks were very hard, trying to show honor to Rebbe in the hospital, when we knew he showed little chance of recovering. During each visit I was confronted by a question: How do I leave his bedside when I'm not sure I'm going to see him again?
>
> Yet he tried to make life easy for me. He knew I wanted to come to visit him. I wanted to stay there as long as I could. Yet he would say, "I think I'm going to take a nap now." This was his way of saying, "You know, Chaim. You can go. You don't have to go on your own. I'm suggesting it."
>
> That was very special. Looking back, I think this was Rebbe's way of sparing me the decision. I didn't even know how to say "OK, Rebbe, feel better. I'm going to be back tomorrow." I mean, to tear myself away from the bed of someone I loved so much was very hard. Yet he found a way to take the burden off me.

During the last weeks before Rabbi Milikowsky passed away, his daughter Malke and his son Chaim flew in from Israel to be with their father, whose situation was now deteriorating. Thus, all of his children were able to be with him during his last weeks.

Three days before his passing, Joseph Friedman went to visit Rebbe. There were others visiting also. Though weak and wracked with pain, Rebbe was alert but not talking. When the nurse came in with a popsicle for him, he raised himself up in the bed and with great effort made the *shehakol* blessing. Though he was not speaking to anyone in the room, he was still speaking to Hashem.

During the last few days of his life, Rabbi Milikowsky remained conscious, but his eyes were closed and he could not speak. The students in the high school of the Talmudical Academy and in various other institutions recited Psalms for him. The following is Rabbi Akiva Houghtling's recollection of his visit to Rabbi Milikowsky towards the end.

I had already graduated when he got very sick. I was studying in New York and was in Baltimore during Chanukah. Rabbi Milikowsky was in the hospital on a respirator. Not everyone was being allowed to see him. I phoned Rabbi Milikowsky's daughter and obtained permission for myself and Lonnie Bork to visit him.

Although his eyes were closed and he looked unconscious, his daughter told us that he could hear us. We spoke to him for several minutes, telling him we still needed him in our lives. We started crying and asking forgiveness, and the monitor showed that his heart was starting to beat very quickly (a sign that he heard us and understood who we were). We kissed his hand and left. The next day, he died.

The *Levaya*

When Rabbi Milikowsky passed away on the seventh night of Chanukah in December 1990, his funeral was held in the auditorium of the Talmudical Academy where he had played such a central role for more than forty years. Rabbi Aharon Bina, Malke's husband, flew in from Israel for the funeral.

Thousands attended, creating a sea of people spilling out of the auditorium and onto the streets of the Talmudical Academy campus. As more and more people arrived, a man in his fifties, a talmid of Rabbi

Milikowsky, approached Rabbi Joseph Rottenberg to ask him a question. Rabbi Rottenberg, for many years the rebbe of T.A.'s twelfth-grade *shiur*, is an accomplished posek as well. Many people call him for quick and authoritative responses to difficult questions.

The man who approached Rabbi Rottenberg, however, asked him a question for which he did not have a quick answer:

"Do we, his boys, have to tear *kriah*?"

Rabbi Rottenberg stood there, mouth agape. He understood the assumptions that lay hidden beneath this question. On the one hand, there was no biological relationship between Rabbi Milikowsky and his *talmidim*. On the other hand, many hundreds of alumni viewed Rabbi Milikowsky as a surrogate father. In fact, a number of other former students of Rabbi Milikowsky were standing nearby, waiting to hear Rabbi Rottenberg's answer to the question.

After a few minutes, he answered no, that Rabbi Milikowsky's boys did not have to tear *kriah*.

The person who told me this story, having witnessed this exchange, concluded as follows:

"Had Rabbi Rottenberg answered yes, that whole place would have torn *kriah*."

↾ ↽

Rabbi Pinchas Fleishman '60, who was at the *levaya*, reports that Rav Yaakov Weinberg z"l, who was the Rosh Yeshiva of Ner Israel when Rabbi Milikowsky passed away, gave the first eulogy. It was on Chanukah, when we normally do not deliver eulogies. Yet Rabbi Weinberg opened his remarks by saying, "Although normally on Chanukah eulogies are forbidden, in this case it is permissible. A *talmid chacham* is lying before us." He did not use the regular "eulogy formula," the crying singsong that he later used, for example, at Rabbi Benjamin Steinberg's funeral. It was Chanukah, after all. Nevertheless, he delivered a eulogy, setting the tone for all the other speakers.

A number of other prominent personalities eulogized Rabbi Milikowsky as well, such as Rabbi Rottenberg and, of course, Rabbi Avraham Bayarsky, Rabbi Milikowsky's long-time friend and learning partner.

When it came time for Rabbi Milikowsky's son-in-law, Rabbi Aharon Bina, to address the assembled, he tearfully quoted from an idea elaborated on by his own father, Rabbi Arye Bina:

Sifri teaches, "'Teach them to your sons' (Deuteronomy 6:8) – This refers to your students." Yet, as the *ba'alei mussar* ask, if the word means 'students,' why not write 'students' to begin with? They answer as follows: Only if a teacher of Torah views his students as sons will he be able to fulfill his task properly. For Rabbi Milikowsky, every student was like a son."

After the funeral held in Baltimore, the coffin was flown to New York, on its way to Israel. In JFK Airport, a number of students, including Rabbi Yaakov Spivak and Rabbi Dovid Eidenson, had come to the airport to pay their last respects. As the truck slowly carried the coffin out to the tarmac where it would be loaded onto the jet flying to Israel, Rabbi Milikowsky's students had permission from the airport authorities to follow the truck to the El Al plane.

Meanwhile, waiting aboard the El Al plane were two people flying to Israel to accompany the body to its final resting place. These were Rabbi Bina, who had just flown in for the funeral, and Meyer Weinstock, '57, a close *talmid* from Toronto.

After attending Rabbi Milikowsky's dinner in 1985, Meyer had received a copy of the video made of the dinner but had never watched it. When he received a call informing him of Rabbi Milikowsky's passing, he decided to watch the video for the first time. So overwhelmed was he by the memories that it awakened in him that he decided on the spur of the moment to accompany his rebbe on his final journey. He thus flew down to Baltimore for the first *levaya* and continued on with Rabbi Bina to the second.

᠕ ᠖

As Rabbi Boruch Milikowsky's coffin was flying towards Israel, phone calls were being made all around Israel, spreading the news that a Baltimore *tzaddik* was going to have a *levaya* in Jerusalem. Many people stopped what they were doing to attend. Read this testimony by Jerusalemite Shulamit Lebowitz, a long-time neighbor of the Milikowskys:

> The day of Reb Boruch's *levaya*, my mother, may she rest in peace, was moving out of the apartment that she had lived in for years in Petach Tikva, and I was there supervising the packing and moving. My older son Shimon, who lives in Kiryat Moshe in Yerushalayim, called me and said, 'You'd better sit down! I just saw a notice.' And, he told me that Reb Boruch's *levaya* was *that afternoon* in Jerusalem, and here I was in Petach Tikva, two hours before. I hadn't know that the coffin was coming or anything. I left my kids, my younger kids, to supervise the packers with my mother. I got on the bus and Shimon met me at the Central Bus Station, and we *ran* to the *levaya*, which was at the Shamgar Funeral Home. Everybody from Baltimore who heard about it was there.
>
> Chaim, who had just returned to Israel, spoke at the Israeli *levaya*, as did Rabbi Aharon Bina, a second time. Rabbi Hirsch Diskind, Rabbi Milikowsky's predecessor in the Talmudical Academy dormitory, related a story he had just heard. A Ner Israel boy who had gone to T.A. for high school had the previous day asked his *rebbeim* for permission to attend Rabbi Milikowsky's funeral. When they asked him why, he had answered simply, "He loved me."

Rabbi Milikowsky was buried in the Mirrer Section in the cemetery on the Mount of Olives, and Meir Weinstock, together with his brother-in-law, Ritchie Weiner of Rechovot, were privileged to be among the pallbearers. As soon as the funeral was over, Chaim flew to the United States, and all four siblings sat *shiva* together in their parents' home.

Rabbi Boruch Milikowsky had begun his life in the marshy farm country of Belarus, in a home without electricity. His father had traveled to work in a horse-drawn cart. Now he had made a final trip to Israel by jet.

He had arrived in America alone and penniless, in mourning for his family. Now, like the Patriarch Jacob, he had "become two camps," with children on both sides of the ocean, all with large, God-fearing families. Moreover, he had produced hundreds of grateful students. Like his name, "Boruch," he was truly blessed.

Epilogue

WHEN RABBI YOSEF ABRAMS, '64, heard that Rabbi Milikowsky had passed away, he was serving as a Torah educator in Cleveland. As soon as he heard, he made arrangements to go to the house of mourning in Baltimore. He had not seen Rabbi Milikowsky's children in many years, so when he walked in several days later, none of the mourners recognized him. Nobody knew who he was. He walked into the room, wordlessly sat down and started to weep. He sobbed and sobbed. He just couldn't stop. Those present must have wondered, "Who is this person who is crying so hard?" but the answer was as simple as the question: Rabbi Abrams was one of Rebbe's boys.

         ஐ   જી

Just six months later, Rebbetzin Leah was spending some time together with her children and grandchildren in Jerusalem. On Friday night, her grandson Chanan, the youngest in the Bina family and a kindergarten pupil, was talking about *Parashas Beha'alos'cha*, repeating what he had learned from his teacher. Then, when he finished talking about the portion of the week, he decided to hold forth on the portion of the following week, *Parashas Shelach*.

The other children in the family, who all wanted their own turns to say something about the week's portion, tried to hush him.

Rebbetzin Leah objected to their attempt at curtailing free speech. "What's the matter?" she asked. "What's wrong? Is he talking nonsense? What's wrong if he talks about *Shelach*?"

As Rabbi Bina points out, the Talmud teaches that forty days before a person dies, he has a sense that he is leaving this world. Perhaps Rebbetzin Leah sensed that she would not live to hear about next week's *parashah*. Indeed she died in her daughter's home that Shabbos morning, before *Parashas Shelach* ever arrived. Although she was more than ten years younger than her late husband, her time had come.

❧ ❧

The beauty of the relationship between Rabbi Milikowsky's children is best described by Rabbi Milikowsky's son-in-law, Rabbi Yitzchak Koff:

> After Rabbi and Mrs. Milikowsky passed away, the four siblings remained extremely close. There is a really warm relationship between them. It must have been a lesson that was imbued in them from a young age, that this is what is expected, and they have followed through on the lesson later on.
>
> All of them are involved in their communities. Each has picked up magnificent traits, and I think it's a credit to the type of house they had, a warm, open house, where there were always boys going in and out. *They saw that their father was always doing whatever other people needed.*

❧ ❧

That same closeness that existed between Boruch Milikowsky and his young aunts and uncles and that continues between the siblings today finds other modes of expression as well. To this day, Rabbi Milikowsky's surviving sister Minna knows that she can find a sympathetic ear for the deep philosophical questions she has about what her family experienced during the Holocaust. She recalls how pious her younger sister Drezel Matla was becoming in the months before the massacre. Why was this pious fifteen-year-old girl murdered while she herself was spared? Obviously there are no fast answers to such a question, but she knows that Rabbi Milikowsky's sympathetic, learned children are there for her.

❧ ❧

Ultimately, following Rabbi Milikowsky's passing, Mr. Emanuel Friedman was moved to contribute and collect a very large sum for the Talmudical

Academy. In return, he asked that the Talmudical Academy dormitory, where he himself had spent four significant years of his life, be dedicated to his Rebbe, Rabbi Boruch Milikowsky, and that is what occurred. His efforts saved the school from closure.

❧ ☙

The Kollel

I have just related – in two installments – the story of how one man's love for his rebbe saved a school from closing. But the story does not end there.

During the 1980s, as more and more Jewish day schools opened in America, T.A.'s high-school enrollment decreased steadily. Rabbi Milikowsky became increasingly convinced that T.A. should establish a post-high-school yeshiva. He thought that graduating students should have a framework within their own school in which to continue learning Torah. Furthermore, he believed that high school boys should have a yeshiva environment with post-high-school students, or kollelniks, learning right in their own high school.

When Rabbi Yudie Levkovitz became Executive Vice President of the Talmudical Academy in 1987, Rabbi Boruch Milikowsky shared his ideas with him. As Rabbi Levkowitz explains:

"Rabbi Milikowsky's greatest challenge to me was about the post-high-school idea. He said, 'Find sources! Get this going! You've got to have some sort of a post high school program so that the boys will want to stay. Right now the eighth graders have been challenged to continue their learning and their general studies on the highest level. When they reach the ninth grade, many of them leave to find yeshiva high schools that house such programs.'"

Rabbi Levkovitz undertook to meet the challenge set forth by Rabbi Milikowsky. In 1998, eight years after Rabbi Milikowsky's passing, Mr. Emanuel Friedman once more came through and agreed to fund five kollelniks learning full-time in the T.A. *beis midrash*. If his dormitory dedication had been a material shot in the arm, his kollel was certainly just the spiritual shot in the arm that T.A. needed. Rabbi Milikowsky's dream was fulfilled, and the Talmudical Academy has been thriving ever since.

The new kollel was named Birkas Shmuel after Rabbi Samuel and Zehava Friedman, father and mother of Emanuel. Yet, as Rabbi Avraham Leventhal wryly comments, it would be no surprise to hear that the word *birkas* (blessing) is one more way for Mr. Emanuel Friedman to honor Rabbi Boruch Milikowsky, his beloved Rebbe.

Today, five kollelniks learn in the T.A. *beis midrash* all day long. Yet one chair in the *beis midrash* remains empty – Rabbi Milikowsky's red upholstered chair from the left side of the eastern wall. No one has presumed to sit in it. Rabbi Milikowsky's place cannot be filled.

Last Court of Appeals

Rabbi Milikowsky exerted great influence on his boys not only while they were under his care but also through his contact with them after they left T.A. and entered adulthood. Yet even now, following his passing, his very memory continues to exert an enduring influence on his students.

One boy, who had been sent to T.A. by Rabbi Emanuel Feldman of Atlanta many years ago, ultimately returned to Atlanta and became a pillar of the Jewish community there. He continued to *daven* in Rabbi Feldman's shul, where he had been raised and had celebrated his bar mitzvah, even after Rabbi Feldman retired and handed over the pulpit to his son Ilan, himself a dormitory student of Rabbi Milikowsky during the 1970s. A charitable, philanthropic individual, this layman was very active in synagogue decision-making.

Sometime following Rabbi Milikowsky's passing, a disagreement arose between this layman and Rabbi Ilan Feldman over a matter involving the running of the shul. Rabbi Feldman found himself in the uncomfortable position of differing with a person many years his senior. At a meeting of the synagogue board, the issue in question came up for debate, and the layman could not be swayed. Finally, as a last resort, Rabbi Ilan Feldman turned to this layman and said, "What do you think Rabbi Milikowsky would say in this situation? Do you think that *he* would agree with you?" To make his point, Rabbi Feldman had used the common language of T.A. alumni.

The layman's mouth fell open and he had nothing to say. Rabbi Feldman had appealed to the man's moral sense in a way that the man could not ignore. The argument was over.

"It is not so much how much you remember of those particular days. It's after the fact. You look back and then all of a sudden you realize the importance and the beauty of what was. And the appreciation that I have of him and of my years at T.A. as a result becomes more and more special the older I get. It's an appreciation I can see, even though I probably did not recognize it in my high school years or for long after."

—*Rabbi Edward Davis, '64*

Glossary of Yiddish and Hebrew Terms

Acharonim – Talmudic commentators and authorities in Jewish law from the sixteenth to twentieth centuries

ba'al mussar – master preacher; master of the Mussar approach to life (see "Mussar")

ba'al teshuva – a Jew who decides to increase the level of his religious observance and belief

beis midrash – a Jewish house of study

blatt – A two-sided page of Talmud

bochur, pl. bochrim – yeshiva student

chavrusa – study partner, study partnership

cheder – An intensely Jewish elementary school, especially as existed in Eastern Europe

chessed – kindness

chiddush – novel Torah thought

chol ha-moed – the intermediate days of Succos and Passover

Chumash – the Pentateuch or one of the five books thereof

daf yomi – the daily page of Talmud studied all over the world in unison

daven, davening – to pray, prayers

derech eretz – (in this book) worldliness

devar Torah, pl. divrei Torah – words of Torah, a short talk on a Torah topic

erev Shabbos – Friday, the day before Shabbos

erev Yom Kippur – the day before Yom Kippur

frum – Torah-observant

gebrochts – baked items (such as *kneidlach*) made of matzah meal and water or other liquids that Chassidim do not eat on Pesach, but Misnagdim do

gedolim – great rabbis of the era

Gemara – the Talmud

halachah, adj.: halachic – Jewish law

kabbalas Shabbos – Friday evening services

kohen, Pl. kohanim – Jew descended from Aaron the High Priest and charged with the Temple service when the Temple was standing

kollel – yeshiva for married students

kollelnik – student in a *kollel*

keriah – literally, tearing. The mourning practice of tearing a section of one's shirt upon hearing that a loved one has passed away

le-havdil – literally, "to distinguish." Figuratively: "Forgive my mentioning them together."

levaya – funeral

ma'ariv – The evening prayer

mamash – really

mashgiach; mashgichim – spiritual guidance counselor in a yeshiva

Mashiach: the Messiah

maskil, pl. *maskilim* – Jewish supporters of the European Enlightenment; Jewishly-educated persons who were also at home with the modern literature, ideas and isms of the nineteenth century. In many cases, the maskilim were not as observant of Torah as members of the yeshiva world. Some were actually opposed to Torah Judaism

melave malka – meal eaten on Saturday nights to extend the atmosphere of the Sabbath into the week

mensch – person of quiet integrity.

minchah – the daily afternoon service

minhag, pl. minhagim – religious customs, especially relating to family or geographical background

minyan, pl. minyanim – prayer gathering of at last ten men, or the required quorum of ten men

Mishnah, Pl. Mishnayos – the Oral Law, as put in writing in the third century by Rabbi Judah the Prince

Mishnah Berurah – the Chafetz Chaim's commentary on the *Shulchan Aruch*, the major law code by Rabbi Yosef Caro

misnaged – Today, a non-chassid. Previously, an opponent of the Chassidic movement

mitzvah – good deed

Mussar – ethics, reproof

Mussar movement – A movement started in the nineteenth century by Rabbi Yisrael Salanter that emphasized refining one's character and pondering one's purpose in life

parashah – weekly Torah portion

posek – An authority on Jewish law.

Rashi – Rabbi Shlomo Yitzchaki (1040–1105); also refers to his work, the most important commentary on both the Pentateuch and Talmud

rav – rabbi

rebbe, pl. rebbeim – teacher of Torah

Rishonim – Talmudic commentators and authorities in Jewish law who lived from the eleventh to sixteenth centuries

rosh yeshiva, pl. rashei yeshiva – the director of a yeshiva

schlogging kaporahs – ceremony of symbolically transferring guilt from our sins to a fowl or to charity money. The fowl is then slaughtered and given to the poor

seder – Torah-learning session

sefer – book, holy book

Shabbos, pl. Shabbosim – the Jewish Sabbath, observed on Saturday

shalach monos – Food portions exchanged as gifts on Purim

shaleshudis – "the Third Meal," generally small on food and big on spirituality, consumed late on Shabbos afternoon

sheva berachos – any of the seven ceremonial dinner parties held during the week following a Jewish wedding

shidduch – (matrimonial) match

shiur, pl. shiurim – Torah lecture

shmuess, pl. shmuessen – a lecture or intimate talk. As a verb: to chat *shomer Shabbos* – a Sabbath-observant person

shtender – a lightweight lectern used by yeshiva students

siddur – prayer book

Succos – the Pilgrimage Festival of Booths

Talmid – student, disciple

Talmid chacham – Torah scholar

Tashlich – prayers that refer to casting off one's sins. *Tashlich* is recited on Rosh ha-Shanah afternoon near a body of water

tefillin – phylacteries

Tisha be-Av – the ninth day of the Jewish Month of Av and the anniversary of the destruction of the First and Second Temples in Jerusalem

Torah im derech eretz – philosophy of life that advocates combining Torah study with the study of Western science and thought, especially as espoused by Rabbi Samson Raphael Hirsch of Germany during the nineteenth century

Tosafos – one of the commentaries on the Talmud

Tzaddik – saint, righteous person

tzitzis – Ritual fringes worn by a Jewish man under his shirt

Tzom Gedalya – Fast on the day after Rosh ha-Shanah, mourning the assassination of Gedalya ben Achikam, last Jewish ruler of the First Commonwealth

Yeshiva – A Jewish center for Talmudic and rabbinic studies

Yeshiva gedola – yeshiva for post high school students

Yeshiva ketana – Yeshiva for high-school students

Yom Tov – Any one of the three Festival Pilgrimages, Pesach, Shavuos or Succos or, sometimes, Rosh ha-Shanah and Yom Kippur

zechus – A privilege or merit

Zemiros – Liturgical songs sung at Shabbos meals

Rabbi Boruch Milikowsky was born in Vishnevo, Belarus in 1913. Over a twenty-year period, he learned in Radin, Baranovitz and at the Mir Yeshiva. Together with the Mir Yeshiva, Rabbi Milikowsky fled to Shanghai during World War II. The Nazis murdered most of his family.

After the war, Rabbi Milikowsky became a Torah educator and *mashgiach* at the Talmudical Academy of Baltimore. There, over the course of forty years, he employed his unique, God-given talents to help hundreds of boys to remain Jewishly strong and inspiring many to go on to careers in the rabbinate and in Jewish education. He passed away in 1990 and is survived by four children and many grandchildren who live in both the United States and Israel.

About the author:

Raphael Blumberg, who grew up in Baltimore, Maryland, studied under Rabbi Boruch Milikowsky in Tenth Grade at the Talmudical Academy of Baltimore. He earned degrees at the Johns Hopkins University and at the University of Pennsylvania, and spent four years learning in Israeli yeshivas. He is the translator of more than twenty-five books and hundreds of articles on mostly Torah-related topics. He and his wife Mona and family have lived in Kiryat Arba, Israel since 1984.